# Democracy in Action

*Collective Problem Solving in Citizens' Governance Spaces*

Albert W. Dzur
and
Carolyn M. Hendriks

# OXFORD
UNIVERSITY PRESS

Great Clarendon Street, Oxford, OX2 6DP,
United Kingdom

Oxford University Press is a department of the University of Oxford.
It furthers the University's objective of excellence in research, scholarship,
and education by publishing worldwide. Oxford is a registered trade mark of
Oxford University Press in the UK and in certain other countries

© Albert W. Dzur and Carolyn M. Hendriks 2025

The moral rights of the authors have been asserted

All rights reserved. No part of this publication may be reproduced, stored in
a retrieval system, transmitted, used for text and data mining, or used for training artificial
intelligence, in any form or by any means, without the
prior permission in writing of Oxford University Press, or as expressly permitted
by law, by licence or under terms agreed with the appropriate reprographics
rights organization. Enquiries concerning reproduction outside the scope of the
above should be sent to the Rights Department, Oxford University Press, at the
address above

You must not circulate this work in any other form
and you must impose this same condition on any acquirer

Published in the United States of America by Oxford University Press
198 Madison Avenue, New York, NY 10016, United States of America

British Library Cataloguing in Publication Data

Data available

Library of Congress Control Number: 2024949917

ISBN 9780192870575

DOI: 10.1093/oso/9780192870575.001.0001

Printed and bound by
CPI Group (UK) Ltd, Croydon, CR0 4YY

Links to third party websites are provided by Oxford in good faith and
for information only. Oxford disclaims any responsibility for the materials
contained in any third-party website referenced in this work.

The manufacturer's authorised representative in the EU for product safety is Oxford University
Press España S.A. of el Parque Empresarial San Fernando de Henares, Avenida de Castilla, 2 –
28830 Madrid (www.oup.es/en).

# Acknowledgments

This has been a rich collaboration that began in Canberra ten years ago when we met over coffee and shared stories about our research on democratic practice. At the time it struck us that we were both independently observing practical citizen-led forms of political engagement that did not seem to feature in scholarly and practical discussions on democratic renewal. Indeed, we did not see these self-organizing citizens reflected in the kinds of participatory and deliberative democratic theories we admired and used in our scholarship and teaching. Neither did any of the plethora of conceptual labels attached to them in empirical studies seem apt for those groups we found most interesting.

We wanted to learn more about these groups and people to see what insights they might hold for practitioners and scholars of democracy.

Our project began small and iterative—much like the spaces we consider in this book. We mapped contours of these spaces by exploring scholarship in diverse fields and adding, over time, a growing number of case examples. As our analytical framework came into focus, we dug deeper, investigating what citizens were doing in a select group of cases. These steps led to presentations, a workshop, journal articles, and then a book project. The pandemic slowed our research progress, but it also brought to wider awareness the significance of citizen-led efforts such as mutual aid.

All along the way our project has benefitted tremendously from conversations, interviews and observations, site visits, conferences, feedback, and research and editorial assistance.

*Primus inter pares* for our thanks is the Centre for Deliberative Democracy and Global Governance at the University of Canberra, where this project began. Many faculty members, associates and students of the Centre have offered valuable feedback, ideas and insights that have enriched our thinking in this book project, and we would especially like to acknowledge Hans Asenbaum, Henrik Bang, Nicole Curato, John Dryzek, Selen Ercan, and Henk Wagenaar.

In the early days we were grateful to have some excellent research assistance from Ella Weisbrot from the Crawford School of Public Policy at the Australian National University (ANU), who developed a useful map of diverse literatures, which has proven a valuable resource throughout this entire project.

Our research for this book has been greatly enriched by inputs from, and discussions with, our students. We would especially like to acknowledge students from the Crawford School of Public Policy at the ANU for their case study papers on citizens' governance spaces which have informed our own empirical research and arguments. In particular, we thank: Felippa Amanta (Savy Amira); Abigail Bakker (Nundah Community Enterprise Cooperative); Adina Jordan (Bourke Tribal Council); Nathan Pong (Heart of Dinner); Andita Primanti (Community-based Internet services in Indonesia); Leah Rheinberger (Friends of Canberra Grasslands); Tessa Royal (Landcare); Kyle Salkeld (Orange Sky Australia); Tania Wilson (Totally Renewable Yackandandah, TRY) and Christie Woodhouse (Tender Funerals).

Interviews with citizens and governance practitioners have also shaped our ideas in this book. Special thanks to members of the Goulburn Murray Resilience Taskforce for their willingness to be observed and interviewed, particularly Sarah Thomson (Chair), John Ginnivan, and Carl Walters. We are also grateful to Christie Woodhouse who provided research assistance with this case study.

Thanks to Estelle Zinsstag, Ivo Aertsen, and the other members of the editorial team at *The International Journal of Restorative Justice*, and Mike McGrath of the *National Civic Review* for their support for interviews with innovators such as Lauren Abramson, Fania Davis, and Kay Pranis, who appear in this book.

Our work has been informed by valuable discussions with colleagues including Emilia Aiello, Edana Beauvais, Benjamin Bradlow, Harry Boyte, Archon Fung, Marshall Ganz, Peter Levine, Meira Levinson, Carmen Sirianni, and Marie Ström all of whom participated in the "Citizen Agency in Democracy Renewal" Workshop we convened at the Ash Center of Democratic Governance and Innovation at Harvard University in September 2019.

For their helpful feedback we would also like to thank discussants and participants at the European Consortium for Political Research (ECPR) General Conference in Montreal in August 2015, the ECPR Joint Sessions in Nicosia in April 2018, the Deliberative Democracy and Global Governance seminar at the University of Canberra in July 2018, and the AusPSA Political Organisations and Participation (POP) Workshop held at ANU in November 2019.

We are also grateful to the several reviewers who offered many useful suggestions that have strengthened our arguments.

For his belief and support in our book project we thank Dominic Byatt, our editor at Oxford University Press, along with Jade Dixon for her support in the final stages of the book's production.

Our ideas and arguments have been sharpened by many conversations and insights from colleagues and friends. We are especially grateful to: John Boswell, Rikki Dean, Denis Ginnivan, Sango Mahanty, John McKnight, Sarah Thomson, Richard Reid, and Christie Woodhouse.

We are extremely grateful to Ann Milligan for reading our work so closely and providing excellent feedback and editing.

For our parents and families we thank you all.

And finally, our gratitude also goes to all the citizens who lead and participate in collective problem-solving work. Your efforts have inspired this book, and we hope will continue to create paths for people to make meaningful contributions to daunting problems.

# Contents

1. Citizen Action in Uncertain Times: Contextualizing Citizens' Governance Spaces  1

2. Citizens' Governance Spaces: Characteristics of Citizen-led Problem Solving  25

3. Citizens' Motivations and Governance Practices  51

4. Doing, Thinking, and Sharing: Knowledge Contributions of Citizens' Governance Spaces  81

5. Citizen Agency and Autonomy in Shared Governance  115

6. Risks and Opportunities of Citizens' Governance Spaces: Insights for Democratic Theory and Practice  141

*Appendix: List of Empirical Cases*  173
*References*  175
*Index*  197

# Chapter 1
# Citizen Action in Uncertain Times: Contextualizing Citizens' Governance Spaces

## Introduction

In the early 2000s a group of Baltimore residents began meeting to discuss how their newly established Community Conferencing Center would use restorative justice practices. They wanted to work with the local community by offering alternative ways to defuse interpersonal strife, ensure neighborhood safety, and reduce future harm (Abramson and Beck 2010). Ten years later, across the Atlantic, a group of 150 citizens in north-east Catalonia was putting together plans to create Som Energia—a community cooperative to produce affordable renewable energy for households in their region (Riutort Isern 2015). Around the same time, in Port Kembla, an industrial seaside town south of Sydney, Australia, a group of citizens was setting up a community enterprise, Tender Funerals, to offer low-income people an opportunity to access affordable and personalized funeral services (Wallworth 2013).

From the outside these citizen-led initiatives might appear to be modern-day examples of the kind of community organizing or charity work that common-purpose citizens' groups have done throughout the ages. Yet when one takes a closer look at how these initiatives emerge and what they do, what comes into view is a particular mode of citizen engagement that deserves fuller attention by anyone interested in understanding contemporary democratic practices. In this book we label these kinds of grassroots efforts *citizens' governance spaces*—an umbrella term that captures practically focused citizen-led initiatives working on a collective problem.

In these initiatives, citizens define the problem and rethink it; develop and experiment with feasible solutions; generate knowledge and networks; and evaluate and refine their approaches.[1] While many begin as small-scale initiatives, they can grow into high-impact policy interventions. For example, the Baltimore Community Conferencing Center has diverted felony and misdemeanor cases from the juvenile courts, with judges inquiring into how they can adopt more restorative justice programs (Dzur 2013). Som Energia has defied Spain's oligopolist energy sector by producing, developing, and supplying small-scale affordable electricity from renewable sources (Pellicer-Sifres et al. 2018), now to over 84,000 members nationwide.[2] Tender Funerals has disrupted Australia's profit-driven funeral industry by offering individualized funeral services at affordable prices (Chenery and Rousset 2022). In 2020 it expanded into a nationwide organization that works with communities around Australia to help them establish a Tender Funerals franchise in their local area (TF 2023a).

Citizens worldwide have a rich history of self-organizing to solve collective problems, from well before the emergence of the welfare state.[3] Yet since the early 2000s there has been an increase in citizens' governance spaces across diverse sectors and countries, responding to a mix of economic, technical, political, and social forces.[4] Depending on the context, citizens have felt driven to self-organize to fill governance voids left by inadequate or declining public services; for example, brought about by the marketization of welfare systems, economic crises, and socio-demographic pressures (Soares da Silva et al. 2018). Citizens have also been motivated to find innovative or alternative solutions to complex problems that governments and markets are failing to address adequately, such as accessible welfare services, inequality, substance use, food insecurity, environmental protection, climate change, and homelessness (e.g., Brandsen et al. 2016a; Campbell et al. 2011; Figueroa and Alkon 2017; Mathie and Gaventa 2015; Simon et al. 2020; Soares da Silva et al. 2018). When the global COVID-19 pandemic took hold in 2020, the media raised the public profile of local self-organizing groups providing food and care for those in need (e.g., de Freytas-Tamura 2021; Tolentino 2020).

---

[1] Consistent with other scholars of democratic governance, such as Fung (2006, p. 74), we use the term "citizen" to mean not only "individuals who possess the legal status of formal citizenship but rather individuals who possess the political standing to exercise voice or give consent over public decisions that oblige or affect them." Relatedly, we strive to use those descriptive terms favored by people working in the spaces we are studying. We thus employ words such as "drug user," and "marginalized," and "homeless," even while acknowledging here that these have been historically stigmatizing labels.

[2] Membership figures taken from https://www.somenergia.coop/ retrieved May 20, 2024.

[3] For a historical overview of citizen-led initiatives in western liberal democracies, see de Swaan (1988) and Healey (2015a).

[4] Studies show that the contemporary drivers for citizens' governance spaces are multiple and context-specific (for good overviews, see Borzaga et al. 2016a; Edelenbos et al. (2021b); Mathie and Gaventa (2015); Soares da Silva et al. (2018); Wagenaar and Healey (2015)).

Separately, citizen-led problem solving has been actively promoted and explicitly championed by government directives that call on communities to take responsibility and use their own initiative and ingenuity to address collective problems (e.g., Denters 2016; Taylor 2018). These spaces are also celebrated by global institutions because of their capacity to foster bottom-up forms of social entrepreneurship and innovation (e.g., OECD/EU 2017; World Bank 2016). As governments around the world deal with more frequent and more severe disasters such as wildfires, floods, and cyclones, the vital roles of citizen-led efforts in emergency response and disaster recovery are being increasingly recognized (Cretney 2018; McLennan 2020). In these uncertain times, it seems we have much to learn from the nimble, innovative, participatory, and practical initiatives that citizens are creating and leading.

This book explores why citizens self-organize and lead collective problem-solving efforts, what governance work they undertake, and how they do that work. Drawing on over 30 empirical cases from diverse policy domains and countries we examine what motivates people to initiate citizens' governance spaces, how they engage others in their practical activities, what knowledge and impact they generate, and how their efforts interact with relevant state and non-state actors. Our analysis finds that people are attracted to citizen spaces and are willing to devote time and energy under sometimes difficult conditions, in ways that they are not attracted to traditional political and civil society organizations. Citizens in these bottom-up initiatives are getting on with the practical business of addressing complex issues themselves, often in highly experimental and effective ways; and citizen-led initiatives often work congruently alongside the market and government. This contrasts both to the strategies used in protest and social movement activism to oppose, support, inform, and steer policymakers, and to those community organizing efforts and mutual aid groups that eschew connections with state agencies or private enterprises.

Our analysis of citizens' governance spaces illuminates a specific domain of civil society that has yet to be fully recognized and understood in debates on contemporary democracy.[5] This is not to say that scholars of democratic practice and theory have neglected civil society. Many have explored the roles and diversity of social movements in resistance, mobilization, and solidarity (for example, Berberoglu 2019; della Porta and Diani 2015). Others have studied the roles (and demise) of membership-based associations in

---

[5] Much of the existing knowledge on citizens' governance spaces has been generated by the fields of public governance and organizational studies, and largely overlooked by scholars of contemporary democratic practice and renewal. Two notable exceptions here are Hendrik Wagenaar (2019) and Frank Hendriks (2019).

informing, educating, and building deliberative and civic capacity (Skocpol 2003; Warren 2001), or as conduits for advocacy and representation (Halpin 2006). These studies on the democratic contributions of civil society have had far less to say about the arenas of civic action where citizens themselves are driving forward collective problem-solving efforts in practical ways to address specific public issues.

The findings from our analysis hold important insights for current understanding of how citizens can engage in contemporary governance and democratic systems. We show that citizens' governance spaces engender a distinct form of citizen engagement that is not adequately captured by conventional categories and activities of civil society, such as community organizing, social movements, mutual aid, and co-production. We use examples and empirical material from diverse regions and policy domains to show how people involved in citizens' governance spaces often interconnect their governance work with public and non-public actors, drawing resources and authority on the one hand, and modeling innovation and change on the other. We argue that while these spaces offer citizens a form of participation that can foster agency and autonomy, there are some democratic risks to consider, particularly with respect to inclusion, equality, and effective governance.

In the remainder of this chapter we elaborate further on the concept of citizens' governance spaces, making a case for its analytic and practical value. We then consider the political context in which these spaces are emerging and operating today, focusing on three broad trends: decentered governance, rising distrust, and growing division. We conclude by laying out our methodological approach and normative considerations, and outlining the arguments of the five chapters that follow.

## Citizens' Governance Spaces

In this book we develop and apply the concept of citizens' governance spaces to better capture the novel governance work being undertaken in a range of "spaces."[6] The Baltimore Community Conferencing Center, the Catalonian renewable energy cooperative Som Energia, and the Australian community initiative Tender Funerals are just three examples. From the outset we acknowledge that our new term *citizens' governance spaces* is somewhat ungainly; indeed, throughout the book we use the synonyms *citizen-led*

---

[6] As we describe more fully in the next section, "governance" refers to the complex and networked processes through which state, private, and non-state actors develop and deliver public goods and services (see Jessop 2020).

*spaces, citizen spaces, citizen-led governance,* and *citizen governance* as shorthand. But we think this new language is needed to avoid mis-categorizing actions and actors, and ignoring social, economic, and political possibilities, and trivializing their effects. In practice, most citizens' governance spaces are not understood or labeled as sites of democratic action, or even politics. Some may self-label as a "movement," "community organization," "cooperative," "civic enterprise," or as a "self-help" or "mutual aid" group, creating some conceptual confusion. Not all organizations that carry such labels engage in the kind of citizen-led governance work that we focus on in this book. We use the term citizens' governance spaces to delineate those that do.

As the examples outlined thus far illustrate, citizens' governance spaces can come in many shapes and sizes. The "space" might be a project, a civic enterprise, an organization, or a physical or virtual space such as a community garden, a café, or a Facebook page.[7] Some are platforms of outreach, where the citizens driving the initiative seek to engage marginalized publics by providing vital goods, services, or processes (for example, washing, justice, food, or care), or by offering opportunities for support and connection. These can also be spaces in a figurative sense; they can provide an alternative arena in a given policy domain by offering novel, even disruptive, framings and solutions to public problems. Spaces can also vary considerably in terms of their informality and size; some are formal citizen-led partnerships involving governments or corporate actors; others are loose and local arrangements. Citizen spaces operate outside and often at some distance from formal institutions of the state, market, and civil society; they engage people in problem solving in ways that are fun and attractive, offering them practical opportunities to contribute to public work with impact.

In recent surveys on contemporary modes of political participation, the concept we label here as citizens' governance spaces tends to be subsumed under expressive public actions (e.g., Theocharis and Van Deth 2018), or viewed as part of "pre-political" or "latent" political participation (e.g., Amnå and Ekman 2014). In the diverse scholarship on third sector organizations, public policy, development, planning, and volunteering, citizen-led initiatives sail under many flags.[8] Problematically, most common labels—such

---

[7] Central to the concept is a spatial metaphor carrying different meanings. While it is often the *work* rather than the *setting* that links actors in democracy, spatial metaphors find wide appeal in democratic practice and theory; for example, they are used to distinguish between "invited" and "popular" spaces (Cornwall 2004) and "empowered" and "public" spaces (Dryzek 2010). The concept of space also finds wide appeal in the disciplines of geography and development studies, particularly in research centered on how citizens actually engage and participate in local politics (e.g., Gaventa 2006; Jupp 2008).

[8] Some of these include: community-based initiatives (Edelenbos et al. 2021b; Visscher et al. 2023), citizen-led initiatives (Bherer et al. 2024; Igalla et al. 2019); civic enterprises (Wagenaar and Healey 2015), social enterprises (Laville et al. 2015), social innovation (Brandsen et al. 2016a; Moulaert et al. 2013),

as "social innovation," "social enterprise," and even "co-production"—are too broad to differentiate between governance efforts that citizens lead and governance efforts that state or market actors lead.

The characteristics underscored by the term "community-based initiative" (Edelenbos et al. 2021b; Igalla et al. 2021) come close to the concept of citizens' governance spaces. However, we prefer to avoid the term "community" because frequently citizens leading collective problem-solving efforts are contesting the very boundaries and constructions of "the community." Moreover, we prefer the term "governance" to draw attention to the significance and public meanings of the collective problem solving that citizens are engaged in. They are not only initiating. They are also doing: reframing; generating knowledge; and solving problems.

Citizens' governance spaces are located in what political theorists label "civil society"—a domain of society that is organized through "purpose built, normatively justified associations" (Warren 2011, p. 378). When discussing components of civil society, scholars of democracy regularly rely on broad concepts such as "the public sphere," "social movements," or "interest groups." These umbrella concepts might be useful for political theorizing, but they do not do justice to the heterogeneity of modern associational life (Evers and von Essen 2019; Jessop 2020).[9] Moreover, these broad categories cannot accommodate the changing nature of how people are choosing to engage in community groups and civic associations. Worldwide we see a rise in more informal and sporadic modes of participation and volunteering, while membership and engagement via formal and professionally administered civic organizations are in decline (Aiken and Taylor 2019).

Current understandings in democratic theory of informal citizen-led action fall short of capturing how contemporary citizens are leading and doing *governance* work. For example, Henrik Bang and Eva Sørensen (1999) identified that many citizens engage in "everyday making" where they participate in small "p" politics of day-to-day life when they can, and how they can. In his writing on "public work," Harry Boyte (2004) points out the often overlooked labor of citizens engaged in grassroots action aimed at social problem solving outside conventional community organizing, social

---

citizen-led innovation (Mathie and Gaventa 2015); community self-organization (Denters 2016; Edelenbos et al. 2018), grassroots organizations (Mitlin 2008), cooperatives (Borzaga et al. 2016a; 2016b), community co-production (Bovaird and Loeffler 2012), mutual aid or self-help groups (Gitterman and Shulman 2005; Spade 2020b) and prefigurative movements (Beckwith et al. 2016).

[9] One notable exception here is the work of Nancy Fraser (1993), who draws attention to the implied homogeneity in the term "public sphere" by pointing out the power differentials between different publics. She argues that modern democratic societies contain multiple publics "that are differentially empowered or segmented ... some are involuntarily enclaved and subordinated to others" (p. 93).

movement mobilizing, or political campaigns. While useful, concepts like "everyday making" and "public work" can inadvertently reproduce conceptual divides between government work and citizen work, insiders and outsiders, professionals and lay people. What we find in our studies of citizens' governance spaces is that these divides largely dissolve in practice, as it becomes evident what self-organizing citizens can know and do.

The kind of grassroots problem solving that we observe in citizens' governance spaces is also not fully appreciated in current debates on public participation and democratic renewal. For example, these spaces do not feature in the ideas and designs of participatory and deliberative governance where much of the emphasis is on state-led structured forums for citizen engagement (e.g., Nabatchi et al. 2012; OECD 2020; Warren 2009; World Bank 2018). Typically, citizens in these structured spaces of participation are not independently leading and driving the problem-solving effort. This is also the case in Fung and Wright's (2003) important research on "empowered participatory governance" (EPG) which is state-led governance that involves citizen engagement.[10] In contrast, people involved in citizens' governance spaces are self-organizing and leading collective problem-solving activities rather than being asked by governments, corporations or non-government organizations (NGOs) to provide advice or help make decisions. Rather than serving in supplementary roles to conventional decision-makers, citizens are generating new knowledge about the core problems that are targets of formal action and regulation.

The bottom-up efforts of people active in citizens' governance spaces are also different from so-called "citizen-led democratic innovations" where social movements and activists attempt to improve or embed opportunities for citizen participation within and outside institutions (Bua and Bussu 2020; 2023; della Porta and Felicetti 2019). The main agenda of citizens in governance spaces is not democratic or institutional reform; rather it is focused on practical action on a particular public problem. Citizen spaces are, indeed, typically inclusive, often employing informal participatory methods or community outreach approaches, but participation in them is problem-solving oriented and not an end in itself.

We contend that the concept of citizens' governance spaces is useful for scholars because existing categories potentially overlook and mis-categorize

---

[10] In the case examples of EPG considered by Fung and Wright (2003), the state typically creates the governance program, with agencies and officials coordinating participatory activities. In a community policing initiative, for example, police departments invite citizens to come and assist them. Citizens' governance spaces may have similar governance objectives, but they are led and driven by citizens. A state agency may eventually become involved with a citizen space through funding or collaborative work, but the citizens are self-organizing and leading in the first instance.

the agency of citizens leading these spaces, the diverse actors they engage, and the innovative approaches they develop. For example, if restorative justice initiatives are categorized as a social movement, then we risk seeing them all as local franchises of a multi-national organization, thus overlooking the innovative procedural and substantive work that citizens are leading in criminal justice. Moreover, if scholars misread citizen spaces in terms of protest, activism, community organizing, mutual aid, or co-production, then we risk ignoring their broader social, economic, and political possibilities. For example, some, like the Baltimore Community Conferencing Center, demonstrate that it is possible to challenge and disrupt the status quo policy approaches while also collaborating with the state; others, like Som Energia, show that citizens can work productively with the private sector, either with or without the state. Relatedly, existing categories of social action, such as protest and community organizing, tend to overlook the local and global reach and impact achieved by citizen-led spaces through modeling practices, sharing knowledge, and communicating experiences via practitioner networks.

Our concept citizens' governance space has value outside academia as well. It provides a label, and indeed a set of ideas, to help those involved in the work of citizen-led governance to become more attuned to what it is that they are doing. While practitioners might share tropes or stories about "doing common stuff," "going back to basics," or "restoring" some pre-modern social norms, those narratives do not adequately describe what they are doing, particularly with respect to their innovative procedural and substantive governance work. For those in government, in more traditional voluntary organizations, or in private sector firms, knowing more about citizen spaces will help foster useful connections and better understanding about factors that are motivating active citizens.

We describe the key characteristics of citizen spaces more fully in Chapter 2. We turn now to discuss the broader governance and democratic context within which citizen spaces emerge and operate. This context provides general insights into what motivates citizens to participate in governance spaces and what kinds of collective problem-solving work they are undertaking.

## A Dynamic Governance and Democratic Context

Citizens' governance spaces today operate within dynamic systems of governance and democracy.[11] There is much to say here. For our purposes we

---

[11] This dynamism varies between countries (see Duffy et al. 2023a).

focus on three significant trends shaping how contemporary citizens participate in modern politics: the decentering of governance; rising distrust in institutions; and increasing division.

## Decentered governance

Contemporary public problems are increasingly governed by multiple state and non-state actors via service agreements, cross-sectoral networks and knowledge exchanges, collaborative projects, or public–private partnerships (Jessop 2020). Consequently, governance is decentered across a host of state and non-state actors that are connected and interdependent around knowledge, expertise, resources, capacity, and public legitimacy. As Mark Bevir puts it:

> contemporary government increasingly involves private- and voluntary-sector organizations working alongside public ones. Complex packages of organizations deliver most public services today. The resulting fragmentation means that the state increasingly depends on other organizations to implement its policies and secure its intentions. Further, the state has swapped direct for indirect controls. Central departments are no longer invariably the fulcrum of policy networks. The state sometimes may set limits to network actions, but it has increased its dependence on other actors. State power is dispersed among spatially and functionally distinct networks. (2013, p. 9)

The interdependence of diverse state and non-state actors in governance arrangements disrupts conventional democratic norms, particularly regarding legitimate authorization, accountability, and representation (Hendriks 2009; Papadopoulos 2016).

Important drivers of decentering in modern governance have been the ideas and practices of neoliberalism, the application of market-based principles to public sector organizations, and services purportedly to improve efficiencies and quality. In many countries neoliberalism has had profound effects on how collective problems are addressed, both in the state and in civil society. Specifically, neoliberal reforms have led to extensive market-based reforms of the public sector, including initiatives to make public agencies more business-like and competitive, and outsourcing services to the private or NGO sector. For civil society, neoliberalism has resulted in the state "rolling back" its services, and it has also encouraged a "rolling out" of certain civil society groups to fill in service gaps (Peck and Tickell 2002). The neoliberal context of the modern public sector has resulted in significant changes to the nature of civil society, particularly in terms of the groups and associations that get funded and supported, what they do, and how they relate to their member-base and other civil society groups (Taylor 2018). The market context of public governance has also affected state–society relations, with greater access, resources, and influence going to larger, professionalized groups that can meet all the administrative and accountability requirements demanded by public agencies (Suárez 2011).

Alongside the marketization of public services and its effect in civil society, there has been a call for citizens and communities to be more active in their own governance. For example, in the UK under the discourse of Big Society there has been a push for "active citizenship" and "self-governance" calling on citizens to "step up" and take their own initiative (Taylor 2018); in the Netherlands governments have promoted the concept of "do-democracy" encouraging citizens to not just talk but to be innovative and take action to solve problems (Dekker 2019; Verhoeven and Tonkens 2013). These policy discourses on citizens taking responsibility to "do more for themselves and their communities" often coincide with such citizens facing reduced services or hardships—due to austerity measures and cost of living pressures, for example. Critics worry that these discourses mask attempts by states to off-load the work of government onto citizens.[12]

## Rising distrust in state and civil society institutions

The combined effect of decentered governing and the marketization of public services has left many citizens feeling locked out of policy processes and decision-making (OECD 2022). Contemporary governance unsettles conventions and procedures about what constitutes legitimate democratic governance, because it is not always clear who is doing what, and how they are to be held to account (Hendriks 2009; Papadopoulos, 2016). This extends well beyond matters of procedure and accountability. Recent surveys around the globe reveal that many citizens are distrustful of, and disappointed in, the capacity and effectiveness of modern governments to solve and address collective problems—especially complex issues such as poverty, inequality, crime, climate change, and substance use (OECD 2022). Citizens are also skeptical about the responsiveness of their governments to act on citizen input; and they lack confidence in their public agencies to adopt innovative ideas (OECD 2022).

---

[12] To be clear, our arguments about citizens' governance spaces are not attached to these particular policy discourses about active citizenship and localized self-governance. Instead, our insights are informed by diverse empirical cases of citizens driving problem solving themselves.

Other, broader dynamics of political distrust deserve consideration here as well. Social scientists since the 1970s have drawn attention to what some see as a loosening of attachment to democracy. Drawing on a term used by comparative political scientists to describe the process of "democratic consolidation," in which social and institutional factors coalesce to help countries transition to democracy, they have warned of increasing "deconsolidation" (Foa and Mounk 2016). One factor at the root of their concern is trust in political institutions like legislatures, courts, and executives, which has significantly declined in established democracies. Country by country, survey data corresponding to trust issues reveal a decline from the mid-1960s and early 1970s onward (Dalton 2005). Recent surveys reveal worryingly low levels of citizen trust, particularly in elected representatives, political parties, and legislatures (e.g., Duffy et al. 2023b; OECD 2022).[13] Explanations for global trends in diminishing trust in government are multiple. Two of the most prominent explanations are economic factors—such as the shifts in a globalized labor market, which made many workers less secure in their employment—and modernization factors—such as higher living standards and increased education, which have encouraged citizens to be less deferential and more willing to challenge political elites and state authorities (Dalton 2005).

Another condition that worries social scientists is a decreasing engagement in elections and parties. Citizen participation at all levels—from local to national elections—is low in established democracies, and party identification has dramatically loosened over time. From 1980 to 2000, scholars note, political parties in Europe lost an average of 35% of their members. Britain's Labour Party, for example, had more than a million members in the 1950s; by the 2000s it was down to 200,000 (Keane 2009, p. 754). Dealignment from parties continues in many countries as contemporary citizens are increasingly frustrated with partisanship, and cynical about "politicians and … the political process as an efficient means to mediate between different values" (van der Steen et al. 2011, p. 320). Politicians are seen as being out of touch with citizens' needs, which are not adequately heard and represented (Allen 2018; Boswell et al. 2019).

---

[13] Low levels of citizen trust in democratic institutions is borne out by both country specific and cross-country surveys (see Cameron 2020; Citrin and Stoker 2018; Stoker et al. 2018; Valgarðsson et al. 2021; Whiteley et al. 2016). The Organisation for Economic Co-operation and Development's (OECD) inaugural Trust Survey (conducted in 2021 across 22 OECD countries) found that citizen trust is especially low in political parties and in representative legislative institutions, such as parliaments and congresses (OECD 2022). According to the World Values Survey, public confidence in the legislature has declined steadily in the UK, the US, and Australia since the early 1980s, although it has remained steady in Canada and even improved in Germany since 2006 (see Duffy et al. 2023b, p. 13).

Citizens, increasingly frustrated over lack of action, have lost trust in the capability and sincerity of politicians and institutions to tackle local and global problems. A recent comparative study found that a majority of citizens in France, the US, and the UK believe that elected officials are out of touch with ordinary citizens and "do not care what ordinary people think" (Pew 2021, p. 5). The study found that "roughly two-thirds of adults in France and the US, as well as about half in the United Kingdom, believe their political system needs major changes or needs to be completely reformed" (Pew 2021, p. 4). It is no surprise that electorates are less willing to stick with establishment candidates and are more favorable to single-issue movements, populist candidates, and anti-system parties in opposition to the status quo.

Recent survey research shows increasing cynicism not just about political officials but about the value of democracy as a political system. Generational differences are concerning to some scholars, who point to age gaps in attitudes toward democracy in a host of countries. In the UK, recent survey data find that Gen X, Millennials, and Gen Z are less likely to have confidence in parliament and government than pre-war and baby boomer generations (Duffy et al. 2023b).[14] Comparative research suggests this is a widespread phenomenon. Surveys across Western Europe and North America find that young people are less likely than previous generations to get involved in conventional forms of political participation as well as nonconventional political action such as protest, activism and social movement mobilization (Foa and Mounk 2016, p. 11). In the US, for example, 72% of people born before World War II select 10 (the highest value) when asked "On a scale of 1 to 10, how essential is it for you to live in a democracy?" In the Netherlands, 55% of that cohort do the same. People born since 1980 think differently: only around 30% of Dutch and American millennials choose 10 (Foa and Mounk 2016).

Members of the public are also increasingly distrustful of civil society organizations (CSOs), particularly large centralized non-profit institutions (such as charities, religious organizations, and high-wealth philanthropy) that often operate at national rather than local level. In comparison to government and market-based organizations, CSOs have enjoyed relatively high levels of public trust. However, contemporary views are changing as people become concerned about the increasing professionalization of CSOs, and their impact and accountability. As studies have shown, many professionalized associations lack any meaningful engagement or connection to their members (Skocpol 2003).[15] In both the Global North and South charities and

---

[14] Gen X typically refers to people born between 1965 and 1980; Millennials are people born between 1981 and 1996; Gen Z are people born between 1997 and the mid-2000s.

[15] We are reporting here on general trends in membership-based groups in civil society. We acknowledge that some highly professionalized CSOs actively engage members (e.g., Heylen et al. 2020).

not-for-profits are increasingly struggling to attract volunteers (e.g., Grimm and Dietz 2018; UNV 2021). Recent surveys in the US find that public trust in the non-profit sector is in decline.[16] In 2023 a survey of over 3,000 Americans concluded that non-profits face the "largest trust decline of any American institution in 2023" (Independent Sector 2023, p. 13). People were especially distrustful of high net-worth philanthropy. Large, centralized organizations were the least trusted (Independent Sector 2023, p. 7). Conversely, public trust was highest for civil society organizations that are "small and locally operated." The public "… feel that as an organization grows so too does its internal bureaucracy—and the danger of misappropriated funds or ulterior motives from staff members increases …. They also see small, local non-profits as more agile, understanding of and responsive to the communities they serve" (Independent Sector 2023, p. 7).

## Increasing division

Contemporary democracies are also plagued by deep polarization and division. In some countries polarization has reached extreme levels, as in the US, where divisions are ideological and partisan.[17] According to Finkel et al., the two major parties in the US:

> … have sorted along racial, religious, educational, and geographic lines. Although far from absolute, such alignment of ideological identities and demography transforms political orientation into a mega-identity that renders opposing partisans different from, even incomprehensible to, one another. (2020, p. 534)

In contemporary America people deeply dislike and distrust the views of those who support the other major party (Iyengar et al. 2019). Commentators have labeled this kind of deep partisanship a form of "political sectarianism" where opposing partisans view the other as not just different but alien. Both groups are strongly opposed to each other, and divided on almost every policy issue, regardless of the objective facts. Research shows that this kind of "fear and loathing across party lines" is also prevalent in Europe (Reiljan 2020).

The influence of this "partisan affect" extends into many areas of contemporary politics: it compromises the norms and standards applied to elected

---

[16] Since 2020, the Independent Sector has commissioned annual surveys (in partnership with Edelman Data and Intelligence) on trust in (American) civil society, see https://independentsector.org/resource/trust-in-civil-society/

[17] Scholars distinguish between ideological and affective polarization, with the latter relating to the deep animosity felt between people that support the opposing political parties (see Iyengar et al. 2019).

representatives, it shapes if and how they are held to account, and it fuels distrust in electoral procedures and results, all of which threaten the legitimacy and stability of representative systems of democracy (Iyengar et al. 2019). More broadly, comparative research has found that when democratic systems are under threat and stressed, citizens fracture along partisan lines over core citizenship values such as the rule of law, tolerance, forbearance (mutual tolerance), vigilance, and being politically informed (Goodman 2022). In uncertain times, such as those we are currently experiencing, individuals are responding "not as citizens but as partisans, acting to protect what's best for 'their side' even if it means sacrificing democracy in the process" (Goodman 2022, p. 183). The nature of modern political communication, particularly on social media, can fuel divisions on contested issues and inhibit listening across differences (Hendriks et al. 2019; Mansbridge and Latura 2016). It is not just that social media funnels like-minded people into discrete echo chambers (Sunstein 2018); research has also found that even when people are exposed to opposing views social media tends to further exacerbate polarization (Bail et al. 2018).

## Citizens' Governance Spaces and Democracy: Neither Dupes nor Heroes

Where do citizens' governance spaces fit into these trends in modern politics? Are they products of these trends, or do they represent avenues out of the democratic malaise in which we now find ourselves? In responding to such questions scholars to date have formed two broad intellectual camps. Both camps' arguments have some merit, but a more nuanced perspective on the democratic implications of citizens' governance spaces is needed.

The more critical camp sees citizen spaces as democratic dupes. Rightly pointing to the recent history of government austerity, shrinking social welfare budgets, increasing public–private partnerships to deliver public services, and the dominance of private-sector norms of efficiency and entrepreneurialism, some scholars worry that the rise of citizen governance is a mark of declining social commitments to marginalized populations. The arguments in this camp run as follows: the macro-level neoliberal environment underpinning citizen-led governance efforts is symptomatic of how states and markets off-load collective responsibilities (Eliasoph 2013; Lee et al. 2015). People involved in citizen-led governance are dupes of a neoliberal political rationality that asks the public to do more for itself and for less (McQuarrie 2013). Far from a democratic renewal, citizen spaces herald the emergence of do-it-yourself (DIY) democracy where the devil takes the hindmost. Under-resourced and unregulated bottom-up efforts to deliver public services, such as welfare, risk reinforcing inequalities and increasing competition between groups in civil society (Martinelli 2013). Worse still, citizen spaces' practical problem solving does nothing to build social solidarity, teach effective protest strategies and nurture activists who might press for universal citizen rights to a decent standard of living, against a state increasingly beholden to powerful economic interests (Spade 2020a; 2020b). A citizen space that builds new houses for the unsheltered, for example, may very well be helping people at a rate that cannot keep up with the real estate speculators and hedge funds foreclosing and tearing old houses down (Eliasoph 2013).

In the other camp, people active in citizens' governance spaces are celebrated as democratic heroes. Advocates of this position draw on scholars from Tocqueville (2004) through to Putnam (2000) and their followers who emphasize the social capital formation made possible by citizen-led initiatives. In this framing, citizen spaces are a testament to the capacity of communities to self-organize and solve collective problems outside the formal political process (Boyte 2004; Ostrom 1990). Such activity enhances civic life, representational capacity, legitimacy, and de-polarization (de Souza Briggs 2008; Sirianni and Friedland 2001; Warren 2001). Local-level social action develops skills of collaboration and dialogue, norms of compromise, and trust. By working together in civil associations, citizens grow to recognize common interests and act on them, even if they are separated by other aspects of their lives, like religion or occupation. In this camp, citizen spaces are viewed as quite distinct from the state. It is assumed that because citizens are the ones schooled in constructive participation in their communities, they prefer to tackle collective problem solving alone without support and resources from the state.

In this book we contend that, although both interpretations have merit, they significantly misidentify the motivations, challenges, available resources, and distinct democratic work of citizens in these spaces of bottom-up governance. In the following chapters we show how neither narrative is suitable for explaining the emergence of citizen governance in the last generation. While austerity has been a factor, citizen spaces are better seen as active responses to shrinking resources, and not as dupes of state off-loading. As we will see, the norms followed by many are the opposite of neoliberal political rationality, and they encourage solidarity rather than individuation. At the same time, the cases we will describe do not show that people involved in citizen-led spaces are social-capital heroes: many recognize the need to connect with the state and with the private sector, to secure resources but also to shift policy and funding priorities, and to alter the way the state and market actors think about public problems. And citizen spaces frequently dissent from and chafe against community norms; breaking, not reinforcing, common ties of local ownership; challenging divisions between same and other; rejecting conventional labels. Neither democratic dupes nor heroes, participants are active, organized citizens focused on solving a particular set of collective problems. The opportunities and risks a specific citizen space might present depend on whether it goes about problem solving in inclusive, reflective, meaningful ways, or whether its work raises barriers, represses critique, and thwarts creative energies.

## Building on a Fertile Foundation

A central goal of this book is to offer a fine-grained and empirically informed interpretation of the implications of citizens' governance spaces for contemporary democratic systems. We examine *why* citizens are motivated to participate in these spaces of collective problem solving, and *what* governance work they are doing and *how*, and then we consider the implications—in terms of both potential benefits and potential risks—for democracy. A closer look into these spaces of citizens' governance, we contend, offers important lessons for projects that aim to deepen the quality and reach of citizen participation in modern systems of democracy. Knowing more about citizen spaces should open doors through which scholars, practitioners, and citizens may enter.

As a starting point, our analysis is informed by tranches of empirical and theoretical studies emerging from diverse fields, such as community development, planning, geography, social innovation, and public governance. One tranche of relevant research consists of early studies on citizen participation in development contexts, which drew attention to how citizens themselves can lead and organize participation and problem solving on their own terms (e.g., Cornwall 2004; Gaventa 2006; Mitlin 2008). Another tranche of relevant research can be found under the broad topics "social innovation" and "social economy," which explore the type of policy experimentation driven by non-state actors (Moulaert et al. 2013; Parés et al. 2017). Closely related is the diverse literature on "civic enterprises" and "social enterprises," particularly scholarship on their associative and informal qualities (Laville et al. 2015; Pestoff and Hulgård 2016), their innovative and experimental problem solving (Mathie and Gaventa 2015; Wagenaar 2019; Wagenaar and van der Heijden 2015), and their capacity to empower highly marginalized citizens (Bakker et al. 2012; Borzaga et al. 2016a; 2016b; Campbell et al. 2011).

We also draw on empirical studies from the field of public governance that considers citizen-led collective problem solving under various labels (see note 8). Research on community trusts, local planning, and "do-democracy," makes another important contribution to this field (Dekker 2019; Healey 2015a; Wagenaar and van der Heijden 2015).

From this fertile starting point we then inject insights from 31 empirical case studies that stem from countries in the Global North and South covering a range of policy domains—such as health, energy, substance recovery, disaster response, food insecurity, homelessness, elder care, funeral services, and technology infrastructure (for full list, see the Appendix). Although citizens' governance spaces are ubiquitous, finding cases for research purposes is not straightforward because in practice many are informal, localized and lack a strong public profile. To help identify possible cases we drew ideas from our local, national and international networks, social and mass media, practitioners, colleagues, and students. A handful of our cases have come from empirical studies conducted within a particular field of practice, for example, social work, community development, or substance recovery. Our guiding principle for case selection was that the initiative was led and driven by citizens undertaking practical governance work to address a collective issue. We also sought to ensure that our cases were diverse in terms of emergent contexts, public problems, and countries.

Our analysis of the 31 cases centers on the *citizens* in these spaces—an important point of contrast to existing studies. We ask: what motivates citizens to instigate and participate in these problem-solving efforts? What challenges do they face? And what resources do they use? We also examine how and when citizen spaces generate and diffuse knowledge, influence policy, and partner with state, market, and civil society actors. To answer these questions we draw on a mix of primary and secondary sources, including qualitative interviews with citizens and relevant policy makers; media and secondary accounts; policy reports; and digital materials.

The book brings these grounded empirical perspectives into dialogue with pressing debates in democratic theory and the practical project of deepening the quality and reach of citizen participation in modern systems of democracy. Our goal here is to render more visible an arena of civil society that is not well understood or appreciated in contemporary debates on democratic practice. Our analysis draws attention to the goals, motivations, organization, knowledge, and partnerships that citizens develop as they engage in concrete activities to address complex societal problems. This kind of community driven problem-solving work is often denigrated as "amateur," "unprofessional," "unrepresentative," "discretionary," "local," and "unscalable." But we argue that the functional policy work undertaken in citizen spaces resets expectations for what can be done by citizens, and adjusts our understandings of crystalized divisions of labor in public governance between citizens, officials, and the market. While attentive to the potential benefits of citizen spaces, we also take care to note the risks identified in our own research and through the work of other scholars.

Our inquiry into citizen spaces aims to improve scholarly and practical understanding of citizen spaces by exploring their complex realities. We think knowing more about citizen spaces will shed light on the possibilities and limitations of citizen-led approaches to addressing complex social conditions for marginalized people or those who lack endowments of social or economic influence. Our broader argument is not that these largely hidden spaces of civil society can resolve all the dysfunctions that ail modern democracies, but rather that they present both democratic opportunities and risks. To this end it is important to acknowledge, early on, that not all citizens' governance spaces have the same normative weight.

## Normative Considerations: The Good, the Bad, and the Ugly

As we will see in the coming chapters, it is not uncommon for groups made up of marginalized citizens to push back against and evade norms, laws, and regulations that endanger or immiserate them. This can have vital democratic importance, since non-compliance can be a form of voice, and unsanctioned actions may serve as valuable policy experimentation (Gofen 2021).[18] Moreover, it is difficult to judge, at one point in time, factors that might facilitate democratic development in the future. Indeed, some of the groups we will discuss have dramatically different views of how to work on the same social problems. Still, the fact that some citizen-led initiatives can violate social norms and break laws, yet also have value for democracy, raises the question as to whether "anything goes" when it comes to citizens' governance spaces. Does the mere existence of a citizen space grant it democratic value, or is it the case that some types of spaces are more worthy of attention than others?

Scholars studying citizen-led governance typically avoid addressing this question directly, but their answer can be seen in the organizations and practices they choose to research. Those who have attempted explicit answers

---

[18] See also Bayat (2013) for discussion of non-compliant citizen *inaction* as a kind of voice and an important force for change.

offer two different approaches. One is to make distinctions on the basis of procedural values: that is, citizen spaces are "good" when they foster social change, generate debate over contemporary issues, provide alternatives that would otherwise be missing in conventional state or market approaches, and model practices that can be reproduced elsewhere (Brandsen et al. 2016b). They are "bad" when they fail to deliver on these objectives; when they are not genuinely separate from state or market actors; or when they have no efficacy or staying power.

Another approach is to stress substantive values, most commonly progressive, left-leaning values. Citizens' governance spaces are "good," in this framework, when they exemplify "the values of solidarity and equity, fostering research and actions that aims at building a more socially inclusive society" (Klein 2013, p. 9). A "good" citizen space appears as "an alternative to the neoliberalist societal vision. Favouring solidarity over individualism, integration over sectorization, and collaboration over division, it distinguishes itself through epistemological, ethical and strategic approaches" (Klein 2013, p. 11). These are organizations that seek to discover and act upon "progressive solutions for a whole range of problems of exclusion, deprivation, alienation, lack of wellbeing, and also to those actions that contribute positively to significant human progress and development" (Moulaert et al. 2013, p. 16). Citizen spaces are "bad" when they are "conservative forces that are eager to strengthen or preserve social exclusion situations" (Moulaert et al. 2013, p. 17).

The procedural approach allows in too many groups and practices, because concepts like "change," "debate," and "alternatives" lack concrete specificity. These concepts do not explain why most scholars prefer to focus upon groups which do not, for example, promote *reactionary* change, *demeaning* rhetoric, or *exclusionary* policy alternatives. Yet the more substantive approach is also problematic, ruling out groups motivated by conservative or neoliberal ideas. What counts as "division," "exclusion," "human progress," and "development" is often in dispute.

We favor a position between the procedural and substantive approaches, with an emphasis on the ways citizen governance practices can contribute to democratic competencies on the part of citizens and governing institutions. Drawing upon and expanding on Martinelli (2013, pp. 348–349), who develops such a list of goals and aims, we can say that good citizen governance practices:

- identify and respond to basic needs (including self-realization and recognition),

- increase democratic governance,
- empower people,
- improve governance processes,
- reproduce and spread to other locales,
- create and transmit knowledge.

Though most of the cases of citizen-led governance we discuss in this book share all these goals and aims, a citizen space does not have to produce all the previous objectives successfully to be considered "good."

"Bad" citizen governance practices thwart the previous goals and aims. In addition, they condone or promote:

- coercion or the threat of physical force,
- deception and non-transparency,
- highly exclusionary or dehumanizing rhetoric,
- proselytization rather than dialogue and debate.

At the root of "bad" citizen governance practices is a refusal to treat certain groups of citizens as deserving of respect, as being equal members of political society. Chambers and Kopstein, in defining "bad civil society," refer to this as the denial of reciprocity, which they see as "the recognition of other citizens, even those with whom one has deep disagreement, as moral agents deserving civility" (2001, p. 839). Citizen spaces that promote "hate, bigotry, racism, anti-Semitism, and aggressive xenophobia" are "bad" in this way (Chambers and Kopstein 2001, pp. 839–840).

While racist or anti-Semitic motivations and practices are obvious examples of what "bad" citizen spaces look like, there are many others that regularly operate using the practices noted previously. Crisis Pregnancy Centers (CPCs), for example, are citizen spaces set up, ostensibly, to serve the needs of pregnant women. In Indiana, the Wabash Valley Crisis Pregnancy Center owns a mobile medical van and parks it in publicly accessible places, like shopping center parking lots. Clinicians offer non-diagnostic ultrasound reports and medical information useful for supporting a healthy pregnancy. Yet CPCs routinely use deceptive tactics to recruit pregnant women as patients, "often advertising themselves as abortion providers" and sometimes "established next to abortion clinics and were designed to resemble them" (Griswold 2019). CPC staff frequently mislead clients about the hazards of abortion, claiming "increased risk of breast cancer, infertility, miscarriage, and/or the made-up 'post-abortion depression' that results in suicide" (Griswold 2019). Griswold's reporting suggests that the citizens organizing and staffing CPCs have no intention of hearing and acting upon women's interests as the clients themselves see them, but only support a particular view of the "right" approach to an unwanted pregnancy—namely childbirth and adoption. This, in our view, is a bad citizen space, not because it is anti-abortion but because it deliberately and not accidentally uses deception and proselytization in its work.

There is reason to deplore rather than merely ignore citizen governance practices such as these. The same can be said for some of the militia groups which patrol the southern border of the United States and routinely use the threat of force to further the public policy they favor; or groups that draw upon and nurture hatred of others, to attract members. They are "bad" citizens' governance spaces, just as state officials operating in the same ways would be bad state officials: not because of their conservative ideology, but because their version of that ideology condones violence and hatred. A healthy civil society ought to weed these out through media scrutiny, market incentives, and disincentives, and even through state regulation.

## Chapter Outline

We turn now to articulate the logic of the five chapters to follow. Chapter 2 further develops the concept of citizens' governance spaces. It draws on diverse empirical cases to identify and examine five defining characteristics of citizens' governance spaces. The chapter then situates the concept of citizens' governance space alongside related social science concepts, including social movements, community organizing, mutual aid, and co-production. We argue that while citizen spaces share common elements with these existing social science concepts, they engender a distinct form of citizen engagement focused on practical agency and governance work. The concept of citizens' governance space provides practitioners and scholars with a useful analytic category for identifying and making sense of citizen-led arenas of collective problem solving.

Chapter 3 examines the reasons why citizens come together to lead and work on collective problem-solving efforts, what functional policy work they do, and their inclusive and participatory attributes. Our analysis considers the various reasons why citizens are motivated to self-organize and lead a governance space, for example, because they believe traditional state, market, and civil society organizations have withdrawn or failed for some section of society, or because they want to provide an alternative governance pathway to a public problem that is too complex, persistent, or emergent. Using rich empirical material we showcase some of the governance activities and practices that citizens undertake in these spaces, including 1) goods and services production and delivery, 2) social order, conflict resolution, and adjudication; and 3) planning and development. The third part of the chapter considers four democratic attributes of citizens' governance spaces, namely, power sharing, giving voice, building capacity, and broader public engagement. These attributes, we argue, are integral to how citizens in these spaces self-organize and go about their practical governance work.

Chapter 4 discusses the kinds of knowledge and skills being generated in citizens' governance spaces, and how these are being reproduced and shared. Drawing on diverse empirical examples this chapter illustrates how citizen spaces reframe problems and solutions, and how they generate and transmit substantive policy knowledge. Cases reveal that through their problem-solving efforts citizen spaces also accumulate considerable expertise on procedures, organizations, and governance systems. In some instances, citizens working in these spaces share their knowledge with experts and non-experts, and across sectors and borders. Knowledge produced in citizen spaces can challenge conventional community attitudes and disrupt settled practices among public and private sector actors.

Chapter 5 examines how citizens in governance spaces interface with administrative, political, and market systems, and the opportunities, complexities, and dilemmas they encounter. The chapter develops the concept of "congruence" to describe how citizen spaces use autonomy and agency in their collective problem-solving work, while also being open to working across boundaries between sectors, institutions, and types of actors. Using diverse examples we illustrate different types of congruence in action. Examples demonstrate how congruent citizen spaces negotiate with more powerful and resourced entities without compromising their agency, organizational autonomy, and grassroots credibility. They avoid co-option while also gaining access to system resources such as funding, data, and information, and formal legal authority. The final section of the chapter examines the tensions and dilemmas that can arise when citizen spaces interface or partner with relevant state and non-state actors.

Chapter 6 draws out key opportunities, risks, and lessons citizens' governance spaces present for scholars and practitioners. In terms of opportunities, the preceding chapters have demonstrated how citizen spaces can foster a practical mode of political agency in which citizens instigate, lead, and drive policy work; how they offer a space for citizens to rethink and reframe issues, to push forward innovative experiments and solutions, and to work nimbly across sectors, networks, and boundaries. The earlier chapters have shown that although citizen spaces are small-scale, they can have systemic reach by attracting the attention of relevant state, market, and civil society actors. On the other hand, in terms of risks, Chapter 6 considers how citizen spaces might reproduce inequalities, co-opt civil society, behave unaccountably, or push the governance of essential public goods onto the work of under-resourced or unrepresentative citizens. A broader worry is that they can distract citizens; keeping them busy on the "small stuff" as they reconcile gaps in the market or state, when they could be contesting bigger structural causes. Related is the concern that citizen governance solutions can temporarily mask the severity of some public problems, and thereby weaken calls for government action. From here, the chapter reflects on the theoretical implications of citizen spaces, arguing that their problem-solving governance work is partly reflected in more pragmatic, Dewey-inspired democratic theory yet core concepts such as "democratic experimentalism" need to be reconstructed with insights from citizen governance practitioners. The chapter concludes by drawing out key lessons from our analysis for citizens and for diverse state and non-state actors involved in public governance.

# Chapter 2
# Citizens' Governance Spaces: Characteristics of Citizen-led Problem Solving

In 2014 two 21-year-old men—Lucas Patchett and Nic Marchesi—decided to retrofit a simple van with two washing machines, a dryer, and water tanks. They then traveled around Brisbane, Australia, offering a free mobile laundry service to those living on the street. Their motivation was not just to help homeless people by offering clothes washing services, but also to start conversations and build connections with those feeling isolated and forgotten by society. These initial steps seeded what is now Orange Sky Australia (OSA)—a large social impact organization that engages around 2,800 volunteers each year to provide free weekly laundry and shower services to homeless people in 37 locations across Australia (OSA 2023).

As scholars of participation and democracy we are intrigued by what citizens are doing in initiatives such as OSA. Their collective work is disrupting norms and ideas around homelessness across Australia but not in the way that activists might, through protests, nor in the way that an advocacy group might, through lobbying government or mobilizing citizens. The citizens leading and participating in OSA are volunteers who are willingly offering their time to help address a collective problem.

These are not conventional volunteers tasked by a large, professionalized charity organization to "help and hand out." Terms such as mutual aid or community organizing also misrepresent what is going on in OSA because the citizens involved are not rooted in a place and are not anti-state nor anti-system. Today OSA partners with diverse businesses and government agencies to offer laundry and washing services, as well as training and employment opportunities for the homeless (OSA 2021, p. 41).

In this chapter we draw on OSA and other citizen-led initiatives to flesh out the concept of citizens' governance spaces introduced in Chapter 1.[1] We

---

[1] This chapter builds on and extends the ideas and arguments presented in Hendriks and Dzur (2022) and Dzur and Hendriks (2024).

begin by elaborating on five defining characteristics of these spaces, which we conceptualize as diverse grassroots initiatives that are: 1) led and driven by citizens, who 2) undertake practical governance work to address a collective issue, 3) in innovative, experimental, and disruptive ways, 4) by engaging inclusively with affected publics, and 5) by working autonomously and congruently with relevant state, market, and civil society organizations.[2] Next we discuss how citizens' governance spaces differ from related social-science concepts, including social movements, community organizing, mutual aid, and co-production. We show how some concepts are either too capacious (e.g. social movements), while others do not adequately capture the agency or autonomy of citizens in citizens' governance spaces (e.g. co-production) or the nuanced way that citizens willingly work with or alongside existing state or market systems (e.g. community organizing and mutual aid). Overall, we contend that the citizens' governance space concept has both practical and scholarly utility: it helps identify initiatives that are citizen-led and aimed at collective problem solving; it offers a heuristic for scholars and practitioners to make sense of what citizens do in these spaces, in order to understand the benefits and risks they present to contemporary democracy.

## Defining Characteristics of Citizens' Governance Spaces

### Characteristic 1: Led and driven by citizens

Citizen spaces emerge from civil society through the actions of everyday people, and are wholly independent (at least initially) from state or market support. This self-driven aspect differentiates these participatory spaces from other social innovation projects that are seeded and propelled by solo "high value" entrepreneurs, corporations, or philanthropic organizations. In citizen governance the problem solving begins through the interventions of citizens themselves, who self-organize to address a problem, and then drive and lead the collective effort by bringing other citizens along with them.

Citizens instigate problem-solving spaces for various reasons (see Mathie and Gaventa 2015; van Meerkerk et al. 2021). For example, they might self-organize a group or project because they believe public sector agencies have

---

[2] These characteristics have emerged through a combined analysis of our own cases together with insights from empirical studies published in diverse fields such as organizational studies, social innovation, volunteering, planning, public policy and administration, sustainability studies, criminal justice, substance recovery, disaster studies, development studies, geography, and social movement studies. Our five characteristics overlap with the features of "citizen initiatives" that Igalla et al. (2019) developed from definitions found in their review of 55 empirical studies of grassroots, self-organizing community initiatives published in journals on public administration, volunteering, and the broader social sciences.

withdrawn from or failed to address a complex, persistent or emergent public problem. In some contexts, the state may be absent or weak, so there is no alternative other than for citizens to step in (Mitlin 2008). Market failure can also drive citizens (Mathie and Gaventa 2015). Citizen spaces can also emerge to address holes not adequately filled by conventional civil society organizations. Citizens may choose to act because they can no longer bear witnessing the human costs of ineffective or counter-productive policy, and channel their frustration into practical experiments that seek to address the issue at hand. Some citizens self-organize to help address problems faced by voiceless or highly marginalized groups, such as the homeless, drug users, Indigenous people, or victims of violence and crime. We discuss these and other motivations further in Chapter 3. In the present chapter we characterize the key features of these collective problem-solving spaces, and show that they represent a distinct associational form in civil society.

Most citizen spaces begin as small-scale experiments or local initiatives. Typically, a group of citizens might start a practically focused project with the aim of tackling a particular collective problem—for example, food waste, mental health, homelessness, opioid addiction, repeat crime, or the production of clean energy. Citizens leading a governance space often start in a small way to test their idea; for example, they offer an act of kindness, set up a local project, or start an online group. In these early days, citizens work their way into the problem; they collect information and start tinkering and experimenting with different practical options.

At some point the citizens leading the initiative might decide to formalize into a group, organization, or enterprise. To widen the governance space, citizen-leaders typically need to find more leaders, especially those with time and energy as well as relevant expertise, skills, and resources. Citizen-leaders often do this by leveraging their personal networks and trust in the community to ask people to join in the effort (Adams and Oeth 2020; Bherer et al. 2024). Some make use of social media and social messaging platforms, such as WhatsApp, to connect and mobilize others to join their problem-solving effort (e.g., Manning and Brook-Rowland 2023). Depending on the size of the governance space, citizen-leaders might establish a website, hold a community workshop, form a governance structure, and source support through local donations, fundraising events, or crowd funding. In time, their small practical efforts begin to generate impact, and this can attract interest in the community through local and social media, schools, and actors in relevant policy networks. In some cases, citizen-leaders are able to draw in funds and support from private and public sector organizations (Evers and Brandsen 2016).

An example is the evolution of OSA, which was small at first as Nic and Lucas experimented with different ways to construct a viable mobile laundry service. They tried various washing machines, vans, and tanks, and discovered new ways to work with volunteers, as well as how to partner with local residents, charities, businesses, and governments. About a year after they had trialed their laundry service in Brisbane, they were awarded a small grant from the airline operator Jetstar,[3] which enabled them to expand their operations interstate. By January 2016 OSA had done over 5,000 washing cycles "for their friends on the street" and engaged over 260 volunteers. When Lucas and Nic won the 2016 Young Australian of the Year award their idea of a mobile laundry service was shown on national news.[4] By 2022, OSA had evolved into a large organization providing washing and showering services to around 24,000 people per year in multiple locations all around Australia, including in remote Indigenous communities (OSA 2023). To help coordinate their 2,800 volunteers the OSA team has also developed a new volunteer app, Volaby (together with Google), which they now share with other volunteer organizations (OSA 2023). OSA has expanded to a location in Aotearoa New Zealand (OSA 2022).

To kick start a practical collective project such as OSA demands considerable citizen-leadership. In the first instance Nic and Lucas had to believe in their concept, and then "give it a go." They needed to have the resources to allow for experimentation, and for making mistakes and then trying again. They also had to have the skills and energy to bring other citizens with them, the confidence to push ahead despite the naysayers, the knowledge and expertise to apply for funding and seek partnerships, and the leadership skills to steer a team that could successfully develop the initiative. Importantly, citizens are the ones who initiate the space; they are the ones who choose the practical activities to undertake and decide on the resources and partners they need. While Nic and Lucas expanded OSA by sourcing external funding and partners, the governance space only came into being through their initiative, drive, and leadership. They came up with and "ran with" the mobile laundry idea; retrofitted the van and experimented with variations; and mobilized and then inspired an army of volunteers to connect and have conversations with people on the street.

In sum, citizens' governance spaces emerge from civil society, linked to but also separate from personal, work, and formal political spheres of action. Typical of civil society associations, participants in these spaces freely take up

---

[3] https://www.jetstar.com/au/en/flying-start-winners
[4] https://www.youtube.com/watch?v=ORzX9-dtWmU "Nic Marchesi and Lucas Patchett - 2016 Young Australian of the Year."

their tasks without thinking of them as familial responsibilities, jobs, or strict duties (Warren 2001). While initiated and led in the first instance by citizens, over time these spaces interface with relevant state, market, and civil society institutions—a theme we explore in detail in Chapter 5.

## Characteristic 2: Doing and rethinking practical governance

Citizens in governance spaces do functional public work, providing public goods and services such as care, shelter, food, energy, environmental protection, conflict resolution, social order, and social welfare.[5] As pointed out in Chapter 1, some scholars label this self-driven collective effort "everyday making" (Bang and Sørensen 1999) or "public work" (Boyte 2004). Yet we think the term "governance" more precisely identifies the way people in citizen spaces take on some of the most serious tasks confronting society without being invited and, indeed, under conditions where citizen action may have been actively discouraged by conventional civil society and government actors.

The term "governance" in this book refers to the complex and networked processes through which state, private, and non-state actors develop and deliver public goods and services (Jessop 2020). The collective work of citizens' governance spaces fits into this expansive understanding of how public problems are governed in contemporary democracies, but it also goes well beyond conventional government tasks. In contrast to Igalla et al. (2019, p. 1182) who suggest that "citizen initiatives provide and maintain an alternative form of traditional governmental public services, facilities, and/or goods themselves, such as water distribution, education and training, and residential care," we contend that citizen spaces disrupt and sometimes reconfigure conventional definitions of problems, solutions, and ways of working. Other scholars point more broadly to a "governance form in which citizens mobilize energy and resources to collectively define and carry out projects aimed at providing public goods or services for their community. Citizens control the aims, means, and actual implementation of their activities" (Edelenbos et al. 2021a, p. 9). We go further and argue that citizens' governance spaces are not just *doing* places, where old and new governance work is taken up, they are

---

[5] For empirical examples of citizens self-organizing to solve collective problems in a range of policy areas, see Alkon and Guthman (2017); Bherer et al. (2024); Borzaga et al. (2016a; 2016b); Brandsen et al. (2016a); Soares da Silva et al. (2018); Denters (2016); Duijn et al. (2019); Edelenbos et al. (2021b); Frantzeskaki et al. (2016); Igalla et al. (2019); Mitlin (2008); Parés et al. (2017); Wagenaar and Healey (2015).

also *thinking* places, where wrongs or inadequacies in current practices in the private, public, and civil society sectors are confronted.

The governance work that citizens lead and enact centers on trying to address a complex public problem in practical ways.[6] They identify and define the problem, form feasible plans, implement solutions, and make evaluations and refinements. Consider the problem-solving activities of OSA. Rather than ask people to sign petitions for governments to do more about homelessness, Lucas and Nic decided to develop some practical interventions to assist homeless people in direct ways. The underlying motivation here was that if the state or market was unable to provide basic human services such as shelter, then they could "step up" and offer homeless people some of life's basic needs: clean clothes and a conversation.

A focus on practical activities that "make a difference" by achieving substantive outcomes differentiates citizens' governance spaces from "insisted spaces" where citizens participate in lobbying, advocacy, and protest work, for example via a mobilized group or social movement.[7] The kind of claim-making that occurs in "insisted spaces" is not a central motivating force in citizens' governance spaces. For example, though citizens working for OSA might interact with state officials to deliver or align multiple services to people on the street, they are not making claims on officials to do their work better.

OSA produces manifold public goods and services. In the first instance they provide accessible facilities where homeless people can clean and dry their clothes and have a shower. They partner with state and non-state organizations so that people on the street are also easily able to access other services such as food, counseling, medical support, training, and employment opportunities. It is true that OSA has not been able to solve or indeed govern the complex problem of homelessness; and that on one level the work of OSA might be interpreted as a superficial "charity" effort, that does little "problem solving" let alone governance, as some argue (Parsell and Watts 2017). Yet that critique mistakenly sees OSA as a failed social movement rather than as a robust citizen space.

From our perspective, we see that citizens leading and engaging in OSA are trying to tackle two practical problems that face people on the street, which government and non-state actors (such as churches and formal charities)

---

[6] Frank Hendriks (2019) labels the action-oriented political work in these practical initiatives as "pragmatic activism." We prefer not to use the term activism because of its strong association with adversarial protest politics, which is a long way from the kind of backstage political work that many citizens undertake in citizens' governance spaces.

[7] The term "insisted spaces" refers broadly to efforts by citizens to mobilize and advocate to push an idea or proposal into the political process (see Hendriks and Colvin 2024). The term was inspired by Carson's (2007) discussion of how citizens and nascent social movements can "insist" for a seat at the table by pushing forward democratic reforms.

have either neglected or at best struggled to address. The first of these is hygiene. When you are homeless the tasks of cleaning clothes and oneself are challenging and expensive. While critics might see the work of OSA as middle-class do-gooders cleaning up people on the street (Parsell and Watts 2017), the underlying motivation for Nic and Lucas is about dignity. When we are clean we can feel positive about ourselves; and clean clothes can potentially open doors, whether that be to a conversation or to a job interview. The growth of OSA around Australia is testament to the fact that people on the street value and make great use of their services. People living rough are often wary of government and institutional support. So, rather than visit a costly laundromat or seek assistance from a large charity where they might get questions and judgment, they are willing to trust a group of nimble locals to wash their clothes in an efficient mobile service. Though critics worry that OSA is distracting advocacy and volunteer effort away from addressing "housing" and inadequate welfare support (Parsell et al. 2021), for Lucas and Nic OSA is about offering something today, right here and now, that can improve the lives of people on the street. Their primary motivation is not to mobilize a social movement, nor to advocate for a particular policy change that might take years to realize.

Social isolation is the second, more complex, problem that OSA is seeking to address. A central part of the OSA model is to enable people on the street to connect to people in their community. They do this not by inviting people to step through a church door or asking them to fill out a government form, but by engaging in conversation with people as they wait for their washing to be done:

> In the one hour time it takes to wash and dry someone's clothes there is absolutely nothing to do but sit down on one of our 6 orange chairs and have a positive and genuine conversation between our everyday volunteers and everyday friends on the street. (OSA 2016, p. 5)

The term "friends" marks a distinction from conventional language of state-sponsored social work which stresses distancing terms—"clients," "the needy," "the homeless"—that can label, disempower, and marginalize (Kretzman and McKnight 1993).

## Characteristic 3: Innovative, experimental, and disruptive interventions

Citizens in governance spaces do not know the answers in advance. They tackle complex problems with unknown solutions and fluid governance pathways, and find that they must revise and adjust both strategies and objectives as they go along. Typically, citizens in these spaces proceed into the unknown: they experiment as they go; take risks; learn about possibilities along the way; and sometimes upend established policy concepts and objectives. Indeed, the empirical case studies analyzed in this book reveal that citizens are not operating from a tacit community consensus on what needs to be done; instead they are often sailing against the wind. Through their experimental work, citizens push boundaries and expose problems or inefficiencies in existing structures, community norms, and formal rules.

The solutions and actions that citizen spaces develop—however seemingly simple—often demand considerable experimentation and innovation (Mathie and Gaventa 2015). For example, when Lucas and Nic came up with the idea for a mobile laundry van, there was no blueprint to follow, nor any obvious civil society organization or government agency to whom they could "pitch" their idea. Instead, they themselves decided to take action to realize their idea. They began with small steps, tried different things, made mistakes, and learnt new skills and practices along the way. Eventually "Sudsy"—OSA's first mobile laundry van—was created. Over time OSA has become a master at experimentation, pushing boundaries, and developing novel ways to do things. As Lucas explains:

> When Nic and I first started Orange Sky, we had no idea about budgets, impact or scalability, but we sure are thankful that we gave it a go anyway ... [and learned to] support that very idea of "giving things a crack." ... From building our very first van "Sudsy," to upgrading our laundry vans to include shower capability, to our work in remote communities and the launch of Volaby—we are constantly looking for ways to innovate and help more people in our community. (Patchett 2020)

The rethinking of conventions and standard practices is at the heart of what most citizens' governance spaces do. Citizens are typically wrestling with policy problems that are ill-defined, ill-structured, or even invisible, and that have a history of failed and sometimes stigmatizing official interventions (Evers and Brandsen 2016). In contrast to many classic co-production projects where citizens are self-organized to generate solutions to discrete problems known in advance (Ostrom 1990; 1996), in citizen spaces people are trying to address problems whose solutions are not well understood in advance of their action. Sometimes through their attempts at problem solving they stumble across other problems, for which they then develop solutions. For example, Lucas and Nic realized early on in their experimentation that their "friends on the street" were seeking not only clean clothes but also connections:

> The most important thing in our van isn't the washing machines, driers, generator, water tanks or even bubble machines on the roof! But our 6 orange chairs that we pull out at every location. These chairs are now symbolic of hours and hours of conversation between every day volunteers and every day friends on the street, every single day. (OSA 2016, p. 5)

Unusually, the innovations developed by OSA have been well received, celebrated, and supported by governments, businesses, and civil society organizations alike. They have received corporate and government funding and have won many awards, but this kind of public celebration of citizens' governance spaces is rare. A more common story, especially for more informal, locally-based citizen spaces, is that they fly under the radar of public agencies and civil society organizations that support volunteering and collective programs (see Dean 2021; Woolvin and Harper 2015).

In some cases the innovative and experimental activities of citizen spaces can disrupt established practices and power arrangements. Citizens might push along solutions that challenge existing roles, conventions or knowledge; or their activities might threaten existing funding arrangements; or because they reframe discussions about particular problems or populations (see Mathie and Gaventa 2015). These disruptive aspects of citizen spaces can often mean that they generate politics, even though many citizens involved do not see their work as "political," and do not self-identify as activists or policy advocates.

Consider, for example, the experiences of Serenity Café—a citizen space that emerged to address substance use and recovery in Edinburgh, Scotland (Campbell et al. 2011). The café organizers (who included a community development officer working with recovering substance users) self-consciously crafted a meeting and support space that was drug-free. They wanted substance users to experience an open, celebratory, and positive recovery experience, expanding the image that recovery entails attending discrete, closeted mutual support groups. The organizers wanted to fill a gap in "adult social venues" by providing a place in which recovering users "can form positive, supportive relationships." Importantly, they recognized a need for a bridging space between the "cloistered environment" of support groups (such as Alcoholics Anonymous), and wider social activities with all their challenges and temptations (Campbell et al. 2011, p. 135). In this sense Serenity Café was more than a physical space; it was also a space that altered how recovering users interact, build social connections, and re-engage with the wider world. The value of talking and listening is well recognized in recovery support, but the organizers of Serenity Café created something more. They built a space of support that centers on presence. As one customer put it: "Phoning is not as easy as walking into a cafe. You don't want to talk about what's wrong; you just want to be with someone"(cited in Campbell et al. 2011, p. 147).

The Café was highly disruptive to existing state and civil society protocols and regimes on substance recovery. When the café first emerged around 2009 its emphasis on abstinence as a recovery pathway sat at odds with the then Scottish Government's policy focus, which was to treat substance addiction mostly via short-term detox programs.[8] As the citizens who developed the Café explain:

> We have been directly and indirectly steered away from using the term [abstinence] by potential funders, and yet not using the word to describe the recovery of the people using the Serenity Café would seem to be selling them short, because their abstinence is what they take pride in and what they perceive as keeping them alive. (Campbell et al. 2011, p. 156)

In sum, by offering a space of abstinence, Serenity Café challenged government policy at the time and also challenged the temptations arising from the broader cultural norms in Scotland—which, as in many nations, assume that socializing with friends involves drinking alcohol or using drugs, and the more the better. The café not only addressed some deficits in state and non-government organization (NGO) approaches, but also altered patterns of interaction in the surrounding civil society (Campbell et al. 2011).

Citizen spaces can also cause governance disruptions by working in unconventional ways with marginalized groups or the broader community. An example is the disruptive ways in which various consumer and health cooperatives operate in Japan's competitive service-provider market for elder care. Member-run cooperatives have expanded conventional notions of elderly health care in Japan by offering a range of diverse services well beyond standard home care. They include programs for welfare support, mutual aid, cleaning services, food delivery, and recreation and social activities (Kurimoto and Kumakura 2016). In other cases—for example, in citizen-led syringe exchanges—citizens are prepared to break rules and go against

---

[8] While the Café supported harm reduction approaches such as maintenance prescribing, it was established to demonstrate that social and community support for "abstinence" can be an effective part of supporting former users in their drug and alcohol recovery. The Café's emphasis on abstinence is considered provocative for local drug treatment practitioners and is not the stance taken by the Vancouver Area Network of Drug Users (VANDU), a substance-user governance space we introduce in Chapter 3, and discuss further in subsequent chapters (see Campbell et al. 2011).

conventions to offer a problem-solving response, regardless of the legal consequences (Lupick 2017).[9] In communities that are accustomed to looking away from the bodies nodding off in the alleyways, deaths from overdoses are not a high priority for policy. Here, norm-bending citizens' governance spaces operating experimental needle exchanges can be a matter of life and death.

A broader form of disruption to governance comes from the capacity for some citizen spaces to challenge how knowledge and power operate in contemporary politics. People in citizen spaces experimenting with sustainable modes of production and consumption work in direct competition with corporate-led innovation (Mathie and Gaventa 2015). Empirical studies observe that these grassroots innovations not only contribute "novel ideas and practices for green transformations" but also contest the very principles and character of mainstream innovation processes and ideas about transformation pathways (Smith and Ely 2015, p. 103). Citizen spaces may challenge established roles and relationships among relevant actors and institutions, and—some researchers argue—may have the potential to unsettle or challenge dominant discourses and entire systems of production (Wagenaar and van der Heijden 2015, p. 126). We expand upon this theme in Chapter 4.

Citizens are also self-authorizing their problem-solving work in fields of action that are typically dominated by professionals, specialists, and officials (Evers and Brandsen 2016). Over time, citizen spaces can become productive and reflective zones of civic agency that can, in fact, unsettle conventional assumptions, challenge market practices, and disrupt formal policy positions (Borzaga et al. 2016a). For example, Serenity Café met resistance from health professional and civil society groups working on substance recovery. As some Café volunteers explain: "we encounter[ed] a great deal of prejudice toward it among other professionals involved in drug and alcohol treatment, among funders, and in policy circles"(Campbell et al. 2011, p. 149).

Serenity Café met resistance in large part because the Café was focused "on recovery, not on the substance," whereas in traditional mutual aid recovery the groups focus on specific substances (for example, alcohol, cocaine, narcotics, etc.) (Campbell et al. 2011, p. 148). Some 12-step mutual aid recovery programs also objected to the way recovering substance-users promoted the Café, and worried about profits being made from recovery. Traditionally, 12-step mutual aid groups are committed to non-affiliation; they forbid participants to affiliate with or endorse any outside bodies. According to

---

[9] The title of one memoir of VANDU, a substance-user governance space, celebrates its counter-normative stance: *Raise Shit! Social Action Saving Lives* (Boyd et al. 2009).

Campbell et al.: "some 'traditionalists' have objected to enthusiasts sharing their experience of the Serenity Café as part of their personal testimony during meetings" (2011, p. 148).

In short, as a user-led initiative, Serenity Café offered solutions that some users wanted, although these rubbed up against well-established ideas, traditions, and protocols in substance recovery. While recovery-support groups for particular substances may suit professionals and the needs of some users in recovery, the Café demonstrated that some recovering users also want to step outside groups for their particular substance, and to engage in social spaces that are more open. Café customers placed a high value on how it has brought "people from different fellowships together" or, as one customer put it: "A fantastic idea and a great way to eradicate recovery fascism" (cited in Campbell et al. 2011, p. 149).

## Characteristic 4: Engaging inclusively with affected publics

Citizens' governance spaces are not just citizen-led; they are also open to currently and formerly marginalized citizens taking on productive roles.[10] As we have seen, many address complex problems like homelessness, law breaking, domestic violence, mental health, and addiction, which affect the dispossessed and marginalized (for instance, Abramson and Moore 2001; Borzaga et al. 2016a; 2016b; Campbell et al. 2011; Wagenaar and Healey 2015). They often innovate to include the poor, the elderly, the young, the addicted and formerly addicted, and the disabled, in planning, organizing, and conducting their problem-solving work. Their goal is to work with—not work for or on—those on the margins.

Citizens leading these initiatives often reach out to these marginalized people, actively promoting equality and power-sharing. They recognize people's interest in becoming more civically active—through peer-to-peer work, for example—once they get their lives stabilized. And if citizens have been given opportunities to be involved in the "formulation of their own means and the ends" (Jacobi et al. 2017, p. 267), they are better placed to provide solutions to similarly marginalized others. The small group of citizens that founded the Serenity Café, for example, recognized that former drug and alcohol users were not natural "joiners" of community groups, especially given their history, social alienation, and suspicion of leaders—ex-drug users

---

[10] Founders and routine participants of citizens' governance spaces may have greater access to resources than do members of marginalized groups. Differences such as these do not appear to be as significant as, say, those that stand between state agents or long-time social movement activists and members of marginalized groups.

and their recovery are not promising topics for social movement advocacy; very few people openly carry the identity of an ex-drug user into the public sphere—so their approach to engagement has focused on creating a social and supportive environment, via the Café, where former users could connect and be empowered to help those vulnerable to drug abuse, such as young people(Campbell et al. 2011, p. 140). As the founders explain: "The strengthening of individual social networks of support in turn creates and reinforces a sense of community, and the building of personal recovery capital contributes to and strengthens the collective recovery capital available to the community"(Campbell et al. 2011, p. 142).

People actively engaged in citizen spaces work experimentally on public problems in a collective fashion: they draw on skills, knowledge, and entrepreneurship among their members, participants, and broader community. While the mode of engagement and degree of power sharing vary between organizations, empirical research suggests that many citizen spaces are committed to working in inclusive, participatory, and empowering ways (Pestoff and Hulgård 2016). Many citizens leading a governance space reach out to, and engage with, relevant affected publics to mobilize support or to attract members; for example, via social media, community events, forums, and conferences; they may also hold reflective workshops, train volunteers, or convene online discussions.[11] In some instances this community engagement work can be relatively unstructured. Recall the outreach and connective work of Orange Sky with its orange chairs. Orange chair conversations form connections and reveal possibilities for social change, encouraging people on the streets to become volunteers themselves, to work within the organization, and to learn new skills (OSA 2016). We elaborate further on the participatory aspects of citizen spaces in Chapter 3.

Citizen spaces are not in the explicit business of formally representing the views or interests of constituents or members, as an advocacy organization might. However, over time they can be drawn into policy-making realms where they are asked to provide experiential advocacy drawing on their practical knowledge regarding the perspectives and experiences of the people they work with or seek to assist. Through their practical attempts to address collective problems, citizen spaces render hidden experiences and perspectives—for example, of substance users, the elderly, and victims of domestic violence—more visible to decision-makers. Citizens in these spaces are not claiming to be the "voice of the community," but their practical and experiential knowledge enables them reflectively to challenge stereotypes and uninformed community standpoints.

---

[11] See the special editions of *International Review of Sociology*, 26 (1, 2).

## Characteristic 5: Working autonomously and congruently with state, market, and civil society actors

Citizen spaces work nimbly and flexibly across boundaries between sectors, institutions, and types of actors; for example, citizens, clients, experts, professionals, policy makers, and politicians. Many citizens in these spaces appear willing to work with, alongside, and outside government and civil society organizations. "Citizen initiatives strive for autonomy, ownership, and control regarding internal decision-making" yet they "are often linked to formal institutions, such as local authority, governmental agencies, and NGOs, especially for facilitation and public funding" (Igalla et al. 2019, p. 1182).

While citizens' governance spaces may have boundaries with, and objections to, particular aspects of the system—such as the courts, police departments, or large corporations—they are willing to work congruently with them. Organizational autonomy is not fetishized but it is taken seriously; citizen spaces wish to work with more powerful and resourced entities *only* on the terms established by citizens. Consider, for example, the way OSA has formed partnerships with a range of government departments, religious groups, charity organizations, private donors, and corporations (OSA 2016; 2019). The organization is not anti-government, nor is it co-opted by the government and other elites. Instead, it is willing to work with state or non-state collaborators who support its mission, and this networked approach has enabled OSA to have significant reach and impact (OSA 2019).[12] In some other instances, citizens choose to work actively with the market and bypass the state altogether, as is the case in some community-led renewable energy initiatives (see discussion in Chapter 5).

Partnerships between citizen spaces and the private sector are typically conducted to sustain and enhance citizen governance effectiveness, not for economic gain. According to Igalla et al.: "Citizen initiatives often develop their own business model to increase financial stability, which helps them continue their activities, but they are not focused on private profitmaking (i.e., profits are invested back into the local community)" (2019, pp. 1182–1163). Serenity Café organizers, for example, were determined "that the initiative should be developed and managed by people in recovery" and

---

[12] An external evaluation estimated that the annual social impact of OSA's total outputs (including washes, showers, conversation hours, employment hours, and referrals to other service providers) was around $9.5m (AUD) in 2018/19 (OSA 2019).

sought to be a "fully independent enterprise" (Campbell et al. 2011, p. 135). They communicated "very clear and transparent explanations of how the Serenity Café might attract funds, generate income from the café, and dedicate all funds to further developing opportunities for people in recovery" (Campbell et al. 2011, p. 149).

Sustainability sometimes requires sacrificing organizational autonomy, as Serenity Café organizers came to realize when they experienced tensions between the need for profitability and their objective of providing meaningful workplace experiences for as many of their members as possible:

> [A]t the beginning of our journey, we assumed that we could play this game, with a well-planned business model that would show that the Serenity Café could generate sufficient income from café sales to operate as a viable enterprise. We were wrong. We realized very quickly that most high-street cafés survive because they operate on a skeleton staff and waste no money on supporting people or providing supervised developmental opportunities for volunteers. (Campbell et al. 2011, p. 154)

Resolving these tensions led to a "hybrid funding model—social enterprise with grant aid" albeit with long-range plans to establish a "full user-led operation as an independent entity" (Campbell et al. 2011, p. 155).

As these examples show, citizen spaces emerge in response to failures or limitations of conventional state institutions and market or civil society organizations—such as energy infrastructure, health support, courts and police, food distribution agencies and NGOs—to address public problems. Yet the citizens involved do not necessarily reject or take a stand against these institutions and organizations. Instead, they might choose to carve out a congruent governance pathway that is not in direct opposition to state officials, agencies, and departments and may in fact be in collaboration or coordination with them. Hybridity and liminality seem essential to citizen spaces' identity; the people involved would find them less appealing if they were part of a state agency or traditional civil society association—and also if they were completely detached from them. Success, in other words, is not absorption into a department or institution, nor is it being completely autonomous from the system and shut out from resources and ongoing policy conversations; but a commitment to impact is crucial (Wagenaar and van der Heijden 2015, p. 132). These are themes we explore in more detail in Chapter 5.

## Citizens' Governance Spaces and Related Concepts

Conceptually, the practically focused problem-solving work of citizens' governance spaces might appear to fall awkwardly between the "messy categories" of community organizing, social movements, mutual aid, and co-production. However, we contend that each of these four terms allows in too much that is dissimilar to capture the motivations and governance activities of citizens' governance spaces. In the following discussion we argue that citizens in these spaces undertake a particular mode of participation that is different in significant enough ways to warrant the more precise term we favor.

## Community organizing

Community organizing is a wide-reaching term used around the world in multiple fields and disciplines each with their own meaning. Some define community organizing in very broad terms, as, for example, "localized, often 'prepolitical action' that provides the foundation for multilocal and explicitly political social movements" (Stall and Stoecker 1998, p. 730). Others adopt a narrower definition, viewing community organizing as "a process through which residents come together and build social power to investigate and take sustained action on systemic issues that negatively affect their daily lives" (Christens et al. 2021, p. 3003). Notwithstanding this diversity, the term "community organizing" carries a number of core features for scholars and practitioners of community development and social movements.[13]

Typically, community organizing refers to activities that are strongly rooted in place. While practical and focused on problem solving, such work is oriented toward a specific locality or proximity to a neighborhood, rather than to a particular problem. As Christens et al. contend, community organizing involves "residents of geographic communities and often engaged members of other local institutions such as schools, faith communities, workplaces, and the like" (2021, p. 3003).

---

[13] A related concept here is that of "community development" which is particularly prevalent in the practice of community planning, social work and local welfare delivery (see Kenny et al. 2017). In some contexts, such as in the UK, Australia, and New Zealand, the term community development refers to a range of locally-focused and place-based approaches to planning and policy delivery, which are mostly government-led (see King and Cruickshank 2012; Matarrita-Cascante and Brennan 2012). In the US, community development carries multiple meanings—from activist community organizing, through to more neoliberal varieties where elites establish partnerships between community, state, and market actors (see Stoecker and Witkovsky 2021).

Driven by the interests of local residents living in a common area or neighborhood, community organizing projects might emerge through neighborhood gatherings or residential committees. In short, people are motivated to engage in community organizing to "make their own neighborhood better." These features of community organizing contrast with the motivations and practices of citizens' governance spaces, which often work on problems that transcend a specific place.

In the North American context, community organizing is often facilitated by outsiders to a neighborhood who have received specific training by groups like Asset Based Community Development or the Industrial Areas Foundation (Stall and Stoecker 1998). Organizers conduct "one on one" interviews with community members to identify interests: what they most care about, what they think needs to be done in their neighborhood, and what they are willing to spend their time and effort on to accomplish. Also important is "asset mapping" where the organizer or a community member scans the neighborhood for resources (Kretzmann and McKnight 1993). An artist's talent that could be used for a mural; a youth's energy that can be used for park clean-up; an elder's free time to monitor children after school: these are all "assets" that are ready to hand. A public school in the area might be tapped for its meeting facilities and for office supplies and copying. A church might be a good place for further recruiting and for planning neighborhood projects.

Central to community organizing is a strong sense of self-reliance. Particularly in urban neighborhoods, residents are accustomed to being patronized by social workers and other helping-professionals funded and empowered by state agencies. Asset mapping is a kind of counter-knowledge that insists on the capacity of the marginalized to do something worthwhile for their communities, as long as they are organized to do so and not labeled and expected to be "needy."

Community organizers' relationship to the state, therefore, is wary and oppositional: they are likely to reject partnerships that do not allow the community to call the shots. Because of the history of labeling, and a suspicion that the balance of every state dollar spent in a marginalized neighborhood goes to support the state professionals rather than the locals, community organizers do not seek reciprocity with state institutions (McKnight 2022). This contrasts with citizen-led governance, where citizens might choose to partner with relevant state or market actors if it helps their broader problem-solving effort (see Edelenbos et al. 2018, p. 58).

Like citizens' governance spaces (but, as we will see, unlike social movements), community organizing efforts may attract citizens from across the ideological spectrum who share a common place with many overlapping interests. Another similarity is the overarching concern with problem solving, and the willingness to get one's hands dirty to work on an issue rather than advocate and protest to have elected officials and state agencies work on it. While advocacy and protest are often part of community organizing efforts, their central focus is on what residents can do to improve their lives rather than what they can get officials and agencies to do for them (Alinsky 1971; 1989).

However, unlike community organizing, and closer to social movements, is the way citizens' governance spaces tightly focus on specific problems that often transcend neighborhood boundaries and may very well have broad impacts, with regional, national, and even global meanings. That allows them to develop different kinds of knowledge and to link—on their own terms—to state and market actors rather than remain in opposition.

## Social movements

There are similarities and differences between social movements and citizens' governance spaces. Like citizen spaces, social movements often begin in response to government or civil society failures or dysfunctions, and they are often representative of those on the margins who lack voice and conventional influence. As Moody-Adams notes:

> A social movement is a sustained, organized endeavor in extra-institutional "contentious politics" through which a group either (a) asserts an unaddressed need; (b) demands attention to an insufficiently acknowledged interest; or (c) seeks respect for the dignity or worth of some marginalized or excluded group or project, with the goal of changing relevant institutions, policies, and practices. (2022, pp. 23–24)

When it comes to practical problem solving there are important distinctions between social movements and citizen spaces. Most social movements are primarily focused on making calls for action addressed to the state, corporations, or the broader public. While they may encourage and facilitate practical problem solving, their primary mission is not to undertake the practical activities to address the problem themselves. More common are performative actions that draw media, official, and public attention to the problem of concern to the movement. As Johnston points out, "marches, demonstrations, protest rallies, petitions, and sometimes violence distinguish movements from other forms of claims making" (2014, p. 94).

Of course, social movements are diverse, and some have developed activities with a strong practical focus—referred to as "prefigurative." For example, some environmental movements set up community gardens to grow local food or establish ride-share programs. Here there is some overlap between what people do in citizens' governance spaces and some of the prefigurative work done in social movements. An important distinction, however, is that participants in citizens' governance spaces are typically not driven by an overarching and unifying vision, as they might be in the practical protest activities of "prefigurative politics" (Yates 2015).

The way social movements relate to other actors also differs from citizens' governance spaces. Social movements tend to be wary of, and even antagonistic towards, state actors and to those working in formalized civil society organizations, such as churches, unions, and long-standing NGOs. In contrast, people participating in citizen spaces typically adopt a more pragmatic view; they will work, if necessary, with people holding positions in established institutions, especially if they gain vital resources and support for their problem solving.

Social movements also differ from citizen spaces in how they engage the public. As Christens and Speer assert, "Although they [social movements] may invoke the rhetoric of community organizing, they often offer few opportunities for members or volunteers to play meaningful roles" (2015, p. 216). Social movements frequently link to local community organizing efforts, and recruit from them, but they typically operate by mobilizing citizens to action through issue frameworks and narratives that have been created outside particular communities. In contrast, people are drawn into citizen spaces via their social or professional connections; for example, they learn about a local initiative inviting people to "come along and help out." This invitation to engage in collective work typically centers around practical activities to help address a specific collective problem.

The political nature of engagement also differs between social movements and citizen spaces. Movements tend to be outwardly political and "contentious"; they have strong messaging; powerful public campaigns with emotive language and issue-framing; participants are motivated by anger, fear, outrage, injustice, passion, and ideology. Movement leaders call on people to "get political": to go protest, agitate, door-knock, advocate, and make change. In contrast, the disruption and politics generated by citizens' governance spaces is more subtle; their political work occurs behind the scenes in neighborhoods, boardrooms, and the hallways of policy makers, rather than overtly in the public sphere.[14] Some citizen spaces, such as OSA, intentionally frame their governance work in non-political terms:

> We are not politically or religiously associated, just everyday people in the community .... We believe to have the biggest impact we must collaboratively work together to help our homeless friends .... Our volunteers are not there to fix anything, sell anything or preach anything but purely provide a platform to reconnect people with the community. (OSA 2016, p. 26)

Citizens' governance spaces also differ from two concepts closely linked to social movements. First, the notion of "free spaces" is akin to the autonomous aspects of citizen-led governance efforts (Polletta 1999; Polletta and Kretschmer 2013), but this concept is too capacious to describe the purpose-driven governance work citizen spaces do. Second, citizen spaces are also not captured by the concept of "citizen-led democratic innovation" discussed in Chapter 1, which describes how social movements and activists are building or reshaping participatory institutions (Bua and Bussu 2020; 2023; della Porta and Felicetti 2019; Hendriks and Reid 2023). The bottom-up efforts of people active in citizens' governance spaces are different. Their agenda is not democratic or institutional reform per se; rather it is practical action on a particular public problem. Citizen spaces are typically inclusive, often employing informal participatory methods or community out-reach approaches, but participation in them is problem-solving oriented and not an end in itself.

## Mutual aid

Mutual aid takes different forms and meanings in different political contexts but in broad terms it refers to localized bottom-up collective efforts at "helping" and providing "care" (Gitterman and Shulman 2005). Mutual aid practices are centuries old, often used by socially and historically excluded groups as a way to meet their own needs when systems of governance fail to

---

[14] Zigon aptly calls the kind of political work done in citizens' governance spaces "worldbuilding" and contrasts it with the protest-oriented politics of many contemporary social movements: "this politics of worldbuilding has been able to go beyond the momentary prefiguration, spectacle, and protest that have come to characterize much left political activity today and is now actually building new worlds, which include not only infrastructure, values, and social and worldly interactive practices but the onto-ethical grounds for such worlds" (2018, p. 5). Citizens' governance spaces are "effectively creating and experimenting with potentialities, out of which a future with radically different forms of sociality and politics can emerge" (Zigon 2018, p. 12).

do so, especially in acute crisis (Littman et al. 2022).[15] However, the terminology and practices of mutual aid have been popularized recently, particularly in the context of the COVID-19 pandemic and racial justice protests in the US in the summer of 2020 (e.g., Spade 2020b; Tiratelli and Kaye 2020; Tolentino 2020).

The ideas and practices found in contemporary mutual aid efforts have multiple roots, including the principles of solidarity and mutualism, and theories of social change drawn from anarchist and Marxist political movements (Kinna 1995). In some political contexts mutual aid efforts are prefigurative actions for radical movements that oppose systemic oppression and marginalization. For example, in the US some advocates view local mutual aid groups as spaces that offer radical alternatives to conventional supports (Izlar 2019), and as an entry point to joining social movements against racism, discrimination and marginalization (Spade 2020a, b). Facilitators of mutual aid in the US context also describe how these spaces of assistance not only provide immediate support in the form of care, food or shelter, but how they are motivated by a broader sense of solidarity and a commitment to fight for liberation and redistribution of resources (Littman et al. 2022).

In other contexts, such as in the UK and Australia, mutual aid efforts are less politically radical, at least in terms of seeking to mobilize volunteers into broader movements working against oppressive state and market structures. Many of the thousands of mutual aid efforts that emerged during the COVID-19 pandemic throughout the UK were not anti-state or anti-market, and were willing to work in nimble ways with relevant government agencies, businesses and formal organizations in civil society, to address local needs (e.g., Rendall et al. 2022; Turcu and Rotolo 2022).

While some citizens' governance spaces could be considered "mutual aid," most are not. There are, for example, cases we consider in this book where citizens have self-organized to provide care in a crisis—such as a natural disaster or pandemic—or to fill gaps not covered by existing social support systems. However, the term "citizens' governance spaces" encapsulates a much broader set of governance work beyond plugging holes by offering emergency "help" and "care." Many of the practical initiatives that we consider in this book are working on long-term complex collective problems—such as criminal justice, contested water governance, renewable energy production, substance addiction. Whereas mutual aid efforts might be short lived and emerge in the wake of a particular crisis—for example to deliver meals and

---

[15] For an overview of the history of mutual aid in the US, see Beito (2000).

medication to those in need during a pandemic—the citizen-led initiatives we explore in this book tend to have longer life spans.

Like mutual aid efforts, citizens' governance spaces can be contrasted with top-down policy efforts provided by state agencies or professionalized charity organizations. But this does not mean that the citizens working inside these spaces are anti-state or anti-civil society or even anti-market. In contrast to the self-understanding that is cultivated in many mutual aid efforts, the citizens in the spaces we consider in this book are not typically part of a broader movement seeking to resist the actions of state and market institutions (cf. Spade 2020a, b). In our reading, the concept of mutual aid provides little or no scope to capture the nimble and diverse ways that citizens are partnering with state, market, and civil society actors.

## Co-production

The term co-production has come to mean many things—from community-led problem solving, through to more state-based programs of problem solving that involve the community in some way. It is possible to view citizens' governance spaces as a particular form of community-led co-production (McMullin 2023), but there are differences in how they operate, what they work on, and what motivates the main actors, and those differences make new terminology necessary.

Co-production suggests that it is *how* the work is done that matters most: it is a process of sharing authority between citizens and state actors. While such sharing sometimes occurs in citizens' governance spaces—and is a characteristic that differentiates these spaces from typical community organizing and the efforts of social movements—it is not always the case that citizen spaces work with the state. Some are fully autonomous and do not co-produce at all; some partner with the private rather than the public sector.

Many of the classic cases of co-production discussed by Ostrom (1990; 1996) involve policy problems that are well-defined, while the solutions must be worked out—co-produced—in creative ways. Just as in citizens' governance spaces, the problem-solving creativity in co-production is coming from citizens who are most invested in the issue. However, in citizen spaces, the open-ended nature of their objectives and the fluidity of their work set these spaces apart from many of Ostrom's (1990; 1996) classic cases of community co-production. In those classic cases, the citizens self-organized to generate orderly, efficient and effective solutions to discrete policy problems known in advance, such as providing access to clean water, reducing overfishing, and improving sanitation.[16] In contrast, people involved in citizens' governance spaces are wrestling with chronic collective problems that are ill-defined, and policy problems that are not well understood in advance of citizen action. In citizen spaces, participants work iteratively to re-shape conventional views of issues held by fellow citizens, civil society organizations and government officials. Indeed, this disruptive effect of citizen spaces means that they can be more politicized than typical co-production projects. The motivations of those involved in citizen governance frequently differ from the baseline self-interested rationality that Ostrom identified, and often seek to re-shape collective norms and social expectations (Brandsen et al. 2016a).

In recent discussions on co-production, some scholars and practitioners use the notion of "co-creation"—a term borrowed from the business world (Ansell and Torfing 2021). Though co-production and co-creation are often used interchangeably (Voorberg et al. 2015), advocates of co-creation stress that it places more emphasis on the innovation and creativity that citizens can bring to public governance as joint problem-solvers (Baptista et al. 2020). Co-creation has much in common with deliberative forms of governance—to the extent that it involves citizens coming together with relevant private and public decision-makers for joint sense-making and deliberation about collective issues. But co-creation, advocates argue, is more than mere talk; it involves "joint action based on the design and testing of prototypes, coordinated implementation, and collaborative adaptation" (Ansell et al. 2021, p. 348).

Co-creation has been identified as an important form of co-production for democratic renewal because it connects two sides of governing: inputs (greater citizen engagement) and outputs (improved services, policies and programs) (Ansell et al. 2021). Advocates also argue that co-creation projects create "opportunities for citizens and public and private stakeholders to directly engage with each other in new and pragmatic ways that are different from the ideological cleavages produced by electoral democracy" (Ansell et al. 2021, p. 349). There are motivational and epistemic advantages of co-creation, too, advocates tell us; these projects can bring together "different groups of citizens to engage with each other around specific issues they care

---

[16] Ostrom's work (1990; 1996) has influenced our framing of the distinct ways citizens' governance spaces operate. She showed how grassroots collective action can emerge, without market inducements or state coercion, to handle major matters like scarce resource management, by working together to develop rules and enforcement systems. Citizen governance and Ostrom's community co-production therefore share a common DNA. Where her research centered on efforts to solve discrete policy problems, the contours of which are largely accepted by the actors even though they may disagree on the strategies used to obtain a solution, our focus is on how citizen-led governance often alters the nature of the goods and services aimed for (for example, producing "restorative" justice and "renewable" energy). In citizen spaces, just what is to be co-produced is part of the fluid, experimental, and inclusive work process.

about and around which they have deep experience and knowledge" (Ansell et al. 2021, p. 349).

While the democratic promises of co-creation are alluring, especially in offering a more "bottom-up" and "joined-up" form of co-production, in practice co-creation projects are mostly led by state actors, wherein a government agency identifies "target communities" with which it wants to engage (e.g., Gouillart and Hallett 2015). In other words, co-creation invites citizens into a collaborative process of public-service redesign, along with other state and non-state stakeholders. In rare cases the co-creation is community-based; but these projects typically involve high wealth individuals or large foundations driving the governance efforts (e.g., Rosen and Painter 2019).

We contend that the concept of citizens' governance space draws important analytic attention to three distinct elements that are not always present in co-production activities: (1) they are always citizen-led; (2) they involve shared action to supply a public good or service which could be or has been a government task; and (3) they create or occupy some virtual or physical space over time.

Of course, concepts such as community organizing, social movements, mutual aid and co-production are not hard and fast. Elements found in all these four are also evident in the activities of people involved in citizens' governance spaces. The activities of a given citizen space might be understood as an element of a *translocal* community organizing effort, or a *prefigurative* project connected to a larger social movement, or an effort in *mutual* assistance, or a *citizen-led* co-production scheme. Yet as those four adjectives imply, those standard categories are too broad and do not do enough to distinguish the types of governance work that citizens undertake in citizen spaces and their implications for state, society, and market.

If we continue to understand citizen-led governance as some variant of either a social movement or a mutual aid effort resisting neoliberalism, or as a grass-roots community organizing effort or as community co-production, then we potentially misread the opportunities and risks these spaces pose to policy and democracy. Taking citizen spaces seriously involves giving greater recognition to the ways ground-level citizens are building civic capacity and reshaping governance on their own terms.

## Conclusion

Citizens participate in politics in many ways that are well understood in political science. Yet their engagement in governance outside formal institutions is less fully studied. As the examples in this chapter reveal, citizens adopt a variety of innovative approaches to govern complex policy issues on their own terms—such as to address social isolation, provide elder care, or to support substance-users. In these grassroots policy efforts that we label *citizens' governance spaces*, citizens are experimenting in concert with other mainstream actors, and sometimes they are also challenging and disrupting state agencies and traditional civil society associations. In this chapter we have identified five key features of citizens' governance spaces that create a range of opportunities for action in the public world. These opportunities, which are sometimes unavailable in other roles and organizations, attract citizens who join in and contribute their time and labor.

We have demonstrated that existing social science concepts—such as social movements, community organizing, mutual aid, and co-production—do not adequately capture the practically focused form of participation found in citizen spaces. To be clear, our argument here is not that citizen spaces are more politically or democratically "effective" than these other modes of social and civic action. Instead, we have made the case that citizen spaces engender a distinct form of engagement that is not well captured by existing social science categories. Specifically, because citizens themselves initiate, self-organize and lead these spaces, they exercise a distinct kind of agency in their collective work. Moreover, their focus is on actively doing something about a problem through practical interventions, rather than agitating, mobilizing, or protesting for the state, market or an NGO to fix the problem. In the case of OSA, the citizens could have set up an advocacy group, lobbied their local government representative, or protested online or on the street, asking governments to do something. But instead, they started a small-scale practically focused experiment. Their approach did not rely on loudspeakers in the public sphere but instead invited volunteers to engage in simple interventions—to offer people living on the street clean clothes, showers, and a conversation. These localized efforts have been replicated in cities around Australia, disrupting how everyday people and decision-makers frame homelessness (OSA 2019; 2023).

Having developed the conceptual resources to identify citizens' governance spaces, from here we move on to analyze what motivates citizens to lead and engage in these spaces, what sorts of functional policy work they undertake, and how they engage with others (Chapter 3); how they generate and share knowledge and skills (Chapter 4); and the different ways they partner with state, market, and civil society institutions, and how this affects their agency and autonomy (Chapter 5). In the final chapter we draw together the broader implications of our empirical analysis, offering insights for theorists and practitioners of democracy and public governance.

# Chapter 3
# Citizens' Motivations and Governance Practices

In this chapter we discuss citizens' governance spaces from the perspective of citizens. Drawing on diverse case examples we examine the varied reasons *why* citizens lead and participate in these spaces, *what* functional governance work they undertake, and *how* they engage others in their collective problem solving. Citizens' motivations and the activities they undertake are closely interlinked; people are motivated to find different solutions, and so discussions about how they find solutions, how they self-govern, and how they engage with users, volunteers, and the broader community are also important parts of the story.

Frequently, citizen spaces emerge when individuals facing similar circumstances or "life politics" (Soares da Silva et al. 2018, p. 6) meet and decide to take some practical steps to address their common concern. Citizens are typically responding to a perceived gap in government services or a market failure. But sometimes, as the analysis in this chapter makes clear, citizens are motivated to disrupt status quo governance approaches, in the hope of steering policy reform in a new direction; for example, toward sustainability or more just outcomes.

This chapter proceeds in four parts. First, we consider what motivates citizens to establish and lead governance spaces. Second, we use several cases to illustrate the varied governance work that citizens undertake, especially in producing and delivering goods and services; in assisting with social order, conflict resolution, or adjudication; and in local and regional planning. Our discussion reveals that some citizen spaces support or supplement existing policy programs, while others are wholly non-compliant with established conventions and laws. In the third part of the chapter we draw together four key democratic attributes that citizen spaces engender: namely, power sharing, giving voice, building capacity, and broader public engagement. We conclude by arguing that democratic features are not peripheral but central to how citizens' governance spaces operate.

*Democracy in Action.* Albert W. Dzur and Carolyn M. Hendriks, Oxford University Press. © Albert W. Dzur and Carolyn M. Hendriks (2025). DOI: 10.1093/oso/9780192870575.003.0003

## Motivations: Why Do Citizens Self-organize Governance Spaces?

To appreciate the agency at the heart of citizen spaces, it is useful to reflect on what motivates citizens to initiate and lead a collective problem-solving effort. People could, for example, use other modes of democratic engagement such as advocacy or activism, but for various reasons they are drawn to self-organizing and taking on the complex work of finding practical ways to address a collective problem. According to scholars of community self-organization, the primary motivators for citizens to engage in bottom-up initiatives are citizen discontent with status quo conditions, or external threats such as funding cuts (e.g., Edelenbos et al. 2018; van Meerkerk et al. 2021). Scholars also point out that, in contrast to social movements, citizens involved in community-based governance are motivated mostly by practical purposes rather than by ideology (Healey 2015a). In this chapter we go further, and articulate five different motivations that drive citizens to initiate, lead, and participate in citizens' governance spaces.

### The motivation to address a problem neglected by the state

A group of individuals might initiate a citizen space because they believe traditional state organizations have neglected a complex, persistent, or emergent public problem. In some contexts, the state may be absent or weak, so there is no other alternative than for citizens to step in (Mitlin 2008). For instance, the Indonesian citizens' group Savy Amira (which means "friends of women") was founded in 1997 by three professional women in Surabaya,[1] because there were no local services for victims of gender-based violence (GBV) (Savy Amira 2024). These three women with legal and psychology backgrounds self-organized weekly meetings in Surabaya—advertised through word of mouth—for anyone concerned about GBV. After six months of meetings, they decided to formally establish the Savy Amira Women's Crisis Centre, using finance from a few volunteers and other community contributions (Savy Amira 2024). They began small with an improvised office in a founder's house, where they ran a 24-hour phone hotline offering legal and psychological counseling services to GBV victims (Savy Amira 2024). During the 2000s, Savy Amira's volunteer base grew, and they secured support from individual

---

[1] The three women were inspired by the Philippine Women's Crisis Center (PWCC), after attending a training workshop on counseling where they met the founder of PWCC (Savy Amira 2024).

donors and philanthropic groups. Since late 2019, Savy Amira has been providing services across Surabaya and East Java, including training on GBV prevention (Savy Amira 2024). The group also takes on policy advocacy at the provincial and national levels and it builds networks with similar or relevant organizations, such as other crisis centers in East Java, service-oriented community organizations, large non-government organizations (NGOs), and universities (Savy Amira 2019; 2024).

In other situations, citizens might instigate a governance space on the back of a short-term mutual aid effort or after spontaneously volunteering in the context of a crisis. Short-term projects like these are opportunities for people who have a shared experience—of a disaster, a crisis, or a health condition, for example—to forge relationships. As conversations and ideas start flowing, a group might decide to self-organize to address an issue or to solidify their preliminary collective efforts. Many such citizen spaces were formed around the globe during the COVID-19 pandemic, particularly in its early phase in 2020. One such initiative is Heart of Dinner (HoD), formed by two residents of New York City—restaurant owners Yin Chang and Moonlynn Tsai—who began cooking hot lunches in April 2020 for "those most vulnerable around Manhattan's Chinatown area, with a focus on providing care and essential nourishment for the low-income and homebound elders" (HoD 2023). This initiative was as much about providing food relief as it was about reaching out to isolated elderly people across the Asian diaspora:

> The under-resourced Asian American older adult population have historically been overlooked across the nation, where oftentimes low-income and homebound seniors live in socioeconomic, cultural, and linguistics isolation. (HoD 2023)

The founders of HoD were also motivated by a sense of solidarity; they wanted to reach out to other Asian restaurateurs and their staff who were being impacted financially and socially in the early months of the pandemic. At the time, many Asian Americans were facing increasing xenophobic and racist incidents as people blamed "Asia" for COVID-19. As the co-founder Yin Chang explains:

> POC [People of Color] have been so neglected by this entire system; the fact that we even have to think about providing food, as the most basic way to survive, is an issue first and foremost ... That's why there are so many small businesses owned by POC who understand this and have jumped in to provide that in a way that the government doesn't. (Quoted in Lang 2020)

Over time, this small local response attracted numerous volunteers and partner businesses, enabling Heart of Dinner to expand to other areas of the city. It now delivers care packages to more than 650 elders per week. The founders have also formally registered HoD as a non-profit organization (Lang 2020) that aims to "fight food insecurity and isolation experienced by Asian American seniors—two long-standing community issues" (HoD 2023).

Sometimes, citizens are motivated to fill a governance void that is opened up by a policy opportunity. Consider how Japanese health cooperatives (which are consumer-led and owned) have expanded their localized health services to provide elder care, following the passing of the Long-Term Care Insurance Act (LTCI) in 1997. This was a major policy reform that allowed aged care to shift from a selective service-provision model (means-tested care provided by social welfare corporations) to a universal service that is based on users' choices and contracts. Since the passing of the LTCI Act elder care in Japan can be delivered by non-government groups, including for- and not-for-profit organizations such as cooperatives (Kurimoto and Kumakura 2016, p. 59).

Traditionally, health care cooperatives in Japan are grassroots consumer organizations that encourage members to learn about and self-monitor their health. Members volunteer to help other members in need, by providing public-health checks, cleaning, and laundry. They also provide training so that members can better support dementia patients. Now, since the introduction of the LTCI Act, many health cooperatives in Japan have expanded their health services into the elder-care business by "opening visiting nurse stations, group homes for dementia patients and short-term stay and health care facilities for the elderly" (Kurimoto and Kumakura 2016, p. 59). Today, health cooperatives in Japan operate for both mutual and community benefit by providing both health care and long-term elder-care services. At the local level, some members are active on resident boards that organize activities for local members—such as health checks, walking, and exercise groups, social occasions such as lunches and dinners, and study groups on topics of interest. Research has found that citizens have been motivated to participate in resident boards out of a sense that they could not rely on government to provide care, and because they were keen to give and serve others, and from a desire to have fun and be among others (Endo 2020).

## The motivation to address a governance void in the market

Citizens can be motivated by market gaps. For example, a group of citizens in Yackandandah—a small regional town in Victoria, Australia—self-organized in the early 2000s to save the town's only gas station from closing down. In 2002 the owner tried to sell it but was unable to get the price he wanted. Rather than protest or ask the state to intervene, seven local residents self-organized to purchase the fuel station and convert it into a social enterprise: the Yackandandah Community Development Company, or YCDCo (Social Enterprise Australia 2023). As one of the YCDCo founders explained:

> We knew that if people started going into the nearest metropolis of Albury-Wodonga for their fuel, they'd be doing their grocery shopping there as well and before we knew it we'd be in a dying town. We said "we can't allow this to happen, maybe we can get the community together and get enough money to buy it and keep it operating." (Quoted in Daley 2020)

Today, YCDCo reinvests 50% of its profits back into the local community and provides seed funding for local community initiatives, such as renewable energy projects, which we will discuss further below.

Some citizens self-organize to change market norms by offering a product or service that is more affordable and individualized than those already in the marketplace. This was exactly what motivated the founding citizens of Tender Funerals—an Australian initiative we discussed in Chapter 1—which began as an idea in 2012 to provide families with compassionate low-cost funeral services. The citizens leading Tender Funerals sought to address what they perceived to be a market failure in Australia's funeral industry, which is predominately run by private for-profit businesses that offer expensive, depersonalized funeral packages. The founders of Tender Funerals set out with the very practical goal of offering personalized funerals at lower-than-typical market cost (TF 2023b). At the time, this was a disruptive idea, and the founders struggled for over seven years to raise money to support their vision of creating a not-for-profit funeral service (Chenery and Rousset 2022). Eventually a film, *Tender*, was made, which helped to attract crowdfunding, donations, and grants.[2]

Since 2016, Tender Funerals has been actively transforming the funeral industry in Australia, by reframing funeral services from an experience delivered by professionalized funeral directors to an empowerment process whereby families are supported and given agency. Alongside its provision of funeral services, Tender Funerals advocates for broader structural change in the funeral industry, such as reforming industry norms and increasing

---

[2] The award-winning film, *Tender: A Documentary*, which is written and directed by Lynette Wallworth (2013) follows a group of citizens as they build Tender Funerals from the ground up, while also caring for one of their own, Nigel, who dies in the film.

transparency on funeral pricing. In a submission to a policy inquiry by the New South Wales state government, Tender Funerals argued:

> Industry norms are ... being set by corporations creating a product or package approach which in turn informs the culture of what funeral services should look like. ...
>
> The Funeral industry has been built primarily around the moving and storage of bodies. The value to the community of a funeral is much broader.
>
> The value should lay in the experience rather than the cost and the pressure of a sales-based approach [that] doesn't empower families to make choices that are aligned to their values. It can undermine it. This can lead to funerals that don't truly honour the purpose of the gathering and in some cases impact the ability for people to have a healthy bereavement. (TF 2020)

Here we see how the practical efforts of Tender Funerals to offer respectful and affordable funerals are informing its policy advocacy to reshape market norms and practices.

## The motivation to fill a governance void left by civil society

Deficits in existing civil society infrastructure and programs can motivate citizens to self-organize a governance initiative. The Serenity Café (which we discussed in Chapter 2) emerged to address substance use and recovery in Edinburgh, Scotland (see Campbell et al. 2011). The Café, while open, created a physical space and social and employment opportunities for marginalized substance users in recovery who were not well served by existing services run by the state and NGOs. For organizers, state agencies often employ "know-it-all" professionals and, even when working in concert with NGOs, provide only patchwork support. But an equally crucial motivating factor for Café organizers was the failure of civil society to offer pathways for substance users to reintegrate successfully. Family and neighborhood dynamics, along with deeply rooted cultural norms about alcohol use and the good life, threatened to push recovering substance users back to the margins where there were strong temptations to use again. Café organizers self-consciously crafted a new kind of entity that provided recovery support, addressed deficits in state and NGO approaches, and altered patterns of interaction in the surrounding civil society (Campbell et al. 2011).

## The motivation to rectify dysfunctional state or market-led responses

As well as citizens' governance spaces responding to perceived voids in state, market, or civil society institutions, many citizen spaces emerge in contexts where there is an *abundance* of governance infrastructure. In policing or in energy and food production systems, for example, many people see the dominant approach as conducive to undesirable outcomes such as overincarceration, marginalization, carbon emissions, food waste, or inequality. In these contexts, citizens self-organize to provide a particular public good or service via an alternative governance pathway (Smith and Stirling 2018).[3] This is not a story of citizens taking up the slack from off-loading done by state agencies, as noted by critics (Eliasoph 2013; Lee et al. 2015). Rather, citizens are often motivated to form and work in governance spaces that operate in terrains scattered with the bones of failed policies.

Citizens can be motivated to address a problem where existing state and market approaches are not effective, or are creating negative side-effects. In thousands of community energy projects that have emerged worldwide over the past two decades, citizens have formed groups to produce, store, distribute, and sell renewable electricity from local solar or wind infrastructure (Brummer 2018). Many of these community-led energy projects are driven by popular frustration with the failure of large energy companies and state regulators to provide affordable renewable energy (Caramizaru and Uihlein 2020; Hicks and Ison 2018).

One such initiative started in 2014 in Yackandandah, the small Australian town mentioned previously. In the face of rising concerns over climate change, the residents held a community forum together with the local government to explore possible pathways in their region to produce and use renewable energy (Salathiel 2014). Rather than wait for the state or a large energy corporation to determine their renewables pathway, the residents decided to set up a community group, Totally Renewable Yackandandah (TRY), to accelerate the energy transition in their town. The founders of TRY were not just interested in reducing the town's carbon emissions; they also wanted to "increase the reliability of the network, and save residents and businesses some money" (Smith 2022). To kick start this venture, TRY received some seed funding from YCDCo, the local civic enterprise discussed previously (see Smith 2022).

---

[3] Such pathways are typically more substantial governance experiments than the demonstration activities or "prefigurative politics" of social movements (see Yates 2015).

TRY set an ambitious target: to produce 100% of the town's energy needs from renewable sources by 2022 (Fogarty 2014)—a goal they almost reached (Smith 2022). TRY has sourced and installed affordable solar infrastructure (through bulk buys) for local businesses and residents, and helped them with energy efficiency measures.[4] TRY has also worked with local public institutions to install rooftop solar; for example, at the local medical center, fire brigade, kindergarten, swimming pool, and wastewater treatment plant. The money saved on electricity bills is then used on improving services in the town (Smith 2022). As one of the founding members of TRY, Matthew Charles-Jones, explained:

> We're not experts in energy, all we're doing is working alongside a whole community…. This isn't about the activity of a handful of people or TRY, it's the enterprise of a whole town. (Cited in Driscoll 2017)

## The motivation to replace state or market-based approaches that marginalize people

Citizens can be motivated to lead a governance space because they distrust the capacity or right of the state or market to tackle a collective problem. In some cases, citizens want the state to withdraw its dominant approach which they believe is marginalizing certain populations, such as refugees, the homeless, drug users, or victims of violence and crime. An example is the Vancouver Area Network of Drug Users (VANDU). This citizen space was activated not only because state inaction and neglect had led, in the 1990s, to some of the highest rates of overdose fatalities in the world, but also because the state was doing too much that was coercive and paternalistic and contributing to further death and marginalization. Policing practices in Vancouver pushed substance-using citizens into back alleys where overdoses would go unnoticed. As an early leader of VANDU noted, "It's always the issue…It doesn't matter where. We [addicts] don't have drug problems, we have cop problems" (Lupick 2017, p. 293). Strict anti-narcotic laws forced users to re-use needles, leading to alarmingly high rates of human immunodeficiency virus (HIV) and hepatitis. VANDU was motivated to create safe injection spaces and clean needle exchanges, to save lives and to push back against the effects of an overbearing policy approach.

---

[4] TRY has conducted numerous bulk buy programs for local residents and community buildings; for example, sourcing "highly efficient solar hot water systems and natural refrigerant (CO2) heat pumps" (PoV 2020, p. 142).

Working on substance-use issues without acknowledging the voices and realities of the substance users themselves had led, in Vancouver, to a wide gulf between officials and marginalized citizens. Early meetings of VANDU record members' frustrations:

> We want detox, treatment, showers, etc. They ask us what we want with public consultations and we tell them. We never get these. Money instead goes to the service-providing agencies who hire people with university degrees who get $30,000–40,000. They set you down and tell you, "You have a drug problem," and then they have nowhere to send you anyway for detox or a place to live that won't kill you. Service-providing agencies and their staff lack the political will to change things. They are not for us. (Boyd et al. 2009, p. 51)

> I'm involved in organizing these meetings and would like to see users organized to have a strong voice. I'm homeless. I look around to see which house of horrors I'm going to move into next. Every time we come to the table, the agencies are on the same agenda as three to five years ago. A meeting is called to make an action plan, and when it's all over, there is no action. I believe this is because the situation is very top-down—the people with the power in the community organizations face losing their funding if they take the action necessary to make our lives better. I believe users can get organized to insist on peer-based support systems, community kitchens and community space. People's nutrition is severely lacking in this neighbourhood. We can solve this ourselves because we realize that it is essential to have meals at night for our more nocturnal population. (Boyd et al. 2009, pp. 57–58)

A central motivating goal, therefore, of citizen spaces like VANDU is to de-marginalize: to humanize people who have been acted upon by providing the means and spaces for self-determining actions to better their conditions even if—and necessarily so—these actions do not comply with the law—a theme we discuss in the following section.

Citizens can also be motivated to form a citizens' governance space because they can no longer bear witnessing the human costs of policies. They channel their frustration into practical experiments that seek to address the issue at hand. Citizen-led restorative justice programs, for example, have emerged around the world to address both crime and criminal justice responses to crime (Blad 1996; Dzur 2019; Zinsstag and Vanfraechem 2012). In the case of the Baltimore Community Conferencing Center introduced in Chapter 1, citizens were motivated to help their neighbors handle situations where police interventions were often unproductive. Indeed, police sometimes made harmful situations worse by giving young people criminal records that made them less employable (Abramson and Beck 2010; Abramson and Moore 2001).[5] Similarly, Restorative Justice for Oakland Youth (RJOY) was founded by citizens motivated to intervene in school disciplinary practices that had become punitive and were contributing to a "school to prison pipeline" for Black youth:

> [O]ver the last decades, U.S. schools have been criminalising children instead of educating them. Use of exclusionary school discipline has doubled during this period, and for youth of colour, the use of suspensions has grown eleven times faster than for their white counterparts .... As we design whole school implementation along with training and coaching strategies, consciousness of the need to interrupt the school-to-prison pipeline throughout our practice is paramount. (Davis 2018, p. 431)

Having explored several reasons *why* citizens might decide to form and lead a space of collective problem solving, we next examine some of the types of functional policy work that citizen spaces undertake.

## Functional Policy Work: What Governance Practices Do Citizen Spaces Undertake?

Citizen spaces address a range of policy problems, and three types of functional policy work are particularly common: 1) goods and services production and delivery; 2) social order, conflict resolution, and adjudication; and 3) planning and development.[6] We elaborate on these three types, illustrating the governance practices and activities of citizens who lead and engage in these spaces. We show how some governance practices enacted by citizen spaces comply with current legal norms, while some do not (Gofen 2021).

### Citizens produce goods and services

The most common governance practice undertaken by citizen spaces is the provision of goods and services. Many of the cases we have discussed in the

---

[5] For more on the early development of Baltimore Community Conferencing, see http://www.restorativeresponse.org/how-we-got-started/. Accessed January 29, 2024.
[6] A recent survey of citizens' governance spaces across the world identifies eight prominent sectors in which they are active: community development; education; employment and training; safety; social well-being and health care; sustainability; urban development; and water management (Igalla et al. 2019, p. 1183).

book so far fall into this category, where citizens self-organize to provide a particular good or a service, such as alternative care or health service (e.g., Tender Funerals, Serenity Café, Orange Sky, Japanese health cooperatives) or a more desirable or affordable good, such as renewable energy (e.g., TRY, Som Energia). In those examples, citizens are doing disruptive work, but their governance activities are compliant; that is, they operate within the existing governance and legal frameworks.

There are also instances where citizens develop and deliver goods and services in a way that is non-compliant, such as via the governance practices of VANDU, introduced previously. In 1995, Vancouver community activist Ann Livingston began organizing regular meetings of substance users:

> Our goal was to get involved with local people's issues, listen to what their issues were, and then help them fight for their issues. So we started organizing bi-monthly meetings of addicts themselves. We always tried, as much as possible, to let the addicts run it themselves. (Lupick 2017, p. 85)

The group, which would come to be called VANDU, started meeting at a storefront Livingston had rented. They called the place "Back Alley" and it became "their own space, a first for drug users, certainly in Vancouver and likely in North America—people could just hang out" (Lupick 2017, p. 86). "Word went out that cocaine and heroin users could inject drugs there without having to fear they would die of an overdose alone on the street" (Lupick 2017, p. 88).

By early 1996, Back Alley had become a supervised injection site, which "included a front room and a back room with three injection booths, couches and a reception desk" (Boyd et al. 2009, p. 29). Back Alley was mostly peer-run; aside from Livingston and a few others, "the group's membership was entirely drug users. It wasn't long before casual use at Back Alley became the site's primary function" (Lupick 2017, p. 89). While such practices were illegal, the contributions the VANDU site made to community well-being did not go unnoticed by the police. As one visiting officer noted, "We're not condoning what you're doing. But as long as there is no trafficking going on in here, and as long as we're not getting called here a lot, we're not going to do anything about it." Even in the face of non-compliance, new rules were formed: "No dealing and keep the worst of it out of the cops' sight" (Lupick 2017, p. 89). "The police unofficially tolerated the Back Alley because it was not creating problems; it was reducing them by bringing people into a safe place instead of using in alleys and other unsafe places" (Boyd et al. 2009, p. 29).

While this site only lasted one year, it provided a type of proof of concept for later harm-reduction practices, as noted by a local newsletter: "The idea that users can organize themselves is starting to grow, and even if… the Back Alley were to shut down tomorrow, the idea that we must take control of our own lives, and that we have the numbers and the knowledge to do so, is here to stay" (Lupick 2017, p. 98). Moreover, for the time it was in operation, it served a crucial function: "During the year it was open, there were drug overdoses at the site, but not one fatality" (Boyd et al. 2009, p. 29). VANDU and its allies also staffed portable public toilets in alleys, making sure to monitor them for people overdosing, and offered clean needle exchanges. Their peer-to-peer service delivery and participatory decision-making bridged a longstanding gulf between marginalized citizens and needed resources.

Citizen spaces can also undertake governance practices that do not comply with market regulations. Consider community-based Internet service networks in Indonesia. In the late 1990s and early 2000s, many residents throughout Indonesia had poor access to Internet services, especially those on low incomes and people living outside major cities (Suyatno 2007). A national law introduced in 1999 permitted only licensed operators to build telecommunications infrastructure and transmit radio waves, including frequencies for wireless Internet connection. Lack of supply and competition pushed up prices for Internet services, resulting in many residents without affordable and reliable Internet access (Wagstaff 2007). In response, some citizens pooled resources in their local neighborhoods to set up their own low-cost community-based Internet service (Suyatno 2007; Wagstaff 2007). Many groups adopted a low-tech network called "RT/RW-Net" that had been originally developed in 1996 by university students using walkie-talkies to share Internet connections across campus (Purbo 2015). One such community group, AngkringanNet, that formed in a village near Yogyakarta, established a local Internet service using a computer and a wok (*wajan*) as an antenna. According to Jurriëns, this group:

> … deliberately chose the wajan [wok], a basic piece of cookware that can be found in almost every Indonesian kitchen, to put people with no prior exposure to modern communication technology at ease, and to make it clear that browsing the Internet or sending an e-mail was as easy as frying an egg. The choice can also be seen as a symbol of local resistance against business monopolies dominating the computer and Internet industries. (2009)

In the early 2000s similar neighborhood-based groups self-organized all over Indonesia to form their own local RT/RW networks providing residents with affordable internet services. Eventually the government succumbed to popular pressure and legalized these scofflaw networks.

## Citizens work on conflict resolution, adjudication, and social order

Citizens' governance spaces also form to resolve or adjudicate conflict or to address issues of social order. An example is the emergence of citizen spaces working on restorative justice, such as the Baltimore Community Conferencing Center discussed previously and in Chapter 1. In this case the citizens have developed practices to resolve interpersonal and community conflicts, and to adjudicate disputes. Offenses dealt with range from personal slights to property damage to physical assault. In Baltimore, the Community Conferencing Center seeks to keep people out of the formal criminal justice system by providing "a highly participatory community-based process for people to transform their conflicts into cooperation, take collective and personal responsibility for action, and improve their quality of life" (Dzur 2013). The center has helped thousands of people address problems in their communities before they become formally designated as crimes to be handled by the justice system.

The Community Conferencing Center organizers have developed simple but effective practices to mediate conflicts in the community. First, they invite everyone affected by a harmful action to meet together in one place. This can involve weeks of door-to-door canvassing participants. At the meeting, they encourage each person, one at a time, to tell the group what happened. Then, in a second round of contributions, each participant tells the group how the harmful action affects them personally and how they feel about it. Finally, participants are asked to say what they want to do about the action, to move forward. Facilitators are trained to give participants the freedom to be passionate, sad, and even angry.

According to the Community Conferencing organizers, the process does not repair social problems for people, but rather serves as a medium for them to handle their own problems in their own way. Conventional public and official attitudes have grown comfortable with the typically hierarchical decision-making in criminal justice, and the Community Conferencing process challenges that:

> if our institutions are top-down—if we need a judge in a black robe telling people how they should be punished—then we're going to get one set of outcomes. But if

we engage people with this alternative structure—in a circle where they acknowledge what happened, share how they've been affected, and then decide how to make it better—then we will get a whole different set of outcomes. (Dzur 2013)

Citizens also undertake governance practices to improve social order. The citizens' group, CAHOOTS—an acronym for "Crisis Assistance Helping Out On The Streets"—was founded in Eugene, Oregon, in 1989 to train and field emergency responders. CAHOOTS aims to provide free services to people who distrust conventional social welfare and criminal justice staff. As one CAHOOTS responder notes, "the program started after people in the community expressed feeling alienated from police and health-care providers, and wouldn't seek help because they were scared" (Brenna 2020).

CAHOOTS often intervenes in situations involving members of marginalized populations, and engages in ad hoc problem solving. CAHOOTS workers provide a quick fix, and they also prevent troubles from escalating into issues that would trigger police and criminal justice system responses. "We're there to listen, we're there to empathize, and we're there to really reflect on what they're going through," notes a CAHOOTS operations coordinator (Smith 2020, p. 16). Eugene has one of the largest per capita homeless populations in the US, so more than 60% of the people served by CAHOOTS are homeless and 30% are living with mental illness (Brenna 2020).

CAHOOTS owns and operates three vans equipped with medical supplies and staffed by two emergency medical responders who take 12-hour shifts. The vans continuously travel the streets of Eugene and nearby Springfield, ready to respond at all times to calls coming in from local police or from their own hotline. Responders handle a range of mental health, social welfare, and interpersonal issues. An average shift might include:

bringing several people to the university hospital's emergency room, picking up used syringes whose locations were called in as tips, transporting unhoused people to shelters for the night or giving others blankets and extra shirts, dressing wounds for people living in motels and shelters, rousing a woman who had overdosed on a stranger's doorstep in a residential complex, talking a young trans girl through her suicidal ideation, and counselling a man who had gotten too drunk to go to his scheduled detox program and had to make it through another night at home with his beleaguered wife. (Varagur 2020)

In 2019 CAHOOTS handled 24,000 such calls, with only 150 of these requiring police backup (Brenna 2020).

CAHOOTS staff are given 500 hours of training in medical care, conflict resolution, and "non-judgmental approaches to de-escalation" (Brenna 2020). Their practices are deliberately distinct from those police would use in similar circumstances, and are meant to avoid "harmful arrest-release-repeat cycles, and ... violent police encounters" (Smith 2020, p. 16). CAHOOTS workers do not wear uniforms or carry guns. They dress casually; their white vans lack the sirens and flashing lights common to official emergency and police vehicles, and instead they display a prominent white dove symbol. Their emergency response practices are highly circumscribed: they handle specific crises and offer concrete help, but do not try to solve longer term issues that may be in the background, such as chronic mental health or addiction problems, or insecure housing. "CAHOOTS members can transport people to staffed services and hospitals, or counsel them, or give them food or shelter supplies, but the list is not much longer than that" (Varagur 2020). "We're an intervention team," one emergency responder notes, with "deliberate limits, honed over decades of operation, as to the degree and duration of that intervention" (Varagur 2020). The work done by CAHOOTS—and by the Baltimore Conferencing Center—is compliant to the extent that they are not seeking to circumvent or undermine existing legal institutions.

In other cases, citizens undertake non-compliant governance practices to resolve conflicts or to address social order. Consider the case of civilian border patrols along the US southern border. Motivated by concerns over illegal immigration, the drug trade, and cartel violence, as well as property damage for ranch owners and other border residents, citizens have been self-organizing into groups, both to police the border and to monitor the effectiveness of official border control efforts. Like other non-compliant citizen spaces, civilian border patrols are not sanctioned by the state; they operate in ways that encourage law breaking. It is not illegal to carry firearms and patrol the border, but it is illegal to trespass on private property, carry firearms without permits on federal land, unlawfully detain people, and to impersonate official agents by wearing clothing and insignia that mimic law enforcement (Viña et al. 2006). Indeed, some civilian border patrols also veer into the category of "bad" citizens' governance spaces, as noted in Chapter 1, when they use violence, deceptive techniques, and promote racist ideologies.[7] Civil rights organizations like the American Civil Liberties Union and justice officials alike decry what is often characterized as vigilante action (Caldwell 2019).

---

[7] One scholar notes, "While I am not suggesting a direct connection between civilian border patrol groups and racist, white nationalists, the construction of an 'enemy' that is widely disseminated across many social spaces provides fertile ground for extremist, supremacist groups" (Doty 2007, p. 128).

"Border Watch," a citizen space monitoring the Arizona–Mexico border, organizes operations every two months (Parsons 2022).[8] Groups of around 20 members, who have been subjected to background checks, first conduct reconnaissance missions, then use that information to determine where to place teams to interrupt and detain migrants.

> At the outset of each operation, teams of up to four volunteers conducted reconnaissance missions that scouted the area, looking for fresh 'sign' of clandestine border crossers. Border Watch used this information to build a narrative of what had occurred throughout the week and inform their plans. The ever-present threat of the cartel meant security of the volunteers was of utmost concern. Every volunteer was armed with a pistol and an assault rifle. Many carried personal armor in the form of plate-carriers, vests with ceramic or metallic plates on the chest and back. Once Border Watch established the most likely smuggling routes, they chose specific trails to set up teams of 2–4 volunteers in ways that would trap anyone on the trail. The teams remained in situ for up to 48 h to further reduce the potential for detection. (Parsons 2022, p. 9)

The duration of the operations, the fact that most Border Watch members live some distance from the border, and the need to take time off from paid work, mean that people can participate in only a few operations a year (Parsons 2022).

"Vigilante," a normatively loaded term, which implies "taking the law into one's own hands" in a way that undermines the rule of law, no doubt describes some civilian border patrols. Most patrol members would not be taking part in them if they were not critical of the official border patrol and skeptical about the state's ability to ensure social order. Yet many civilian patrols see themselves as assisting or helping the state, albeit in an uninvited way: "these groups engage in popular sovereignty, or sets of practices aimed at complementing and correcting the state in hopes of restoring its capacity to legitimately use physical force, in this case, over the borderlands" (Elcioglu 2015, p. 439). The motion detecting cameras set up by Border Watch, the reconnaissance information, and any illegal actors detained are meant to supplement official border control and enforce, not challenge, the rule of law (Parsons 2022).[9] One civilian border patrol group, the "Engineers," is based

---

[8] "Border Watch" and "Engineers" are pseudonyms used by the scholars studying these groups, typically to grant research access to civilian border patrol members concerned about legal repercussions of their actions (Elcioglu 2015; Parsons 2022).
[9] Some scholars use the term "neo-vigilantism" to describe contemporary groups acting in ways that support the state (Brown 1975). Elcioglu notes that the groups she studied "try to cultivate collaborative relationships with different parts of the state—Border Patrol, DHS [Department of Homeland Security]

in "a ranch that they use as a laboratory" and "scrutinize the Border Patrol's methods, assemble new technologies, and test them in hopes of redesigning the way the state conducts surveillance on the borderlands" (Elcioglu 2015, p. 439).

> From the ranch, the civilian organization scrutinized the Border Patrol's practices of detection and apprehension. Based on this close study, the Engineers drew on interdisciplinary knowledge, from engineering to seismology to computer programming, to develop technologies for alternative systems of border surveillance. To publicize their new system, the Engineers conducted live demonstrations for the media and local supporters, including immigration restrictionist politicians. (Elcioglu 2015, p. 452)

Using thermal cameras, ground sensors, solar-powered seismographs, drones, lightweight manned aircraft, and sophisticated software designed to sort accumulated data into usable information, the group sought to "document" both the activities of US Border Patrol agents as well as the smugglers and migrants seeking to evade them. As we will discuss further in Chapter 4, like many other citizens' governance spaces, civilian border patrols are interested in *knowing* as well as *doing*: "the Engineers embarked on an iterative process of dismantling, reassembling, and testing technologies that they hoped would let them acquire comprehensive information about the border region" (Elcioglu 2015, p. 454).

## Citizens work on local and regional planning

Another common set of governance practices involves citizens self-organizing to manage aspects of local and regional planning. There are many well-documented cases of this kind of citizen-led planning work especially at neighborhood level, where citizens self-organize a group to develop plans for a particular neighborhood or to self-govern a piece of common land or natural space for conservation or public amenity (see examples in Edelenbos et al. 2018; Edelenbos et al. 2021c). In-depth research, for example on community-led initiatives to address urban decline, has found that citizens are often better placed than siloed administrative government agencies to deal with complexity and long-term local planning (Wagenaar 2007).

---

officials, and local politicians—in an effort to bolster it" (2015, p. 441). They "have taken it upon themselves to help 'restore' the government's capacity to legitimately use physical force to detect, detain, and deport those who do not belong" (2015, p. 442).

Sometimes citizens lead policy work at the regional scale, where their efforts go well beyond local neighborhood initiatives. For instance, the Glendale Gateway Trust (GGT) emerged in the late 1990s to tackle a specific regional issue in the remote north-east of England. Since then, the Trust has grown into a community-led regional organization involved in a range of housing and economic development projects. According to planning scholar Patsy Healey, who has been involved in the Trust as a local resident, it offers substantial "non-state governance infrastructure":

> We manage a community and business centre, several commercial and residential units, and a youth hostel, which we consider as individual social enterprises. We are also a significant player in the effort to expand affordable housing provision in Glendale and promote rural business development. Our direction of travel at present aims to expand our housing and economic development role, strengthen our asset base, and develop our role as a community hub for the area. Over time, the GGT has also become a governance site to which people turn when they want to see something done, or to get a voice heard. (2015b, p. 14)

In some cases, citizens self-organize regionally to promote place-based strategic planning. An example is the group of citizens who developed a strategic plan for the Goulburn Murray region in Victoria, Australia, where irrigated agriculture is widespread. They were frustrated with the short-term and piecemeal approaches to planning taken by multiple agencies and layers of government.[10] For decades, their region has faced successive problems including salinity, farm debt, and cycles of extreme drought and major flooding (see Walker et al. 2009). The impacts of changing climate are creating considerable uncertainty for farmers and businesses; predictions suggest much drier and warmer conditions in the future. The region also faces numerous other issues, such as government schemes to recover water for the environment, technological changes, dynamic markets, energy challenges, and biosecurity risks. In the face of all these challenges, a group of citizens started to explore and discuss how they could promote resilience and long-term thinking among residents, farmers, and businesses in the region. These are goals that piecemeal policies by successive local, state, and federal governments had failed to promote.

The citizens' group formed in 2017, and with some government seed funding it employed consultants to work with the broader community to explore ideas on resilience and planning for climate adaptation. In 2018–19 the group

---

[10] Based on interviews with members of the Goulburn Murray Resilience Taskforce, conducted by Carolyn M. Hendriks between June and November 2023.

then led a consultative process which involved a series of "vision workshops" which engaged people from various local communities, as well as relevant local, state, and federal government agencies, farmers, and the agribusiness sector (for details, see RMCG 2019). Here, the citizens were leading the consultation and inviting relevant state and private actors into their collective problem solving, not the other way around as is common in state-led participatory governance.

From this consultative process emerged a community-led strategic plan, the *Goulburn Murray Resilience Strategy*, which was launched in December 2020. The strategy has since received the support of the relevant state government agency, Regional Development Victoria, and is promoted by the citizens involved as a path-breaking community-led intervention that has the potential to respond to the complex challenges the region faces due to climate change. To guide the implementation of the Strategy the community has established the *Goulburn Murray Resilience Taskforce*, which is a community-led collaborative body composed of community members, farmers, private sector companies, and a variety of local, state, and federal government actors (GMRS 2020). This is an example of citizens seeking to ensure that in highly uncertain times their region is guided by a strategic vision, rather than by short-term siloed interventions from the state.

Citizens in both Glendale and in the Goulburn Murray region were undertaking governance work that complied with the existing administrative and state-based governance arrangements. In other cases, citizens undertake governance practices on planning issues in ways that are non-compliant. An example is the squatters in Lingewaard, Netherlands, who decided in June 2001 to occupy an abandoned military installation, Fort Pannerden, alongside the Rhine and Waal rivers. Although declared a national monument in 1969, this 19th century fort had fallen into disrepair after a number of failed attempts at restoration by the municipal government and the State Forest Service, which had become the site's owner. Squatting was legal in the Netherlands and the occupiers followed the routine procedures: "after entering the fort the squatters called the police, who officially established that the building was empty and the squat peaceful" (van Dam 2016, p. 61). Once in place, the group began repairs and held open houses for the public on the first Sunday of every month:

> Besides making the fort accessible to the public, the squatters also made it fit for habitation. The squatters had their own ideas about what they wanted the place to be: a cultural haven, a social center, and a refuge for people looking for a way of life different to what is widely perceived in society as 'normal'. Many travelers,

an estimated 150, stayed at Fort Pannerden during the squatters' occupancy of the site. (van Dam 2016, p. 61)

The squatters took care to preserve the cultural heritage of the site as they renovated, using appropriate tools and materials in their repairs (van Dam 2016, p. 64). Over time, initially suspicious local residents living nearby came to see the squatters as providing a public good—through the monthly openhouses, tours, and renovation.

Nevertheless, official planners in the municipal government had other plans for the site, and arranged to have the squatters removed—calling on the army to do so (van Dam 2016, p. 61). Two weeks later, however, after the military had left, a group of 80 to 100 squatters returned and re-occupied the fort. Public opinion and widespread media attention favored the squatters, with local residents strongly objecting to the use of military force in the eviction. In light of the public response and the re-occupation, the municipality decided to negotiate an agreement in which the squatters became "the official keepers of the fort" with responsibilities for management, maintenance, and tour provision, though they were not allowed to live there (van Dam 2016, p. 62).

## Democratic Attributes: How Do People Engage in Citizens' Governance Spaces?

We turn now to consider aspects of *how* citizen spaces undertake their governance work. Our discussion focuses on four particular democratic attributes that citizen spaces typically engender in their governance work, namely they: (1) share power; (2) give voice; (3) build capacity; and (4) engage and mobilize the broader public.

### Citizens share power

Most citizens leading governance efforts recognize the importance and value of sharing power in core administrative and strategic decisions. Rather than push forward their own vision and set of solutions, they set up procedures and structures to involve a broader group of citizens in making core decisions about the group's administration, funding, partnerships, and future direction (e.g., Borzaga et al. 2016a; Pestoff and Hulgård 2016). These arrangements vary from highly formal oversight structures such as committees or boards with appointed members, to quasi-formal advisory councils, through to more informal or even ad hoc processes of advice and oversight, such as peer support. Citizen spaces that carry a particular organizational or legal status—such as a cooperative or community trust—tend to have relatively formal oversight arrangements. In some jurisdictions, the specific form of the citizen space requires a particular type of formal oversight, such as a governing board. Member-based cooperatives, for example, are typically required to provide opportunities for the membership to be engaged in decision-making.

Consider the self-governing arrangements in the Spanish renewable energy cooperative Som Energia, which we introduced in Chapter 1. The founding citizens of Som Energia adopted a cooperative organizational model offering multiple opportunities for member engagement in local and central decisions (see Pellicer-Sifres et al. 2018; Riutort Isern 2015).[11] Members all over Spain are encouraged to participate locally in groups of between 5 and 20 people that regularly meet to discuss and debate issues (Pellicer-Sifres et al. 2018, p. 104). Som Energia's decentralized model also fosters power sharing by enabling local groups to have a degree of agency and autonomy over their own activities and events.

Informal power-sharing arrangements are common in citizen spaces; for example, citizens establish leadership groups, peer advisory teams, or steering groups. Some arrangements are particularly sensitive to inclusion and are extremely open, with no requirement to offer dues, or to reside in a particular locality, or to be clean from substance use. The substance-support group VANDU in Vancouver is so committed to inclusion that it mandates that only substance users can be members. As it developed as an organization, it held regular meetings and formed leadership roles for members. "A VANDU AGM [annual general meeting] is a special event to witness. There are elections for board positions that can involve a little money so everybody is competing for them hard. And because drug use is a VANDU requirement for membership, a lot of the people there are high" (Lupick 2017, p. 182). Dean Wilson was drawn into the organization by the offer of a sandwich and three dollars at the end of the meeting. Within four months he was president of VANDU: "It was exactly what I wanted. I wanted to have a voice" (Lupick 2017, p. 183). VANDU embodied a principle of being "The community of everyone who arrives" (Zigon 2018, p. 80).

Other citizen-led spaces committed to inclusion might actively recruit more marginalized perspectives onto their internal governing bodies. For

---

[11] For example, see https://blog.somenergia.coop/som-energia/proceso-participativo-reflexion-estrategica-organisativa/

citizens leading and participating in spaces aimed at providing services for marginalized people (such as the homeless, former and current substance users, prisoners, and ex-prisoners), it matters that these "service users" are also included in core administrative and strategic decisions. For example, the citizens leading the Serenity Café substance-recovery initiative in Edinburgh, discussed in Chapter 2 and earlier in this chapter, established a steering group to engage and empower highly marginalized people in recovery to help lead and govern the Café. As some of the organizers explain:

> Although tempting at times, we did not want to install a higher echelon of people in recovery who are professionals with the skills and experience to easily form a token committee, to lead the process. We felt a more genuine empowerment could come from demonstrating that people whose addiction careers started at an early age—cutting them off from learning and employment—and who are now in recovery can learn, develop, and achieve their full potential with the right opportunities. (Campbell et al. 2011, p. 139)

Here we see how some citizen spaces actively seek to include user perspectives in their own internal governance arrangements; going well beyond the inclusion of "internal stakeholders" such as members or volunteers, as emphasized by scholars of social enterprise (e.g., Larner and Mason 2014).

Power sharing can also be fostered in more subtle ways; for example, by enabling diverse forms of communication within the citizen space. For example, the Baltimore Community Conference Center, discussed previously, places few limits on the expression of emotions. Organizers believe that public expression of emotional remarks can bring emotions out in a safe space where they can be observed, felt, and become part of a collective practice:

> Conferencing is elegant. There are three questions that the group's going to talk about. And they can talk in whatever way they want. We don't go in saying, "You can't make racist comments," because if you do that then the person who is racist is never going to get a chance to change. We let the group decide. So once something offensive comes up, the facilitator will say to the participants: "There is a request to not say these kinds of things, is this something everyone can agree to?" It lets people be who they are and then lets that group decide for itself the norms for their behavior from this time forward. (Dzur 2013)

Even angry words are acceptable in a conference because facilitators think it is better to have them out in public—and potentially subject to contestation—than withheld and simmering inside individuals.

## Citizens give voice

In addition to power-sharing arrangements, many citizen spaces take steps to ensure that the views of their members and users are considered in specific decisions. For example, the energy cooperative Som Energia provides opportunities for its members—who own and operate the cooperative—to have a say on major strategic issues through a voting procedure at its annual General Assembly. Other citizen spaces convene forums or meetings to facilitate discussion amongst members and the broader community on key issues or new directions, or to address particular challenges. For example, when exploring the possibility of partnering with corporate energy actors, the energy cooperative TRY, which we introduced previously, ran a series of community meetings with its members.

Some citizen spaces use processes to elicit specific input and feedback from users, volunteers, or members: they might undertake a survey or run a workshop aiming to understand how people experience a particular collective problem, or to explore their views on an existing service. These insights enable citizens' governance spaces to improve their problem solving and inform their broader policy-advocacy work. For example, Tender Funerals regularly surveys its users to understand their experiences of its funeral services and to explore areas for improvement (see TF 2022; 2023b; 2023c). Similarly, Som Energia runs reflective workshops with its members to explore how they think the organization should grow and evolve, and to identify priorities for advocacy in that evolution (e.g., Som Energia 2017). The cooperative also finds that its devolved structure with local groups has enabled people from different age groups to provide input:

> In relation to Local Groups, these have been seen as a space that has facilitated the participation of young people, generating an intergenerational diversity and also as a space to launch projects of their own initiative …. (Som Energia 2016)

## Citizens build capacity

Many citizen spaces are committed to working "with" marginalized and vulnerable people in ways that can promote new skills. This is less about offering solutions *to* marginalized people—as is often the case in charities—and more about generating and delivering solutions *with* the marginalized. There are citizen spaces that explicitly use engagement to build the capacity of those traditionally excluded from conventional spaces of governance and democracy, such as the homeless, substance users, the hungry, and those on the frontline of climate disruption. The Serenity Café's way of involving Café users in the steering group is one example; and its organizers also encourage users to volunteer in the preparation and service of food and drinks to gain employment skills.

The citizens involved in Orange Sky Australia—offering washing and showering services to homeless people—build capacity by encouraging people living on the street to sit down on an orange chair and have a chat with community volunteers while they wait for their washing, as discussed in Chapter 2. Volunteers are trained to engage with homeless people and start conversations. Connections form, and possibilities for social change open up:

> The humble orange van and six orange chairs have broken down barriers in communities all over Australia. Powerful bonds have positively changed the lives of many people, some are friends on the street, some are our volunteers. There are many stories, some are heartwarming and empowering, others are surprising and confronting. Unfortunately, many stories are heart-wrenchingly sad. (Orange Sky Laundry 2016, p. 3)

People on the streets are also now becoming volunteers themselves and are working within the organization and learning new skills (Orange Sky Laundry 2016).

Some citizen spaces also focus their capacity-building efforts on their members, volunteers, and users to ensure that they feel empowered and supported in their governance work. For example, Tender Funerals supports and involves its users by enabling them to wash and dress "their person" (Chenery and Rousset 2022). It also offers support for its volunteers through a variety of social activities such as choirs and sewing circles, as well as running an artists- and musicians-in-residence program. In its efforts to change the norms and practices of the funeral industry, Tender Funerals has partnered with a philanthropic foundation to design and run a tertiary-level qualification for funeral directors—one that emphasizes the "importance of compassion, informed decision making and consent-based mortuary care" (TF 2023c, p. 12).

In-depth qualitative research on the member experiences of the energy cooperative Som Energia finds that its participatory opportunities have developed members' skills: "the capacity to deliberate, express their own voice, respect other points of view and learn from conflict," for example (Pellicer-Sifres et al. 2018, p. 107).

Capacity-building can also be about building connections and encouraging people to share their existing skills and learn new ones. Consider how the Common Unity Project Aotearoa (CUPA) in Wellington, New Zealand, uses simple everyday practices—such as growing food, cooking, mending, and making—to engage people from a range of backgrounds and multiple generations in accessible practices for climate-adaptation. Like all citizen spaces, CUPA started small, beginning in 2012 as a community-garden project to feed school children three times a week. Since then, it has spawned a wide variety of projects and social enterprises, including:

> growing food on micro-farms; making meals for purchase to support meals for school children; a koha café; repurposing and reselling bikes at affordable cost; collective sewing from repurposed donated fabrics; a waste-free affordable grocery collective; and a beekeeping and honey collective …. CUPA also partners with people in the justice system, who are either currently in prison or serving probationary and community services. These participants may for instance, do their community service time by working on one of the micro-farms, or undertaking general maintenance and building work. (Simon et al. 2020, p. 93)

The expansion of CUPA has been made possible through funding from philanthropic and corporate sources as well as from state grants. People can participate in CUPA in various ways: volunteering, engaging in workshops, donating goods and resources, or purchasing products from one of the enterprises. Particular emphasis is placed on encouraging multiple generations to participate in CUPA activities. Observations at The ReMakery—the building that houses CUPA—found that:

> on any given day at The ReMakery there may be a family bringing in its newborn, a group of teenagers coming by for community service work, or one of the regular elders dropping off knitting or helping with the odd fix-it job. The different social enterprises appeal to different ages and offer various ways to participate. This intergenerational aspect also helps to foster an acceptance of different physical abilities and skill levels and promotes the transfer of ecological-social knowledge across generations …. (Simon et al. 2020, p. 98)

The informal and social aspects of CUPA are attractive to people, some of whom "described themselves as distrustful or disengaged from local and national electoral politics" (Simon et al. 2020, p. 97). CUPA is also accessible to newly arrived immigrants, who are attracted to the practical and connective aspects of volunteering, doing, and learning together. As one participant explains:

> This is why the ReMakery is really good for finding new skills or experience. For somebody like for me too …. I think I'm introvert but in here I am able to be more open and talk more. Before I was really shy, I wanted to say something but I was worried people wouldn't be able to understand what I say. But because of here, volunteering here, I meet different people and it teaches me and I learn a lot and I can improve … so many different things. (Simon et al. 2020, pp. 98–99)

## Citizens engage with the broader public

Most citizen spaces are not inward facing groups. Instead, they seek to connect and engage with the broader community to share knowledge and to attract new participants and volunteers. As we argued in Chapter 2, citizens involved in these spaces of collective governance recognize people's interest in becoming more civically active and the benefits that flow from this engagement. In addition to the participatory activities discussed previously, citizen spaces also run broader community outreach and engagement activities aimed at building public awareness about the public problem they seek to address, and opportunities to participate. Common examples of this kind of engagement include:

- community events
- online webinars
- information events and open days
- stalls at local shows
- workshops
- fund raising events
- site visits and field trips.

For example, Tender Funerals runs death-literacy workshops and holds stalls at local shows and markets to broaden public awareness about funerals. It has also worked with journalists and media groups to produce films to document and share their story. In June 2022, Tender Funerals featured on the Australian Broadcast Corporation's (ABC) program *Australian Story* (ABC 2022). This episode, which was also accompanied by a feature article on the ABC news website, has been viewed over 1.4 million times (TF 2022, p. 10).

According to Tender Funerals, this publicity prompted an influx of interest and comments from families and communities around Australia on how they could create their own Tender Funerals franchise in their local region.

Public awareness raising and educational activities are especially common in citizen spaces addressing sustainability issues, such as renewable energy. Som Energia runs energy-conservation/energy-saving workshops via its local branches. Participation has also generated a broader awareness among members of the social and political context of energy policy in Spain, raising second-order issues such as social justice, power imbalances, and citizen agency. This broader governance awareness of rising energy poverty in Spain has stimulated many Som Energia members to take action in their local area; for example, by engaging in workshops with social workers, and by running training sessions on how to reduce energy bills, and by proposing projects for local authorities (Pellicer-Sifres et al. 2018, p. 107).

The targets of these information and outreach campaigns can also be decision-makers such as elected representatives. For example, the energy group TRY hosted a site visit for members of the Parliament of Victoria as part of its parliamentary inquiry into communities and climate change. This site visit informed decision-makers about the opportunities and challenges facing local communities taking practical steps to address energy insecurity and climate change (PoV 2020).

## Conclusion

In this chapter we have considered citizen spaces from the perspective of citizens. Our diverse case examples have demonstrated the varied reasons *why* citizens lead and participate in these spaces, *what* functional governance work they undertake, and *how* they engage others in their collective problem solving. Our analysis finds that citizens in these spaces are contributing to public policy not because they have been invited to provide advice or to co-design a solution with state officials or a civil society organization. Instead, citizens participate in these governance spaces because they are motivated to address a problem neglected by the state or market, or to rectify dysfunctional or inadequate responses by state agencies, corporations, and civil society organizations. We have also shown how some citizens are motivated to self-organize a governance effort because they want to address a particular problem faced by a marginalized group such as the homeless, drug users, or victims of violence and crime.

The citizens leading these governance spaces are typically not ideologically motivated, as they might be in a social movement or in activist activities. Nor are they asking the state or the market to fix a particular problem, as they might in a protest or in a piece of advocacy, for example. At the same time this form of citizen participation is not antagonistic toward the state or market; rather, citizens want the state and market to work on terms at least partly defined by citizens themselves. "By us" and "with us" rather than "against us," "to us," and "for us" is a common rallying cry.[12] Traditional political power, such as electing officials more sympathetic to a group's interests or perspectives, may be an objective, but is not the overarching or dominant goal.

Even more important are the ways that these spaces allow citizens to have productive, functional power. Citizens leading these spaces want to own the solution, and have agency in the process, and reap the benefits of the outcomes. Our case examples demonstrate that citizens in these spaces do not simply aim to plug holes or fill gaps. Instead, we have shown how citizens themselves are driving forward "functional policy work" through various compliant and non-compliant practical problem-solving initiatives. In many instances the citizens are actively changing the way "the problem" is understood, and experimenting with alternative ways it might be addressed. For example, they are coming up with practical methods to provide more affordable and accessible energy, funeral, and Internet services; they are finding novel ways to resolve or mediate conflict or to address issues of social order; they offer innovative solutions to local and regional planning.

In exploring the democratic attributes of citizen spaces we have shown how participation is a way of working, rather than an added-on mechanism. As citizens go about their collective problem solving they engage others in practical projects where people *do* things. They might also establish internal governance structures and decision-making to share power, or actively seek to listen to and include the voices of relevant members and service users. Beyond practical governance, voice, and inclusion, we have shown how citizen spaces can also be venues of social connection, learning, and capacity building.

Overall, we see how the forms of citizen engagement enacted in bottom-up governance spaces are conceptually and practically a long way from the structured participatory forums constructed for and by governments to bring citizens into policy decisions (Nabatchi et al. 2012). In the first

---

[12] For example, a key underlying value of many community or social enterprises is that they "are done by the community for the community" (Simon et al. 2020, p. 97).

instance, participation is led by citizens, not experts; citizens determine the scope of the problem, the subject matter, priorities, and plans under which engagement takes place (Edelenbos et al. 2018, p. 53). In terms of format, citizen engagement in governance spaces tends to be more informal, fluid and less rules-based than structured participatory and deliberative forums (cf. Nabatchi et al. 2012). Recall for example the informal outreach and connective work of Orange Sky with its orange chairs.

The participatory practices discussed throughout this chapter—such as local committee structures, conversations, community conferences—are relatively simple, which means they can be easily replicated or adapted by citizens in other contexts and locations. They are just some of the many kinds of knowledge that citizens in governance spaces generate and share, which is the topic of Chapter 4.

# Chapter 4
# Doing, Thinking, and Sharing: Knowledge Contributions of Citizens' Governance Spaces

The knowledge landscape surrounding contemporary public problems is complex and contested. Internet and digital technologies, while making it easier to find out about collective problems and learn about possible solutions, also carry communicative risks such as information overload, and the viral spread of misinformation and disinformation. Meanwhile, user data from phones, internet usage, bank accounts, and public transport patterns are collected and used by corporations and public authorities to predict behaviors and preferences, via algorithms and machine-learning technologies. Also significant is the way knowledge is not just a "thing" out there to be collected but is an "emergent property" of the practices and processes of governing (Wagenaar 2007).

Thus, as citizens lead and engage in their governance activities, they can encounter an epistemic jungle; they must learn to navigate through a dense landscape of policies, agencies, and elite networks, and make sense of complex or incomplete information and data. But as they move through this jungle and engage in direct problem-solving work, they develop valuable tacit and experiential knowledge. While skeptics might characterize this citizen-led work as involving merely "local" or "apolitical" knowledge (e.g., Dekker 2019), a closer examination reveals a more dynamic picture of citizens rethinking and reframing social problems, generating new procedural and conceptual tools that can have broad systemic reach (Evers and Brandsen 2016).

In this chapter we consider how citizen spaces develop and accumulate knowledge and skills, and how they translate, reproduce, and share these among expert and non-expert actors, and across sectors and borders. Our empirical cases show that while most people in citizen spaces might be focused on doing practical work, over time they accumulate extensive substantive, procedural and systemic knowledge. In some instances,

*Democracy in Action.* Albert W. Dzur and Carolyn M. Hendriks, Oxford University Press. © Albert W. Dzur and Carolyn M. Hendriks (2025). DOI: 10.1093/oso/9780192870575.003.0004

this accumulated practical knowledge draws citizens into policy advocacy and advisory work, where they share and "represent" the perspectives of those they work with or seek to assist. Citizen spaces can also usefully bring together and distribute different forms of knowledge across wider networks. Sometimes this knowledge sharing breaks down siloed policy approaches and facilitates cross-sectoral connections and partnerships that form to address complex issues. Perhaps most powerfully, when citizens in these spaces reframe problems and develop alternative solutions, the knowledge they generate can disrupt and re-shape community, state, and market norms and practices.

The chapter has five sections. We begin by discussing existing ways to understand, value, and access citizens' knowledge in collective problem solving. Next, we use diverse empirical cases of citizens' governance spaces to demonstrate how they generate and transmit not only substantive policy knowledge but also vital expertise on a host of procedural, organizational, and governance issues. Then we show how citizens working in these spaces reframe problems and solutions, and how they develop and tinker with procedures to generate ideas and foster stake-holding. Next we give examples of citizen spaces sharing their procedural insights with citizens in other places, as a kind of shared democratic intelligence. Finally, we consider the broader implications of the knowledge generated in citizen governance for scholarly and practical debates on public engagement and democracy.

## Citizen Knowledge in Collective Problem Solving

The valuable contribution of citizen knowledge in public policy is well recognized. Scholars and practitioners wrestling with complex and intractable policy issues have long argued that multiple forms of knowledge must inform judgments on collective problem solving (Schön and Rein 1994; Rittel and Webber 1973). They view citizen input as vital to help societies navigate inherent uncertainties and risks in contemporary governance, providing values for collective judgment (Funtowicz and Ravetz 1993; Renn et al. 1995). Rational, functional, and managerial expertise that dominates knowledge production in public policy needs to be supplemented with other forms of knowing, such as practical policy "know-how" and the tacit forms of knowledge from frontline workers (Bergheim 2021; Lipsky 1980), as well as the perspectives and experiences of users, citizens, and communities (Adams 2004). More recently there has been greater recognition of the enormous knowledge potential locked up in the public realm, particularly the capacity of citizens to contribute to novel problem solving and policy innovation, and to help administrators design programs that deliver "public value" (Noveck 2021).

Proposals abound on how to access this kind of street-level and community knowledge, but in general they are instrumentalist in approach—seeking to tap the voices and experiences of those implementing or using public services through surveys, focus groups, or participatory exercises. Here, knowledge is understood as something that can be "extracted and 'mined' [from citizens] rather than co-produced and iterated" (Adams 2004, p. 40). State agents are seen as the rational planners, the knowledge accumulators, while citizens are the supplementary helpers brought in to offer different perspectives.

In an effort to access this valuable citizen knowledge, governments and civil servants are encouraged to "reach out" to the public for their inputs, through designing and convening invited participatory spaces, such as deliberative forums or mini-publics. While such forums have been celebrated for their capacity to boost deliberation and inclusion (OECD 2020), they typically provide limited opportunities for citizens to engage in the practical business of collective problem solving. Moreover, in most participatory forums, citizens have little say over the remit of the process, or the knowledge and experts that might inform the deliberations. Even if citizens can select which experts they seek to hear from, they are typically choosing from a preselected roster. In terms of tacit knowledge, the citizens participating in forums, especially those forums designed using sortition or random selection processes, often lack any direct experiential knowledge of the focal problem. Indeed, the facilitators of most public forums assume that the public needs to be educated in the topic at hand to provide sound data on reflective preferences to policymakers. In mini-publics, such as citizens' assemblies and citizens' juries, topical experts are brought in so that the citizens might form informed perspectives (see Elstub and Escobar 2019). Designed participatory processes like these can be so choreographed and scripted that there is little room to capture the more dynamic kinds of policy knowledge that can emerge when citizens iteratively work together, over time, on a collective problem of significant meaning to them.

Citizens can also actively reach in to governance to bring important sources of policy knowledge into debates and policy decisions. Activists engaging in a social movement might produce counter-expertise, or they might introduce alternative knowledge into public debate to challenge conventional understandings of an issue (Cox 2014). Citizens also produce knowledge through monitoring and documenting what is going on in formal state bodies—such as court and legislative proceedings—and report that information to a broader public (Rosanvallon 2008). Like the knowledge generation that happens in mini-publics, monitoring done by social movements is centered around what the state is doing and not doing. Unlike in mini-publics, however, the knowledge generation and uptake in social movements tends to be oppositional: citizens develop counter-knowledge and then try and inject this into the state to influence policy outcomes. One vulnerability with this kind of social-movement knowledge is that the state can quickly dismiss or ignore it because it is viewed as biased or ideological, and lacking independence. Insofar as monitoring restricts itself to institutional and official action, the knowledge is limited to what the state can do, without offering any perspective on what citizens might do. For example, while a protest movement might expose officials' ties to business interests or document police killings, this knowledge does not demonstrate how to do better governance, even though it could lead to changes in governing regimes, officials, and ultimately to policy change.

Knowledge production by citizens is not limited to participatory forums and activism. Consider, for example, how people are invited to produce knowledge in citizen science projects, where they might collect samples, record observations, or interpret large data sets (Martin 2017). State agencies like the US Environmental Protection Agency have facilitated the work of citizen scientists to broaden the reach of the agency and gather knowledge it could not have accessed otherwise—about watersheds (water catchments), and about community disparities in environmental hazards, for example (Sirianni 2014). Citizens can also inject their specific expertise into policy by contributing to crowd-sourced innovation projects (Brabham 2015; Liu 2021). These forms of citizen knowledge may be useful for advocacy, monitoring, data collection and innovation in public policy, but they are not generated through the practical process of doing governance.

This chapter explores the less appreciated forms of citizen-generated policy knowledge that are produced as citizens lead and work practically on collective problem solving. We argue that as people work collectively on grassroots projects to address a public problem in practical ways, they generate and share diverse forms of knowledge: about the policy issue and potential solutions; about procedures for organizing and community engagement; and about the broader governance system. Through this practical work, citizens develop and share knowledge that is not only experiential but also constructive. Some people working in citizen spaces may have had bad encounters with status quo norms and conventions, and they may oppose these in their own ways. But the alternative forms of knowledge that they generate in their practical problem solving are constructive and revelatory about citizen capacity, rather than oppositional and merely critical of official action. Viewing these spaces as sites of knowledge generation and distribution gives a better understanding of the numerous ways in which citizens are contributing to governance, and to democracy more broadly. When people work on a collective problem to make their world better, they build democratic capacity by asking questions, reframing social problems, generating new conceptual tools, and developing problem-solving skills.

## Citizens' Governance Spaces as Sites of Knowledge Generation and Distribution

Today, certain kinds of citizen spaces, such as civic enterprises, are often celebrated by governments and global institutions for their capacity to innovate and generate novel ideas (e.g., OECD 2020; World Bank 2018). This aspect of citizen governance is also emphasized by scholars and practitioners interested in the role of citizen-led initiatives in pushing forward more socially just and environmentally sustainable forms of production and consumption (Mathie and Gaventa 2015). In parts of this literature, particularly on sociotechnical transitions, the targets of the knowledge produced by citizen spaces are typically private sector actors or prominent scientists, and the knowledge generated by citizens is viewed as an "active and critical alternative to elite trajectories of innovation" (Smith and Ely 2015, p. 103). While this framing sees value in the knowledge that the citizens produce, it sees it as an added bonus to official knowledge—as something that can help experts do their work, offering fresh or new perspectives on a pre-defined problem.

However, the epistemic value of citizen spaces extends well beyond the development of novel ideas and perspectives. Drawing on a range of empirical cases we reveal that citizens working together on a collective problem draw on *and* generate substantive, procedural, and systemic knowledge. Such citizens often challenge official and private sector frameworks and develop different ideas about the nature of a given policy problem, about people's greatest concerns, about how citizens might contribute to solutions, and how public and private sector power-holders might need to act differently.

### Substantive knowledge contributions

In citizen-led spaces people rethink and reframe complex social problems, and develop practical knowledge about how to address them. Citizen spaces acquire street-level knowledge about what does or does not work. This is experiential substantive policy knowledge "acquired in the process of dealing with everyday situations" (Wagenaar 2007, p. 42). These knowledge resources about how best to improvise with practical solutions can then feed into, or confront, formal governance processes, often challenging status quo assumptions. As citizen governance participants connect with frontline staff, volunteers, government officials, and people facing complex problems, they develop grounded insights of diverse perspectives, including of the most marginalized.

**Substantive knowledge about the "problem"**
A policy problem, seen from the ground level of a citizen space working on it, is broken down into concrete personalized elements. The closer one is to people impacted by poverty or lack of shelter or substance use or mental health issues, the harder it is to reduce the complexity of human beings into routinized concepts—common in social work and law enforcement—which often frame people as "cases" defined by social problems (see Bacchi 2009). CAHOOTS (Crisis Assistance Helping Out On The Streets), the citizens' governance space originating in Eugene, Oregon, and described in Chapter 3, responds to low-level disturbances caused by people without shelter and undergoing mental or other health crises. CAHOOTS staff "meet them where they are" and provide treatment or support without the social disruptions leading to jail time or official sanctions (Varagur 2020). CAHOOTS workers know more about these marginalized people than police or social workers do, because of the horizontal and informal nature of the organization. Their "clients" are neighbors and fellow citizens—not just people with problems.

Because of their horizontality, citizen spaces are less likely to use official frames to understand problems. In the Downtown Eastside neighborhood of Vancouver BC, the official narrative—embraced by city office holders, public health personnel, and police—was that increased drug use via unsafe injection was a major "problem"; that it led to the spread of disease and to some of the highest rates of overdose deaths in the country. The Vancouver Area Network of Drug Users (VANDU), the citizens' governance space made up of current and former substance users (see Chapter 3), saw the problem differently. Via regular structured meetings, VANDU members pointed to the ways their living situations inside buildings, and the policing outside in the streets and parks, increased their risk of human immunodeficiency virus (HIV) and of hepatitis transmission and of overdose. Those who were sheltered often lived in SRAs (single residency accommodations) in hotels or other high-capacity dwellings—where a person who overdoses might not be noticed by others if they use drugs indoors. Those without shelter or whose accommodation was in poor repair sought to use drugs in alleyways—outside the purview of police who would arrest them, but also away from passers-by who might come to their aid.

In research projects on which VANDU collaborated, the terms "safe" and "risky" places were used in ways that complicate and challenge the official policy discourse. Places that could be "safe" were like that because of the actions of other marginalized people living in similar circumstances, while what was "risky" often stemmed from drug prohibition policy, policing, and social stigma:

> [O]ur findings demonstrate how drug consumption in the alleyways is the result of a host of disparate factors coming together including SRAs (which push people outdoors), experiences of stigma (which drive people to hide), lack of supervised consumption sites, drug policies (i.e., criminalization), private security (who prohibit people from loitering in public areas), other PWUD [people who use drugs], and fear of police (which again pushes people into secluded areas). All of these elements (and likely others not captured in the data) assembled in unique ways produce a given effect, such as pushing people into secluded spaces, potentially increasing their exposure to risk and harm. (Ivsins et al. 2019, p. 6)

Another substantive knowledge contribution that many citizen spaces offer comes in the form of conceptual tools that they develop to aid sense-making or to reframe a problem. These tools can come in different forms; for example, alternative metaphors that shift how a particular problem is understood, or a heuristic to guide problem-solving work. For example, a citizen space used and adapted the concept of an "iceberg" to promote resilience and long-term thinking in one of Australia's largest irrigation districts, the Goulburn Murray region. As noted in Chapter 3, this is a region that has faced decades of successive challenges including salinity, farm debt, severe droughts and now a rapidly changing climate. In 2016 some local community leaders began discussing how they wanted to foster a brighter vision for the region—one that was underpinned by ideas on resilience thinking and climate adaptation. As part of their initial work, they adopted and adapted an iceberg model to promote deeper thinking needed for resilience:

> The iceberg model demonstrates that it is most effective to intervene more deeply within our system. Working above the water line will not address underlying patterns, processes and systemic structures that enable us to adapt and transform. (GMRS 2020, p. 10)

The iceberg forms a central idea in a series of community processes that the citizen space convened to develop a vision for the region. The *Goulburn Murray Resilience Strategy* emerged out of these community conversations as a community-led planning strategy (GMRS 2020). According to several community leaders in the region,[1] the iceberg model has provided an important heuristic for facilitating conversations within the community about how best to steer systemic long-term change in their region. Almost ten years on, the "iceberg" continues to shape community leaders' deliberations on the region's strategic direction.

### Substantive knowledge about what works to solve the "problem"

A striking element of citizen governance practice is the peer-to-peer nature of its problem solving: those impacted by a harmful situation can help themselves out of it and can help others as well. Restorative justice citizen spaces bring victims and offenders together, often with family and community supporters, to have simple dialogues about what happened, how it made people feel, and what can be done to make amends and repair damages. Applied research rooted in these practices addresses longstanding concerns that informal justice leads to disproportionate outcomes and revictimization (Rosenblatt 2015). While restorative justice sessions are not tick-the-box proceedings, and will vary with every combination of individuals, that particularity is part of what makes them work: their efficacy depends on whether the voices and agency of citizens are expressed (Aertsen 2015).

VANDU meetings, which were sometimes attended by public health workers and city officials, allowed substance users to collectively think through their situation. Meeting notes record the kind of testimony and consciousness raising that is possible when marginalized people are allowed to have a voice:

> The illegality of the drugs causes damage, not necessarily the drug itself. Did I have to be degraded and criminalized to stop? I think I felt worse about myself and may have used more and longer as a result. People have to have a reason to stop, and degradation is not a reason to stop; it's often a reason to use.
>
> Outreach workers won't go into the hotels because they are afraid. Users from down here aren't afraid—peer outreach then would be much more effective at saving lives. Outreach workers on the streets or in offices don't reach the people most at risk. They don't end up being of help. For the most part, users help each other all

---

[1] Based on interviews with members of the Goulburn Murray Resilience Taskforce, conducted by Carolyn M. Hendriks between June and November 2023.

the time. It's too bad too because you can't get hired as a worker unless you have been clean for a long time. (Boyd et al. 2009, pp. 58–61)

Sometimes citizens possess specialized skills or knowledge that can be applied in a novel way to help address a collective problem. The citizen-led group Elevated Access provides private plane transport to oppressed and disadvantaged people "seeking abortion or gender-affirming care." This group formed in 2022 in response to "extreme healthcare bans being enacted in state legislatures" (EA 2023). This is just one of many citizen-led efforts that have emerged in the US to provide abortion services since the Supreme Court rescinded a constitutional right to abortion by reversing the landmark *Roe v. Wade* decision. Elevated Access brings together people with knowledge and skills in transport, particularly in private and commercial aviation:

Our network of volunteer pilots are matched with and provide transportation for passengers and resources to aid people in need of reproductive or gender-affirming care. We do this through careful coordination with organizational partners and logistical coordinators. (EA 2023)

Here is a citizen space that is offering a practical workaround for women affected by legislative changes on abortion: "We don't like that we need to exist, but we know that we can help." Its approach is not to lobby the courts or healthcare providers, nor to protest on the street, but to connect citizens with aviation skills, knowledge, and resources with individual women needing transport for healthcare. As one volunteer pilot who flies passengers in his plane for Elevated Access explained: "I don't like how some of these people have to suffer for this political game … It's tragic" (Kelly and Schwartz Taylor 2023).

Citizen spaces can also generate "integrative knowledge" to deal with complex public problems. They tend to view collective problems in more interconnected ways than in traditional public policy where issues are compartmentalized and dealt with by discrete departments. Citizens in governance spaces can bring important contextuality to problem solving, and adopt an integrated approach to dealing with complexity; for example, they recognize the "related whole of actions, mutual relationships, rules of etiquette, social trends and policy measures" (Wagenaar 2007, p. 27). Wagenaar's close study of citizens' initiatives addressing complex neighborhood decline in the Netherlands revealed how citizens have a "ready grasp of the developmental trajectory of the problems ... that problems extend in time both backward (problems have a history) and forward (a problem is not solved by a one-time initiative but requires an ongoing effort)" (2007, p. 34).

**Substantive knowledge about the needs and capacities of "the needy"**
As discussed in Chapter 2, many citizen spaces work closely with highly marginalized people in efforts to address particular needs or problems that they face. We have seen how citizen spaces self-organize initiatives to provide food, offer washing services for the homeless, create alternative pathways for recovery from substance use, and enable peer-to-peer support services for vulnerable people. They work alongside and with "needy" people; they sit and talk with them; they listen; and they seek to understand their complex circumstances. In the process of connecting with marginalized people, citizens in these governance spaces can come to develop a deep appreciation of the needs and capacities of the marginalized. This grounded knowledge of the lived experiences and capabilities of marginalized people, which contrasts with what officials and agencies typically know about such groups, can then inform further practical interventions and policy discussions to tackle systemic issues. Consider, for example, how conversations with people on the street informed the expansion of Orange Sky Australia's services from laundry and washing to training and employment opportunities for the homeless (OSA 2021, p. 41).

People who come to the state's attention are often seen through the prism of conventional institutional categories such as "offender," "victim," "homeless," "substance user." Criminal justice caseloads are processed, for example, without much attention to whether those most impacted by a harmful event have experienced "justice" (Holder 2018). Citizens creating space for restorative justice, by contrast, develop knowledge about victims' and offenders' needs; about the impacts of crime and of conventional crime-control on communities; about different forms of resolving harms; and about the capabilities of victims, offenders, and communities for dealing with harmful conduct (Koss 2014). An entire body of alternative knowledge has emerged among restorative justice practitioners from working with people who have experienced small and large harms—from property theft to reckless driving to assault (e.g., Madsen 2004). Practitioners use different terminology, such as "person who caused harm and person who experienced harm" instead of "offender" and "victim"; "conflict" rather than "crime"; and the terminology shapes novel pathways for research and analysis and a burgeoning literature on alternatives to punishment.

Knowledge gathered about the needs of victims and offenders via community-run restorative justice programs has challenged default assumptions about the value of official punishment for victim healing and offender reintegration (Blad 1996). Practical, piecemeal work with both parties has revealed different needs. For instance, many victims want to regain a sense of power in the world, to answer questions about their victimization, and to ensure the offender is aware of harms caused and is committed to future desistence; many offenders want to be released from totalizing labels such as "criminal," and to make amends, and to be recognized as a member of a community (e.g., Cissner et al. 2019). These needs cannot be satisfied by standard punishment policy, which frequently sidelines both parties as active agents, forcing them into prescribed roles. Over time, citizen spaces working on restorative justice have shown that even in serious cases of harm, victims often seek out dialogue with offenders as a part of their healing, rather than formalized punishment (Madsen 2004).

The unconventional goals of citizens' governance spaces mean they generate unconventional types of knowledge, opening the doors to other policy approaches. The practical work done in citizen governance produces knowledge about people's needs and capabilities that is not available to conventional actors such as prosecutors, defense attorneys and judges. More cumulatively, knowledge about successful ways of resolving conflicts, of recovering from the trauma of an assault, of apologizing and providing recompense, builds support for alternative approaches.

**Substantive knowledge about place**

Citizen spaces apply and generate important "place-based" knowledge. While geography remains the basis for determining state jurisdictions and electoral districts, too often these boundaries cut across the landscapes and spaces that make sense to citizens (Scott 1998). Many collective problems are felt and experienced in a place; it is also the basis around which many citizen-led problem-solving efforts are organized (Soares da Silva et al. 2018). Indeed, most of the citizen spaces considered in this book have started in a specific place—a suburb, village, town, region or catchment. Citizens self-organize at this level because it is where they have relationships, networks, and a working knowledge of how to mobilize others, where to leverage resources and where they can exercise agency and have an impact.

We are not trying to celebrate local small-scale knowledge, here; rather we are drawing attention to the deep knowledge that citizens possess of places, their histories, meanings, and their people. "Place" is where people experience governance dysfunction, and also where they participate in and engage in collective issues. When policies or institutions are not coping successfully with worsening circumstances, a group of citizens might self-organize and use their place-based knowledge to find a way to address the issue. This is citizens' "doing" knowledge as much as "local" knowledge, since it emerges from their collective action, but it is often the case that "place" is the unit of self-organization for citizens. Healey gives insightful reflections on the significance of place for a citizens' initiative in which she was involved:

> What I notice[d] … is the continual work of listening, learning, spreading knowledge and evolving ideas in all kinds of social sites—in cafes, pubs, on buses, in meeting rooms, in people's homes, on car journeys. It is in this way that you get to understand the complex ways many different people with a stake in a place notice things, care about things, develop positions and engage in initiatives to change things, or get locked into conflicts over one issue or another. (2015b, p. 24)

Citizens and communities solve problems in place-based ways not just because it can be more practical or feasible, but also because it is where gaps in state and non-state approaches are most apparent. In contrast to actors from siloed government agencies or from corporations, who may come and go, citizens often have long-term interests and knowledge in the places where they live. They care about the outcomes and impacts of state or community-led programs to address collective problems such as unemployment, youth suicide, substance use, or environmental degradation. Local citizens often bring a more contextualized perspective to collective problems; they might have witnessed different government interventions over time, seen first-hand examples that do or do not achieve success on the ground, identified gaps or overlaps in service delivery, or observed potential opportunities to address a collective problem.

Some scholars of democratic governance dismiss this place-based focus of citizen governance, arguing that it distracts them from addressing the bigger issues. Dekker, for example, states: "Focusing on 'making a difference' in a concrete and immediate way in villages and neighbourhoods runs a real risk of putting citizens at a growing distance from wider society and the political world" (2019, p. 82). Yet this argument misses the crucial differences between somewhat passive forms of place-based knowledge and the more dynamic way that citizens in these spaces apply *and* generate knowledge about their place and its connections to a broader system, through working on a collective problem. The former can mean being a repository of ground-level experience, traditional ways of working, and awareness of longstanding social networks. The latter, which we emphasize here, captures how people in a specific locality learn about a problem, about others, about themselves, and about connections to the broader society and political system, and how they generate knowledge of place by working with others, formulating plans, connecting up relevant actors, and reflecting and adjusting strategies. As Healey argues, citizens in these spaces of collective problem solving have a "shrewd understanding of local dynamics and the wider context" (2015b, p. 19).

## Procedural knowledge contributions

In governance spaces, citizens may generate and experiment with procedures and conceptual tools that they then share with others. Our discussion here links with themes discussed in other chapters. In Chapter 3 we described inclusive procedures used in citizen spaces to share power, exercise voice, recruit, communicate, and engage with people they seek to assist as well as with the broader community. Many of these citizen-generated processes and concepts emerge as people within citizen spaces seek to make sense of a particular collective problem, and how they might address it. In the present chapter we focus on three different kinds of procedural knowledge that citizen spaces generate, and how their commitment to wide norms of inclusion affects knowledge production. Then in Chapter 5 we discuss the procedural knowledge and skills that citizen spaces gain as they interface with relevant state and non-state actors and with complex administrative processes.

### Procedural knowledge on how to address the "problem"

At the heart of the problem-solving work driving citizen spaces is the development of, and experimentation with, new practical processes to address a collective problem. Consider, for example, the varied procedural knowledge that has been generated through citizen-led restorative justice initiatives globally, about approaches that do or do not succeed, and about how to support and sustain such approaches in communities that are accustomed to more conventional criminal justice. Since the 1970s, a body of practical procedural knowledge has developed around victim–offender mediation, family-group conferencing, circle sentencing, and related forms of restorative dialogue (Johnstone and Van Ness 2006). All these procedures have been adjusted over time and are used in context-dependent ways that suit the problems faced in a community. A family-group conference, for example, is not simply an adjudicatory space designed to "process" caseloads. Rather, it allows all those involved in the citizen space to learn more about background pressures and issues generating conflict and sparking harmful action, while at the same time they are helping a particular offender and victim deal with the impact of an offense.

### Procedural knowledge about how to self-govern

Many citizens' governance spaces develop considerable procedural knowledge on various ways to self-organize and self-govern. They may also experiment with novel methods of including the voices and perspectives of marginalized people in their decisions and governance work (see Chapter 3). In doing so, citizens leading and participating in governance spaces wrestle with questions of inclusion, representation, and deliberation.

Studies show that it is common for citizens' governance spaces to create internal democratic governance structures to ensure that members, volunteers, and "service users" have opportunities to shape collective decisions of the initiative (Borzaga et al. 2016a; Pestoff 2018). In our discussion on power sharing in Chapter 3 we pointed to self-governing arrangements in citizen spaces, ranging from highly formal structures—such as committees or boards with appointed members—to quasi-formal governance structures—such as an advisory council—through to informal or ad hoc processes of advice and oversight—such as peer support for leaders.

Our focus here is on how citizen spaces operationalize democratic norms such as inclusion and representation in their self-governance procedures. For example, consider the citizens' governance space that emerged after a catastrophic bushfire tore through the small community of Strathewen in North East Victoria, Australia, on Saturday February 7, 2009. The fire killed 23 residents and flattened most of the town including the community hall, the primary school, and over half of the houses in the area. Shortly after the fire the local government held a public meeting and there was a "deep anger" towards authorities (SCRA no date). Many in the community felt that they had been abandoned by government not only on the day of the bushfire but also in the early recovery phase (Leadbeater 2013). Shortly thereafter a group of residents decided to take control before government programs and grants started flowing and generating further tensions. This core group held a public meeting on March 22, 2009 and proposed the idea of setting up the Strathewen Community Renewal Association (SCRA) to ensure that their recovery process was owned and steered by the community (Leadbeater 2013). The citizens leading SCRA were very mindful of ensuring that its self-governance was inclusive and representative. According to one of the founding members of SCRA, David Brown:

> We built ownership and had an election for 12 committee roles … it was important to us that we had elected people on our incorporated association because they could legitimately speak with authority to government about what the people in Strathewen wanted … Of that first 12 committee members we had a really broad level of skills and experience …. It was important because it needed to be a representative committee. It needed to bring to important deliberations that it was considering everything from legal and financial knowledge, right through to how people will feel and do feel about the experience they have been through ….[2]

Procedural knowledge developed by one citizen space is often shared willingly with citizens in other locations seeking to do similar problem-solving work. In some instances, groups might place particular conditions on other communities before they are willing to share (or franchise) their specific model of self-organizing and self-governance. For example, for the community organization Tender Funerals discussed in Chapters 1 and 3, part of its mission is to support communities to set up their own Tender Funerals service, and it willingly shares its original model and learnings with others. It does, however, insist that these local initiatives must place communities at their heart: "Expressions of interest to start a Tender Funerals service must come from a community and the community is involved at every step of establishing, owning, and operating the service" (TF 2023b).

### Procedural knowledge about user and public engagement

Citizen spaces develop vital procedural knowledge about how to engage externally with marginalized people, relevant stakeholder groups, and the broader public. As we discussed in Chapter 3, citizens leading governance spaces use a variety of engagement methods to foster voice, inclusion, capacity building, and mobilization. Many develop and apply simple yet concrete participatory processes—such as local committee structures, online conversations, or community conferences—that act as scaffolding around which

---

[2] Quoted in SCRA (no date).

citizens themselves can make necessary procedural adjustments to suit particular contexts. This flexible approach empowers citizens to organize participatory processes on their own terms, without having to rely on participatory experts. Procedures can also be easily replicated by citizens elsewhere in other contexts and locations. For example, the practices used by CAHOOTS to work with people in crisis, and the organizational strategies it uses to sustain its position in relation to the formal administrative matrix of public health and public safety agencies, have found resonance outside their home base in Eugene, Oregon:

> CAHOOTS had been advising similar projects and pilot programs in cities such as Denver, Oakland, Portland, and Olympia, Washington, which voted to create an unarmed Crisis Response Unit in 2017. But the experiences of CAHOOTS and its spinoffs have gained a new, instructive pertinence as municipalities nationwide look to divest parts of their public safety apparatus from police departments. (Varagur 2020)

Interestingly, leaders in citizens' governance spaces do not appear worried that people might have "limited knowledge or capacity" to contribute.

Overall, we see how citizen spaces generate procedural knowledge: not via experts, but rather through the iterative work of citizens experimenting with different ways of working to solve problems, govern internally, or engage externally. All three forms of procedural knowledge generated in citizens' governance spaces are noteworthy for the simplicity of their procedures, their rootedness in basic elements of dialogue, and their social proximity. These characteristics show the organic, easily replicable nature of many efforts, and also show what is missing from state and corporate action.

## Systemic knowledge contributions

In citizen spaces, participants develop tactical and practical knowledge on how a given policy system works operationally and systemically. This is more than just understanding which agency or department is responsible for each policy area; rather, it means gaining knowledge about how the different parts of the governance system work together on a given issue, and knowing where the overlaps, gaps, and points of intervention lie.

### Systemic knowledge about networks and actors

In their attempts to address collective problems, citizens navigate a complex array of organizations and programs. They build up a working knowledge of the civic and policy landscape that surrounds a given issue, and an understanding of relevant networks and resources (Evers and Brandsen 2016). Consider, for example Healey's personal account of being the chair of the Glendale Gateway Trust, the citizens' governance space in North Northumberland (see Chapter 3) that provides affordable housing and community hubs:

> We have acquired knowledge through individual trustees, through tapping into local knowledge, through working with supportive solicitors and estate agents and increasingly through contacts with university specialists and students. Knowledge also comes through careful network building, in particular through the formal government agencies ... (Healey 2015b, p. 20)

Citizens in these spaces build knowledge and networks not just for epistemic reasons, but to mobilize resources and to generate vital support from communities, professionals, funders, and political decision-makers (Barraket et al. 2019; Evers and Brandsen 2016; Wagenaar 2007, p. 33).

### Systemic knowledge about how governance works on the ground

Citizen spaces develop a grounded understanding of how governance systems work in practice, and where the possibilities and tensions lie. By acting practically in these systems, citizens come to discover and assess what different policy actors *actually do* in practice (not just what they say they do). They also have to make sense of how things are operating, and make practical judgments about actions that are successful, those that are not, and the points of impact. As Wagenaar points out, citizens in these spaces are "drawn into policy-making as well as practical delivery, linking policy and action in a much more intimate way than is common in standard models of invited 'public participation' as part of formal processes of planning and public policy" (2019, p. 320).

### Systemic knowledge about potential connections and interventions

Over time, citizen spaces can identify ways to improve links between organizations, develop policy workarounds, close gaps, and open up alternative ways of working together. Their practical knowledge of how existing governance programs and interventions operate, and where the redundancies and inefficiencies lie, opens opportunities for policy innovation and inclusion.

An example is the connective governance work of the citizens that developed the *Goulburn Murray Resilience Strategy*. As described in Chapter 3, to ensure the strategy is embedded across the region the citizens formed the Goulburn Murray Resilience Taskforce which comprises selected leaders from community, government and business. Members of the Taskforce view their role as trying to make sense of all the "governance stuff" that is coming to them, for example, from various policies and programs from multiple layers of government and different agencies, and then trying to find ways to reshape these amid changing market and climatic conditions so that they foster resilience in their region.[3] Their place-based approach to building resilience affords them a unique vantage point to identify possible collaborative opportunities in their region. Rather than responding to disconnected or ad hoc initiatives from siloed government departments, the members of the Taskforce are able to "identify potential opportunities, and call out the stupid stuff."[4] The Taskforce is promoting circular economy opportunities in the region by connecting local businesses and initiatives with various state and corporate programs. Such programs are often framed not around place, but unhelpfully sit within specific policy domains or sectors, such as environment, water, agriculture, housing or economic development. Taskforce members are also well-positioned to identify voices missing from governmental programs, and how they can ensure that these marginalized perspectives are better included in governance discussions.

Brokering and translating knowledge across and between sectors, actors and levels of governance is another systemic knowledge function that citizen spaces offer, exemplified by this Taskforce. In our research we have observed that many of its deliberations center on keeping its members informed about current happenings, and on examining how government or market-based programs may affect their region; for instance, an upcoming inquiry, a grants program, funding cuts, or a new industry. Through regular sharing of knowledge, the Taskforce is well-placed to identify gaps and overlaps in the region's governance, and to reveal potential challenges and opportunities. A citizen space applying this knowledge brokering and translation role may shift piecemeal policy towards more holistic and cross-sectoral approaches to collective problem solving.

---

[3] Based on observations made by Carolyn M. Hendriks at the Taskforce Planning Workshop, June 16, 2023 in Echuca, Victoria.
[4] Member of the Taskforce, Taskforce Planning Workshop on June 16, 2023, Echuca.

## Knowledge Sharing, Reproduction, and Transmission

As well as using knowledge that is place-based and grounded in lived experience, many of the citizen spaces we have studied also seek outsider perspectives. They aim to connect with private- and public-sector actors, in ways that may be supportive or confrontational. Citizen spaces are learning spaces. They do more than recognize and endorse the epistemic abilities of people who are on the margins, or without university degrees or official roles: they bring different viewpoints together, challenge people to express their knowledge in public settings, and circulate new ideas. Therefore, recognition of participants' knowledge is based both on them being "experts by experience" and also on their collective action and willingness to share ideas.

## Sharing with other policy actors such as active citizens, experts, and politicians

In citizens' governance spaces, people can generate new data or experiences on complex issues, and then feed these into the policy process. In Australia, community energy projects have engaged in policy advocacy and parliamentary inquiries to draw attention to the broader challenges facing renewable energy and energy efficiency initiatives. When Totally Renewable Yackandandah (TRY), the citizen space we discussed in Chapter 3, made a written submission to the Victorian Parliament's inquiry into "Tackling Climate Change in Victorian Communities" it showcased how TRY supports local projects to produce and sell renewable energy, and to improve energy efficiency. In its submission, TRY argued that community-led work to tackle climate change is undermined by inconsistent policies between multiple layers of government, especially between state and federal governments, on planning, energy infrastructure and renewables.

Following TRY's submission, the inquiry committee visited the Yackandandah community solar photovoltaic and battery projects in February 2020. The committee parliamentarians gained valuable experiential knowledge about the negative effects of national policy settings on local communities' capacity to adapt to extreme climates. As a result of their visit to TRY, several inquiry committee members directly questioned senior bureaucrats at the Australian Energy Market Operator (AEMO), in public hearing, about why local community microgrids such as in Yackandandah are not permitted to operate off the grid, even though they could provide communities with vital energy autonomy in emergencies such as bushfires, when the main power grid is down. The parliamentarians asked senior federal bureaucrats to investigate the lessons that local community energy projects hold for national energy policy. They also questioned whether local communities were adequately involved in national energy decisions:

> State Politician: Do you reckon community groups like that, or those aspirations even, are adequately enfranchised in the decision-making process? Obviously the distributors, the generators, they all get a seat at the table, but do you think those other things are in the thinking of the regulator, of the operator?
>
> Federal Bureaucrat from AMEO: I think they need to be more involved. I mean, we do have, as part of some of those discussions, consumer representatives at those discussions, and we have seen that really increase more so as part of our processes on the integrated system plan. I know the Australian Energy Regulator has a consumer challenge panel that is part of some of their decision-making. I am seeing a lot more of consumer voices being part of that conversation, but in terms of resiliency, I think there is absolutely a seat. We need to hear from the communities around their needs to make sure we design for them. (State Government of Victoria 2020, p. 40)

Here we see how a single citizens' governance space can inject substantive knowledge into the policy process, and also trigger questions about procedural matters such as the inclusivity of existing governance processes.

Some citizen spaces generate knowledge for the explicit purpose of sharing information to build support from the community and the state. Restorative Justice for Oakland Youth (RJOY) developed ties with law school researchers to document their achievements, which in turn legitimated their ideas, and ultimately secured greater commitment from school administrators and city government actors. Within the schools in which RJOY was active, citizen practitioners gathered and shared data about key differences between restorative and non-restorative schools regarding rates of suspension, expulsion, and arrest:

> For us, cultivating a good relationship with the research and data division of Oakland's school district has been essential. Also, developing a research-practice partnership consisting of the school district, a university research group and a restorative justice community-based group to track and analyse this data is suggested. (Davis 2018, p. 430)

Doing, thinking, and knowledge-sharing go hand in hand as citizen spaces adjust their work to shifting contexts, and strategize to build support and secure resources.

## Sharing with marginalized citizens

Throughout the book we have shown how citizens' governance spaces are unlike conventional political organizations and movements in the ways they engage and communicate knowledge to—and reproduce knowledge with—people who are on the margins. Various cases have demonstrated how citizen spaces connect with those who are not attracted to traditional civil society organizations or mainstream government-led civic engagement projects, such as the homeless, substance users, or former offenders. These spaces of citizen governance can also allow knowledge held by marginalized citizens to enter mainstream expert research programs on a more even footing. Academic researchers often do not realize how much people in marginalized communities distrust universities, clinics, and other institutions that have historically labeled and stigmatized them. Citizen spaces can provide safe environments in which dialogue and collaboration can take place, confronting and rejecting academic professionals who treat marginalized people as mere subjects, while seeking out and working with those academics who give them respect and power. This can be mutually beneficial, as one drug researcher notes, "The medical model for recruitment will not work …. People trust their dealers more than they trust the medical system. They have been traumatized by the medical system, almost universally" (Lupick 2017, p. 353).

Consider two research studies, both of which compared methadone and heroin. The first was conducted *on* and the second conducted *with* drug users in Vancouver. The first, called the North American Opiate Medication Initiative, or NAOMI, drew 251 participants from a pool of long-term users who had failed with methadone. Results showed that people who used heroin were more likely to stay in the study, and less likely to use street drugs and engage in other illegal activity, than were people who used methadone (Lupick 2017, pp. 346–348). When this first study was over the participants went back to their normal way of life. They had improved their lives over the course of the study but were now back to where they had started: fending for themselves on the street to get their drugs.

With encouragement from VANDU (the Vancouver Area Network of Drug Users), one of the research subjects, David Murray, organized others into a group they called the NAOMI Patients Association, or the NPA. The NPA hosted weekly meetings at VANDU, reached out to other former patients, and lobbied for participation in a second research project, the Study to Assess Longer-term Opioid Medication Effectiveness, or SALOME. The NPA connected with a public health researcher, Susan Boyd, who helped them learn research methodology and frame questions. Murray notes: "during NAOMI, it felt like the power that researchers exercised over him was absolute." With SALOME, by contrast, "We wanted to do something different. We wanted to do our own research with Susan as our mentor" (Lupick 2017, p. 350). Collaborative research papers from the study were published to transmit their knowledge into the public health community.

## Sharing with citizens in other places: local, national, and international networking

Many citizen spaces willingly share knowledge on how to address a given public problem with people in other places. For example, the community-led funeral service Tender Funerals facilitates and supports other communities seeking to establish their own funeral service organization, through its not-for-profit entity, Tender Funerals Australia, and a resource network, the Tender Funerals Network. Tender Funerals binds members of this network to its "unique social franchising agreement" to ensure they work in accordance with the organization's principles, vision, business model, and manual. This is not about ensuring consistency across a franchise, nor even about protecting a brand or intellectual property. Rather it aims to ensure that all Tender Funerals share the common aim: "to ensure that people in financial need are able to access affordable, customisable funeral services."[5]

Some citizens' governance spaces nurture robust networks across the globe to share their experiences and lessons. For example, Baltimore Community Conferencing Center began its activities after visits by experienced practitioners in circle sentencing and family-group conferencing from Canada and Australia. Extended interactions and research collaboration led to joint publications on the psychology of conferencing, on neighborhood peacemaking, and emotions (Abramson and Moore 2001).

---

[5] By 2023, there are many communities around Australia in the process of establishing a Tender Funerals organization in their local area, including in Brisbane, Canberra, Eastern Melbourne, Far North Queensland, Newcastle, Perth, Tasmania, and Western Sydney. The first full replication of the original Tender Funerals model opened on the Mid North Coast in June 2022 (TF 2023b).

In another example of global networking by local citizen spaces, VANDU works with allied organizations such as the Portland Hotel Society (PHS) to visit and host public health workers, practitioners, and fellow organizers and activists. The idea of seeking out public health funding to support VANDU came from the Australian Injecting and Illicit Drug Users League, a group that a few VANDU members later joined. The concepts of "harm reduction" and the related "four pillars" approach, legitimated in a few European countries but on the margins of public health discourse in Canada, were circulated in Vancouver by visits of foreign practitioners and officials sponsored by VANDU and PHS:

> They would invite experts from various fields related to drug policy and health care from cities around the world where harm-reduction programs were already implemented. But instead of hosting the event in a fancy hotel, this conference would take place in Oppenheimer Park. (Lupick 2017, p. 142)

The VANDU and PHS public conference had speakers from Frankfurt, Germany—a drug policy coordinator and a police chief who was a progressive voice from within law enforcement. A Swiss public health official attended too, to talk about their "four pillars" approach as well as a heroin maintenance program that allowed long-term addicts access to controlled doses provided by the health care system. "We knew that in order to save people's lives," a nurse working with VANDU on the event said, "we needed to bring some of these experts in so that people who had the ability to make decisions would listen" (Lupick 2017, p. 143).

## Experiential Advocacy

Though it is not the central objective of citizens' governance spaces, representation of the views of affected publics, service users, and those at the frontline can follow from effective problem-solving work. As argued previously, by tapping into the knowledge and experiences of hyper-marginalized citizens—such as substance users, unsheltered people, and those suspected of causing harm—citizen spaces can include voices that other spaces of participation struggle to access.

The VANDU citizen space has shown, in its work, how it is possible to maintain other ways of relating to, supporting, and "letting be" people who have conventionally been stigmatized, shunned, and penalized:

> The beginning of VANDU was exciting for its members and important for the entire Downtown Eastside community, and it continues, a decade later, to accomplish a multitude of life-manifesting projects, as well as becoming one of the strongest and most highly regarded drug user organizations in the world. Its global contacts have inspired drug users elsewhere to organize and continue to struggle to attain initiatives once considered impossible—such as Insite, the first official supervised injection site in North America, which opened its door in the Downtown Eastside in 2003. Another achievement of VANDU's has been to reveal to the rest of society how lives and institutions look from the bottom and the margins, instead of from the perspective of a privileged elite, and its believers. (Boyd et al. 2009, p. 44)

In creating a space for people to work on their own problems together, VANDU creates opportunities for "outsiders" to become recognized as fully-fledged citizens.

The public policy VANDU is promoting is "harm reduction" that recognizes the complexity of "the problem"—criminalization, housing conditions, poverty, stigma. It places the marginalized in positions of authority and agency rather than accepting their conventional status as "needy" recipients of not only benefits and resources but also of labels and expectations from public health and social workers. As Zigon notes, "harm reduction in Vancouver is beginning to become disentangled from its biopolitical-therapeutic and surveillance and control aspects and is simply becoming part of ordinary life. In so doing it is slowly transforming the possibilities for living that life" (2018, p. 48).

> In most places around the globe, the enactment of this philosophy is primarily limited to rather isolated clinics where a few services are provided. To the best of my knowledge, only the Downtown Eastside of Vancouver has been able to begin to build a world where the harm-reduction philosophy has become a dispersed aspect of the ordinary life of that world. (Zigon 2018, p. 110)

Like the prefigurative politics of social movements, citizen-led governance demonstrates ways of living and relating to others; yet it goes beyond self-enclosed performance to reshape whole neighborhoods and districts. The VANDU citizens' governance space is creating "a world in which such [drug] use does not result in the dehumanization, ill-health, or death of those who do it. In other words, to practice harm reduction is to let-users-be and to build worlds that are open to this letting-be" (Zigon 2018, p. 111).

The various knowledges that citizens' governance spaces generate can also be used for more explicit advocacy and representation. Sometimes this can come in the form of introducing explicit experiential knowledge into independent inquiries on a policy or market failure. For example, Tender Funerals took an opportunity to make a policy submission into a formal review of the competition, costs, and pricing of the funeral industry in New South Wales (see TF 2020). The advocacy efforts of Tender Funerals are generating substantive policy impact, according to the not-for-profit organization, Our Community Project, that helped to establish the initiative:

> We submitted many reports and surveys providing recommendations on changes to our industry. Data from our shrouded burial survey was submitted, along with recommendations around changes to funeral insurance, pre-paid funerals and funeral pricing. We advocated for community participation and home funerals. Some immediate outcomes off the back of this review was new regulation about funeral price transparency and accessibility with all funeral homes in NSW now being required to display their pricing on their websites. (OCP 2021, p. 32)

This shows how the knowledge and experiences gained in the Tender Funerals citizen space are not just an asset for policy makers but also enable the citizens to "constructively disrupt" conventional discourses in the funeral industry around pricing and transparency.

## Implications for Governance and Democracy

The knowledge that citizens add to public policy through their governance work in citizen spaces has implications for governance and democracy. These self-organized citizens are challenging established ways of thinking about public policy issues in criminal justice, planning, social welfare, and many other areas. They also disrupt the provision of some services which have been dominated by for-profit enterprises, such as funeral services or energy production.

Citizens' governance work can challenge epistemic hierarchies between the credentialed, the uncredentialed, and the marginalized. The strength of the challenge depends on the efficacy and inclusiveness of the citizen spaces' problem-solving work, and the different pathways and prospects for living together that these spaces create; it does not depend on how many citizens are involved, nor on who or what they are. Nevertheless, the epistemic contributions of citizen spaces present risks as well as opportunities.

## Opportunities for reframing? Or for misinformation?

Citizens' governance spaces reframe the collective problem, and that reframing often provides creative options. These spaces can also re-orient assumptions about the contributions that regular people can make when they are self-organized, working in highly inclusive ways, and open to those who want to contribute on problems they care about. On the other hand, it is possible for citizen spaces to reframe problems using *mis*information, and to offer solutions that go *against* broader collective interests.

In rural Oregon during the wildfires of 2020, for example, armed citizen patrol groups self-organized in response to rumors on social media that the fires were started by "antifa" militants traveling up into the region. In some towns, citizens' groups ran public meetings to boost volunteer numbers to staff armed checkpoints; in doing so they further fueled misinformation that there were "looters and arsonists" on the loose. These vigilantes' roadblocks complicated the efforts of first responders, fire fighters, and police; their weaponry and their racist comments made many locals feel unsafe (Wilson 2020).

In different contexts with different participants, citizen spaces may arrive at opposing solutions to the same problem. Serenity Café's version of harm reduction for substance users aims to cultivate a social network that supports abstinence. VANDU, by contrast, aims to create safe spaces for substance use. It is possible to hold both positions, but it complicates governance decision-making.

## Opportunities for listening? Or for off-loading?

Knowledge generated via citizens' governance spaces is not necessarily produced for antagonistic ammunition or counter arguments, as is often the case in "insisted spaces" — that is, spaces that aim to shape public policy outcomes through lobbying, advocacy and protest work (see Hendriks and Colvin 2023). The novel problem-solving orientation and epistemic standing of citizen spaces trigger interest—and sometimes open the minds—of policy elites and decision-makers, if those in power are receptive to the actions and knowledge that citizen spaces generate.

For example, when citizens formed the Goulburn Murray Resilience Taskforce, key decision-makers from relevant government agencies engaged and offered support. They recognized the potential value these organized citizens could bring to the region, particularly in identifying opportunities for multi-sector or cross-jurisdictional programs. They also recognized the value of having a community-led Taskforce with members who are well connected and trusted in the rural region—assets that the Melbourne-based bureaucrats lack.[6]

There are instances, however, where citizen spaces make fair and open listening more challenging in structured participatory governance. Citizen governance may offer a way for state officials to shift public debate away from what formal government agencies can and should do, allowing them to off-load complex or politicalized issues onto communities (Dekker 2019). One example is in renewable energy, where in some jurisdictions small-scale citizens' energy projects are proliferating but the broader regulatory and institutional settings needed to accelerate long-term energy transitions are not being reformed (Judson et al. 2020). And in relation to poverty, the state publicly celebrates the efforts of citizens engaged in volunteering activities to assist the homeless, such as Orange Sky Australia (discussed in Chapter 2); meanwhile, critics argue that those efforts draw public attention away from the underlying systemic issues of income inequality, poverty, and the cost of shelter (e.g., Parsell and Watts 2017; Parsell et al. 2021).

A related risk is the potential for a disempowering division of labor: citizen spaces doing the "soft" work of listening and social connection, while officials and private-sector actors—freed from the responsibility of those "soft" tasks—do the "hard" work of handling the budgets, extracting the taxes, and making payments. For example, members of the Goulburn Murray Resilience Taskforce are committed to implementing a community-generated strategic plan for resilience in their region, which is something a state agency might have done in the past. Yet the Taskforce has no budget or secure funding beyond that needed for its own administration and communication. With scant funds to instigate or contribute to projects or programs, the Taskforce is entirely reliant on funds and staff from other sectors to implement its strategy. Its role in implementation is essentially limited to doing the "soft" work of sharing knowledge and networking with relevant actors and programs in the region.

---

[6] Based on interviews by Carolyn M. Hendriks with several government-based members of the Taskforce conducted during June and November 2023.

## Opportunities to expand knowledge? Or to fuel contestation and anti-intellectualism?

Citizen spaces can generate and introduce alternative forms of knowledge into governance systems, but in doing so, citizen spaces can fuel the politics around a particular issue. They are not immune to any of the conflicts that surface when knowledge is challenged, contested, or rejected. How do citizen spaces navigate the politics that arise from the new knowledge they produce and inject? Some explicitly seek to be "apolitical" but they inevitably get drawn into various political conversations and decisions. The political tensions that arise from epistemic and procedural innovations might discourage citizens from participating, and thus undermine the longevity of the initiative.

Another epistemic risk is that citizen spaces may embrace a kind of amateurism that thwarts all expertise that does not emerge from ground-level work. Rather than synergy, there may be a kind of dissonance in working with people with different skills and backgrounds. This would be to default into a crude hyper-localism sometimes seen in community organizing (Einstein et al. 2019).

## Opportunities to transfer knowledge across boundaries? Or to build exclusionary networks?

Citizens' governance spaces generate knowledge that is not just localized; it can have broader network and policy-transfer effects. Citizen spaces can empower experimentation by citizens, non-government organizations (NGOs), and government agencies in other jurisdictions; this, in turn, can attract the attention of decision-makers. The nationwide spread of community energy groups, for example, inspired Dr Helen Haines, an independent member of the federal Australian Parliament, to draw public attention to this phenomenon and to the piecemeal governance and poor state investment in the community renewable sector. In 2020, Haines launched The Local Power Plan campaign, which was "a blueprint to drive investment in locally-owned renewables in regional Australia."[7] Questions surface, however, about who may be left out of such policy networks, and whether they are reaching the marginalized.

---

[7] https://www.helenhaines.org/bills/australian-local-power-agency/

Citizen spaces may not be as ideological as activist groups or social movements, and that may not be good for some issues or policy contexts. Are citizen spaces ignoring certain social problems, such as inequality or discrimination, and inadvertently excluding certain kinds of people? Are citizen spaces suppressing conflict and contentious politics in order to drive forward practical solutions? Are different viewpoints tolerated, encouraged, worked through respectfully? Are procedures in place in citizen spaces to challenge operating norms, and to permit critiques of leadership? Many risks emerge, especially if the citizens leading the initiative exclude "amateurs," thereby limiting a space's democratic potential. Indeed, some citizen spaces might be especially technocratic in their approach, emphasizing particular kinds of expertise and sealing the space off to certain kinds of professionalized or experiential knowledge.

These are important issues for organizers of these spaces to address internally and in their public messaging; alert reporters, scholars, and state officials can also hold them accountable. Ideally, citizen spaces reflect regularly on the diversity and inclusivity of members. This type of reflective practice was observed in the Goulburn Murray Resilience Taskforce. The citizens leading the Taskforce initially selected and invited members from community, government, and business. The people stepping into these roles typically wore multiple hats as community members and as engineers employed in local utilities and state agencies. This mix served the epistemic needs of the Taskforce, but meant that its members were mostly white, well-educated, local people. As it evolves, the Taskforce is keen to expand its membership to reflect and represent the diversity of the region, particularly by incorporating youth, First Nations people, and those from diverse ethnic backgrounds.[8]

Another related risk is that the knowledge people generate in citizen spaces transforms them into "experts," which then draws them into state-led processes and away from grassroots empowerment.[9] Henrik Bang (2005) has noted how "expert citizens" transition from local, community work into formal policy processes that distance them from their roots in local community.

---

[8] Based on observations made by Carolyn M. Hendriks at the Taskforce's Planning Workshop on June 16, 2023 in Echuca, Victoria.
[9] An excellent example of this phenomenon is the local movement *Maulmandeulgi* (MM) in Seoul working on local urban governance. Over time MM activists became quasi-experts who worked very closely with state officials, losing their critical perspective, and their links to local communities (see Doucette and Hae 2022).

## Opportunities for citizens' knowledge to strengthen legitimacy? Or to undermine it?

Citizen-led spaces can add significant social value to communities; indeed, they achieve their legitimacy by working on collective problems. This is especially the case for place-based citizen spaces because their legitimacy is often rooted in their knowledge of the local area and their relational networks. For example, the idea for Tender Funerals, Australia's first community-owned funeral service, was germinated by Jenny Briscoe-Hough after going through the experience of organizing her mother's funeral (ABC 2022; Chenery and Rousset 2022). Even though she had no professional experience in the funeral industry she was motivated to change the all-too-commonly depersonalized and unaffordable modern funeral practices that were negatively affecting people in her community. Briscoe-Hough took her idea to a community charity group, Our Community Project, to start a not-for-profit community-driven funeral service. While she began as a "disruptive outsider," over time Briscoe-Hough's organization has attracted insiders from the industry, such as professional funeral director Amy Sugar, who recognized the change that Tender Funerals could bring to the industry and to her own professional practice. Here, the legitimacy of Tender Funerals' knowledge and expertise in the funeral industry has grown over time, as more and more families choose their services and as public awareness has grown, thanks to a successful film (Wallworth 2013), and to the national media coverage mentioned previously.

Citizen spaces can also be perceived to lack legitimacy, however, because they do not possess the requisite professional or expert knowledge. Their participants can be quickly dismissed as "outsiders" who "don't know what they are doing." In some cases, they generate knowledge and solutions that are undervalued or even discredited. Recall from Chapter 2, how the citizen-led Serenity Café faced prejudice from drug and alcohol treatment professionals. According to the Café founders, who self-describe their governance work as "mutual aid," this prejudice is:

> ... based on a great deal of ignorance about the way mutual aid groups work ... part of the problem we face is that the massive contribution of mutual aid groups to recovery in Scotland is not yet recognized within policies concerning recovery in Scotland. (Campbell et al. 2011, p. 149)

## Conclusion

In this chapter we have examined the range of knowledge contributions that citizen spaces can make to democratic governance. Drawing on contemporary cases we have shown that when citizens work together in practical ways on collective problems, they can generate significant substantive, procedural and systemic knowledge. They reframe problems, challenge status quo solutions, and develop novel practical strategies and procedures. These epistemic contributions are not limited to their own local problem-solving efforts; many groups share resources, insights, and procedures with other citizens, and other policy actors in other locations, sometimes across the globe. Solutions that may be of little consequence ("small potatoes," to use an American idiom) in terms of impact in one locality can, via knowledge generation and transfer, help grow different varieties and fill many truckloads all over the world.

Citizen spaces challenge established ideas about the types of knowledge that citizens can bring to public governance. The knowledge created by citizen spaces needs to be recognized and valued, so as to counter dominant managerial, professional, technocratic, meritocratic, and epistocratic trends in academia, in government, and even in formal civil society organizations. Our spotlight on citizen-governance knowledge reveals a more expansive view of citizen knowledge than is found in contemporary discourses about public participation. One popular discourse in many countries, for example, affirms that "citizens' input is a useful pathway to innovation." In our view, this discourse risks privileging citizen knowledge that is considered novel, high-tech, and "innovative," while devaluing the more simplistic, local, low-tech knowledge that might emerge in a citizens' governance space.

There are also important epistemic lessons here for the design of participatory processes. Citizen knowledge in designed participatory forums is typically valued because it represents a user's—or everyday—perspective, framed as something distinct from expert and bureaucratic knowledge. These modes of public engagement conceptualize citizen knowledge as an epistemic good that is external to the designed participatory process or the policy system. In those processes, the role of public engagement is to access, collect, and collate citizens' "external" knowledge. Yet in citizen spaces, knowledge takes on a more emergent characteristic. As discussed in Chapters 1 and 2, citizens do not always come to these spaces with fixed ideas; over time, as they experiment with possibilities and trial different solutions, they iteratively develop knowledge. Citizens generate and develop knowledge through the process of working together to try to address a public problem.

Our arguments also have implications for more innovative participatory designs, such as mini-publics, which are constructed so that lay citizens can learn about and deliberate on complex policy issues. In those designs, the citizens' deliberations are informed by experts and other policy actors who come in to share their knowledge about the problem and its governance. In citizen spaces, however, this distinction between expert and non-expert knowledge dissolves. As our examples illustrate, when citizens in these spaces work together on practical interventions, they inject not only lay and experiential knowledge, but they also become practitioner experts through their experiences with collective problem solving.

More fundamentally, citizen spaces re-orient expectations regarding what people can do when they take on governance tasks, and the kinds of people who join, and the attributes they bring in and carry out from the work. Their democratization of knowledge production emboldens new concepts and practices, like those seen in the philosophy of harm reduction; but it may also affirm old concepts and practices, like restorative justice sentencing circles.

Citizen spaces are diverse and multifaceted, however, and do not always lead to better governance. Their novel and unconventional contributions, while often constructive, can still weaken rather than improve valuable institutions as indicated by the hazards noted previously. We return to this topic in Chapter 6.

Our discussion of knowledge generated by citizens in problem-solving efforts has identified questions that deserve deeper future investigation. Some of these relate to how knowledge claims are negotiated *within* a citizen space. To what extent are different voices within a given citizens' governance space tolerated, heard, represented? How are insights that run contrary to conventional wisdom—and established civil society organizations and political institutions—surfaced, discussed, and legitimated within citizen spaces? There are also broader questions about how citizen spaces operate in polarized contexts. To what extent, for example, can their practical "how-to" knowledge bridge ideological rigidities?[10]

Many of the empirical cases discussed in this chapter underscore another important epistemic contribution of citizen spaces: their role in sharing,

---

[10] For example, there is some evidence that citizen-led restorative justice programs run by evangelical Christians generate knowledge that is useful for more secular programs (Feasey and Williams 2009). Whether knowledge sharing and collaboration between citizen spaces lead to bridge-building is a topic for more research.

brokering and translating knowledge across sectors and policy silos. By asking new questions or adopting different perspectives, citizen spaces are well placed to identify gaps and overlaps in knowledge, and to reveal epistemic challenges and opportunities. This knowledge brokering and translation role can serve to shift piecemeal policy towards more holistic and cross-sectoral approaches to collective problem solving. Of course, there must be willing actors in other sectors receptive to receiving the knowledge generated and translated by citizen spaces. Experts within and outside the state administration need to take the knowledge from citizens experiments seriously and be willing to learn about alternative ways of tackling a collective problem. These themes are the subject of Chapter 5, where we examine the various ways that citizen spaces interact and partner with state and non-state actors.

# Chapter 5
# Citizen Agency and Autonomy in Shared Governance

In this chapter we explore how citizen spaces navigate their broader governance and market contexts. Often it is the broader dysfunction of existing policy structures and institutions that motivates citizens to initiate and lead problem-solving efforts, as we discussed in Chapter 3. Some citizen spaces might go on to disrupt or alter conventional policy practices, while others might be dismissed by, or invisible to, relevant state, market, and civil society actors (see Eversole 2011, p. 66). Regardless of their impact on the status quo, it is inevitable that at some stage citizen spaces interact with other actors and the rules and institutions that govern them. By "interaction," we mean when the governance work of a citizen space comes in contact with its broader policy context and the various actors involved in governing collective problems—such as state agencies, regulators, service providers, relevant non-government organizations (NGOs), consultants, local business, experts, and corporations.

In the literature to date, much of the scholarly discussion on how citizen spaces interact with their governance contexts falls into three broad camps. The first camp is state-centric and worries that citizen-led problem-solving efforts are hyperlocal, small-scale, haphazard, particularistic, or ineffective (e.g., Bovaird and Loeffler 2012; Larrson and Brandsen 2016). Some in this camp are concerned that citizen-led initiatives can lack public legitimacy and accountability (see Connelly 2011; Edelenbos et al. 2018; Meijer and Thaens 2021).

The second camp is community-centric and worries that when citizens work with government agencies they lose their critical capacity, become depoliticized, or risk co-option (e.g., Ostrander 2013; Dekker 2019). Here, state actors are characterized as lacking an appreciation of the relational and informal ways that communities work (Weir 2010). And when communities interact with the market, these scholars worry that citizens may be beholden to the power and might of capital.

Occupying the third camp are critics of neoliberalism who argue even more strongly that, in a market economy, everyday people and communities

*Democracy in Action.* Albert W. Dzur and Carolyn M. Hendriks, Oxford University Press. © Albert W. Dzur and Carolyn M. Hendriks (2025). DOI: 10.1093/oso/9780192870575.003.0005

are victims of broad economic forces outside their control (e.g., McQuarrie 2013).[1] In a market-based context attempts to engage or partner with the community are tokenistic, since communities have little or no opportunity to have a say, make a choice, or exercise power. It is the corporation, developer, and state agency that set the terms of engagement; not the communities. Others go further and argue that many community-led projects that are advancing "alternative pathways" are active subjects in neoliberalism, perpetuating some of its ideas. In her work on citizen-led food initiatives in the US (such as organics and local food projects), Guthman says that "projects in opposition to neoliberalizations of the food and agricultural sectors appear to have uncritically taken up ideas of localism, consumer choice, and value capture—ideas which seem standard to neoliberalism" (2008, p. 1174).

We contend that these three accounts do not do justice to the diversity of contemporary actors located within the state and the market who actively engage with citizen spaces. As discussed in Chapter 1, most collective problems in contemporary liberal democracies are governed through complex processes involving decentered networks of state and non-state actors, rather than solely through centrally controlled hierarchical bureaucracies or through markets involving competitive interactions between producers and consumers (Jessop 2020).

In this chapter, we step away from these sharp divisions between state, market, and citizen initiatives, and offer a more fine-grained examination of how citizens' governance spaces interact with the broader structures and institutions of government, market, and civil society. Our analysis builds on relatively recent scholarship that shines a light on the complex relationships that contemporary citizens can encounter when they lead their own collective problem-solving efforts (e.g., Bherer et al. 2024; Edelenbos et al. 2018; Rendall et al. 2022). These emergent empirical studies reveal that in practice contemporary citizen spaces must navigate complex policy contexts and make choices well beyond whether to simply go "inside" the policy process or agitate from the "outside."

We extend these studies in this chapter by identifying and analyzing some of the varied relationships and working arrangements that citizen spaces can establish with relevant state, market, and traditional civil society actors. Drawing on diverse empirical cases, we consider the kinds of governance

---

[1] The term "neoliberalism" has come to mean many things in political practice and academia (see Harvey 2005). Here we are predominantly interested in neoliberalism as a set of economic practices that broadly include: "the privatization of public resources and spaces, minimization of labor costs, reductions of public expenditures, the elimination of regulations seen as unfriendly to business, and the displacement of governance responsibilities away from the nation-state" (Guthman 2008, p. 1172).

actors and structures that citizen spaces interact with, and how. Our analysis uncovers the diverse opportunities, complexities, and dilemmas that citizens leading problem-solving efforts can encounter. Our cases illustrate how citizens can and do exercise considerable agency and autonomy in shared governance arrangements. While there can be significant knowledge, resource, and power differentials between citizen spaces and other actors, our analysis shows how citizens can and do find savvy ways within complex governance contexts to advance practical problem-solving work on their own terms.

The chapter begins by introducing the concept of "congruence" to better capture the more nuanced ways that citizens are operating within the complex governance context that surrounds contemporary collective problems. Next we explore and illustrate four different types of congruence that citizen spaces adopt when they interact with other policy actors. Our analysis draws attention to the different pressures, constraints, incentives, and resources that flow from working with state agencies, firms, and traditional civil society organizations. We briefly discuss some of the challenges that arise when citizen spaces work and partner with others. To conclude, we draw together the empirical insights from this chapter and reflect further on their implications for understanding community–state–market relations in contemporary democratic practice.

## Shared Governance as Congruence

As identified in Chapter 2, one of the defining features of citizen spaces is their capacity to work nimbly and flexibly across boundaries between sectors, institutions, and types of actors, including citizens, clients, experts, professionals, and policy makers. We call this capacity "congruence." Many citizens in these initiatives appear willing to work with, alongside, and outside government, market and civil society organizations to achieve their governance or reform goals, even while maintaining some critical distance from conventional policies.

The term "congruence" describes the capacity of citizen spaces to use autonomy and agency in their collective problem-solving work, while being fully aware of other actors. Citizens in these spaces are going about governance on their own terms; not because a state, business, or traditional civil society organization invited, incentivized, or encouraged them to. Yet they are pragmatic; they recognize that to effectively achieve their governance objective—such as clean air, education, justice, health and wellness—at times they may need to need to collaborate, pool resources, and combine expert and local knowledge. In even the most disruptive citizen-led intervention, the citizens leading the problem-solving space acknowledge that they are working within a particular policy and legal context. Congruence is manifested when citizens in these spaces manage their activities in ways that avoid dependence and co-option, by choosing with whom to partner, and how to negotiate the terms and conditions of partnership or collaborative arrangement. For example, a citizen space might partner with a relevant state agency to gain access to system resources such as public funding, data and information, and formal legal authority. Alternatively, they might work around the state and instead form partnerships with a business or philanthropic group committed to investing in social justice outcomes.

Focusing on congruence shifts analytic attention onto how a citizen space and its members or participants are experiencing and navigating the complexities and opportunities available to them in a given governance context. Citizen spaces are congruent when they engage with existing systems to create change, rather than simply accepting them or being victims of them (Burkett 2011). For example, a citizen space might identify where unusual alliances and coalitions could be formed, or they might source potential co-funding opportunities. Drawing on observations of groups working on food insecurity, Wakefield et al. suggest it is:

> important to emphasize the opportunities that could emerge from the convergence of a diverse range of organizations around food issues, and their ability to engage in (admittedly asymmetrical) dialogue with governments and the broader public. Conversations among organizations with different orientations towards social change are sometimes uncomfortable but could ultimately lead to meaningful collaborations and broader coalition building. (2013, p. 445)

Attention to congruence also allows observers to take seriously the heterogeneity within sectors. Rather than view "the state" as a monolithic entity, our discussion of congruence recognizes that some actors within the state do champion and support community-based problem solving, and actively help citizen spaces find their way through administrative rules and blockages. The market is similarly diverse, with some actors taking active steps to partner with citizens to address collective problems; for example, in the context of climate change, or poverty, or inequality, or Indigenous issues. Throughout this book, we recognize that actors within sectors are not homogenous, and that in practice some individuals within the public or private sector might support the activities of a citizen space, while others might resist them.

Our concept of congruence also acknowledges that citizen spaces work increasingly closely with market actors and economic structures. By taking up such strategies and relationships, citizens and communities are starting to work with, and reshape, aspects of the economic system and its structures (Bridge et al. 2014; Murtagh and Goggin 2015). In her reflections on the past 50 years of community development in the UK, Taylor asks:

> As governments across the world seek to shrink the state and look to the market as a principal mediating factor in society, is partnership with the state a meaningful option for community development and the communities it seeks to serve? Or should they be looking to the economy and the market? (2018, p. 21)

Congruent citizens' governance spaces are not naïve to "power over"; that is, situations where they might be controlled, dominated, or manipulated by others (see Lukes 2005). Many citizens leading governance spaces adopt a more differentiated view of power; they seek strategic opportunities in partnering and working with state and non-state actors, but are also cautious about the dependencies and constraints that these relationships can create. Noticing the subtle ways that citizen spaces navigate power draws attention to some of the overlooked ways in which communities are managing their administrative contexts and forming productive partnerships—on their own terms—with state and market actors. They are empowered to act on particular issues; in a context of low trust, communities can exercise considerable collective power that the state and the market lack.

## Congruence in Action

Citizen spaces enact congruence with state, market, and civil society actors in various ways. In some spaces the citizens' governance work is fully congruent with existing frames and programs of state and market systems, and the citizens leading the space have significant autonomy to self-style partnerships and relationships in ways that work for them. In other instances, congruence is more compromised; for example, when citizen spaces have limited autonomy to generate their own solutions because they push against the norms and approach of the state or market. Below we draw on empirical cases to illustrate four different types of congruence in action. These four types are by no means exhaustive.[2]

---

[2] This typology emerged inductively through our in-depth analysis of over 30 citizen spaces. Whereas other relevant typologies focus on different kinds of relationships that citizens or community groups might form with the state (e.g., Edelenbos et al. 2018; Thiery et al. 2022; Young 2000), our typology is broader in two respects. First, we center the analysis on degrees of congruence rather than on relationships, and thereby provide analytic scope to consider the agency and autonomy of citizens when their problem-solving efforts rub up against existing systems and actors. Second, our typology considers how citizen

Before we discuss different types of congruence in detail, it is important to note the dynamic nature of state–society–market relationships. The way a citizen space navigates its engagement with relevant policy actors is shaped by relevant policy settings and political circumstances, which change and evolve over time. For example, in the UK in the past 50 years there have been various governance approaches and discourses on community engagement (including Big Society, co-production, partnerships, and social entrepreneurship) where the state has oscillated between actively reaching out to engage with communities, and actively retreating (see Taylor 2018). A contemporary case of this dynamism occurred during the COVID-19 pandemic when government support for communities and mutual aid groups in the UK waxed and waned over time (Cook et al. 2023; Cullingworth et al. 2024). Similar trends have been observed with state agencies elsewhere.[3] Today some states are actively celebrating and championing citizen-led initiatives to work in areas such as local environmental or amenity projects, or to provide care (see Dekker 2019; Soares da Silva et al. 2018; Wagenaar 2019).

As policy responses and interventions change over time, citizen spaces adapt their relationships with relevant public-sector, market-based, and civil society organizations. This dynamism is especially evident during crises, where community-led initiatives are typically the first responses but then these collective, often localized, efforts adapt as more and more state and civil society organizations come in to "take charge" by offering larger-scale support. During the COVID-19 pandemic, emergent mutual aid groups in Scotland adapted their support services and relationships with relevant public-sector and charity organizations over time, moving between what Rendall et al. (2022) call "supplementary," "adversarial," and "complementary" modes.

While acknowledging the dynamic and historical governance context of citizen spaces, our discussion of empirical cases below focuses on how particular citizen spaces interact with relevant governance structures and actors at a point in time, unless otherwise indicated. While some of our cases are necessarily brief for the purposes of illustration and comparison, this is not to deny their rich history and their dynamic policy context.

---

spaces interface not just with the state but also with systems and actors located in the market and civil society.

[3] For example, on changing community–state relationships in Australia, see Onyx (2018), and in New Zealand, see Nowland-Foreman (2018). For a general discussion on different waves of civic engagement in Western liberal democracies since the 1960s, see Edelenbos et al. (2021a).

## Full congruence

In full congruence, citizen spaces willingly work, cooperate, and partner with relevant actors located in the state, market, and civil society. Here we are referring to collaborative arrangements or partnerships that citizens themselves initiate and drive, as opposed to being invited into state-led or market-led collaborative arrangements.[4] Other features of full congruence include: a mutual understanding of the collective problem and how it can be solved; and an appreciation of the value of sharing knowledge and resources, and a willingness and capacity to do so.

Full congruence between citizen spaces and other actors can be found in many areas of public policy but is especially common in nature conservation, where citizen-led efforts (for example, to protect a particular habitat or species) can align well with environmental goals of the state. Consider the collaborative working relationships that the citizens of the south-eastern Australian conservation group Friends of Grasslands (FOG) have established with relevant governments. FOG was set up in 1994 by a group of people in Canberra who saw a need to conserve and rehabilitate the threatened native grassland ecosystems of the region. Grasslands were becoming degraded through poor land-management practices in weed control, fire regimes, grazing, and recreation, and were at risk of being cleared for development (FOG 2014). Over the past 30 years FOG has organized and engaged local volunteers to deliver targeted on-the-ground conservation efforts to conserve and rehabilitate native grassland ecosystems and has undertaken extensive advocacy and community organization. Throughout this period FOG has been able to establish strong cooperative relationships with relevant state and federal agencies and with other non-government organizations.

Today FOG is a valued partner for these actors because its volunteers are trusted native grassland experts with extensive scientific and experiential knowledge. Moreover, FOG can deliver cost-effective conservation through its on-the-ground volunteer programs and its ability to attract grants (FOG 2021, 2022). While this could be interpreted as state off-loading, it is more accurately described as congruence since FOG is strategic in choosing who it partners with, and how it works with them. FOG targets its work at particular sites and development projects, and this enables it to increase its influence when advocating for grassland protection and policy change. Through its partnerships FOG has encouraged relevant government

---

[4] Some scholars of public administration refer to citizen-led partnerships as user or community co-production or citizen-led co-creation (see Bovaird 2007; Loeffler 2018).

agencies, such as the National Capital Authority (NCA), to engage in native grassland conservation and to change their management regimes. Government agencies like the NCA now manage their own native grassland sites for conservation outcomes, rather than simply for future development with no conservation focus. FOG's mix of practical work, expertise, and advocacy has changed land-management practices in the region. As the citizens driving FOG explain: "Friends of Grasslands was created to build community support for grassy ecosystem recovery. A focus on ecosystem conservation is now more common-place, and FOG has contributed to that" (FOG 2024).

Full congruence can also be achieved when a citizen space partners with relevant civil society organizations. For example, the Bourke Tribal Council (BTC) is a citizen space that collaborated with the not-for-profit group Just Reinvest New South Wales (NSW) to design and implement successfully an Aboriginal-led place-based model of justice reinvestment in Bourke, a remote town in north-western New South Wales, Australia. Bourke has a population of about 2,500, of which approximately 30% are Indigenous, compared to 3% nationally. The BTC is a citizen space that emerged to address the over-representation of Aboriginal youth in local justice systems, offering an alternative to the NSW state government's emphasis to fund punishment, more prison beds and incarceration facilities (HREOC 1997).

In the early 2000s Bourke Elders observed that youth offending programs designed in the state capital, Sydney, some 800kms away, were not meeting local needs and were doing little to change the drivers of crime in their town where numbers of Aboriginal youths in the local justice system were increasing (ABC 2020). In response to these trends, a local Aboriginal man, Alistair Ferguson, worked to establish the BTC, which was envisaged as platform for local Indigenous Elders to discuss and guide community decisions, especially those impacting young people (Milliken 2018). Today BTC is an Aboriginal leadership group that represents the 24 clan and family groups living in Bourke (Maranguka 2024a). In 2013 the BTC formed a partnership with the not-for-profit organization, Just Reinvest NSW to develop a justice reinvestment model for their community to prevent Indigenous people from entering or re-entering the criminal justice system.[5] Together with Just Reinvest NSW, BTC set up a *Maranguka* Aboriginal Community Hub[6]—a local, Indigenous-led organization—to coordinate justice reinvestment activities such as "programmes that partner with local agencies and organisations

---

[5] "Justice reinvestment" aims to redirect public funds out of the justice system (police and prison budgets) into preventative measures, such as improved social and community services and infrastructure (Bryant and Spies-Butcher 2022).

[6] *Maranguka* means "caring for others" in the local Ngemba language.

as well as Aboriginal-controlled and run legal, cultural, family and health services" (Bryant and Spies-Butcher 2022, p. 6).

Bourke's *Maranguka* project on justice reinvestment involves a complex ecosystem of partnerships and coalitions with local service providers, anchored by the BTC, the key decision-maker on community-designed solutions. The Elders in the BTC have engaged with a range of stakeholders including citizens, businesses, government actors, and philanthropists (including Dusseldorp Forum and Vincent Fairfax Family Foundation) to identify solutions informed by local lived experiences (Maranguka 2024b). While the *Maranguka* project has not been driven by the government, the NSW state government has funded specific reinvestment activities, and representatives from relevant state government agencies are involved in working groups and expert committees. Frontline government employees and non-state service providers have also adjusted their service delivery practices to ensure expertise and resources are shared with the community; for example, there are now daily "check-in" meetings at *Maranguka* with relevant police, health and education professionals, and social workers (Bryant and Spies-Butcher 2022).

It is important to underscore that the collaborations at the heart of Bourke's *Maranguka* project are citizen-led, and this is what makes them so powerful and effective for the community. Whereas many justice reinvestment programs in the United States are top down, the approach taken in Bourke is "bottom-up" because priorities and processes have been "identified at the local level through community meetings and community-based organisations" (Bryant and Spies-Butcher 2022, p. 5). As the citizen leading the initiative, Mr Ferguson explains:

> What is unique now is sitting at the table—be it with the philanthropic sector, the corporate sector or government—the community is sitting in the driver's seat. It's the first time in history that I'm aware of that Bourke is actually in the driver's seat and making those decisions. (Just Reinvest NSW 2019, p. 28)

Today *Maranguka* is heralded as a success story not just for realizing positive justice outcomes for Indigenous people, but as an example of how governments can support effective community-led place-based change.[7] In 2023 Australia's most senior public servant, Professor Glynn Davis, Head of the Australian Government Department of the Prime Minister and Cabinet,

---

[7] See for example, Riboldi and Hopkins (2019) and Sydney Policy Lab (2021). For details on national awards, see https://maranguka.org.au/

called on the public sector to take inspiration from *Maranguka*, and allow communities to lead:

> [*Maranguka*] only works because the NSW government agreed not to lead but to follow; [agreed] not to impose the standard public sector accountability over the top, but to put funds in and allow the community to make decisions, including bad decisions.[8]

More radically, in-depth research on *Maranguka* has found that its "bottom-up" approach to justice reinvestment, and its diverse collaborations, have enabled it to rework the tools of marketization "to claim fiscal resources, develop bureaucratic capacity, and institute territorial governance" (Bryant and Spies-Butcher 2022, p. 15).

In some instances, citizen spaces work in congruence with market actors and bypass the state altogether—as is common in community-led energy cooperatives or community-led disaster recovery projects. Indeed, this has been the experience of many community energy projects in Australia. In the context of policy uncertainty for renewables, citizens have pushed ahead reforms by establishing local projects to produce solar and wind energy, in partnership with energy retail or distribution companies to assist them in selling and distributing renewable electricity. Many communities are actively creating the conditions under which energy companies may come into their localities, and are directly negotiating not only the engineering and financial arrangements but also the terms of community engagement (Curran 2021). The citizens leading the energy group Totally Renewable Yackandandah (TRY)—discussed in Chapters 3 and 4—invited various energy and water utility companies to come and interact with the broader public in local community forums. According to citizens in TRY, partnerships with industry were important from the very beginning:

> Very early in our journey we reflected carefully about the diverse range of organisations needed to help us toward 100% [renewable electricity]. We therefore reached out to a few key stakeholders to understand both how we might support them and to inform our own practice. This notably included, AusNet Services, North East Water and Indigo Shire. We have been very impressed by each of these organisations and their readiness to engage in the new opportunities and challenges offered with renewable energy—and importantly, supporting TRY in its infancy and beyond. (TRY 2019, p. 3)

---

[8] Excerpt from Professor Glynn Davis's speech to the Australian Public Service, delivered on December 7, 2023, Canberra (see Coade 2023).

Since TRY was formed in 2014, it has gone on to establish productive partnerships, including one with AusNet Services, a multi-national energy corporation that owns and operates the electricity transmission network (or grid) in parts of Melbourne, Victoria, and the eastern part of the state. TRY's partnership with AusNet Services helped it create Australia's first commercially operated community mini grid—a small energy system in which a group of households can generate and store energy using solar panels and batteries. Yackandandah's mini grid, which began operating in 2017, boosts the energy autonomy of its residents by enabling households to function as a unified energy unit that can generate, store, and share electricity across the community (AusNet 2017; TRY 2017).

TRY's partnership with energy companies is not a story of citizens being bought out or overpowered by corporations. On the contrary, this is a citizen space actively building partnerships with private companies because it recognizes that congruence with the companies that have the technology and infrastructure to distribute electricity is vital to its problem solving. Consider the following reflection from TRY citizens on the value of its partnership with Mondo, a subsidiary company of AusNet:

> TRY strongly believes the scale of climate change requires new conceptions of partnership that we can only yet imagine, and it will require new trust, and new collaborations across all sectors. We feel very strongly we have been given some insight to the possibilities with a very substantial relationship between Totally Renewable Yackandandah and Mondo. We think this partnership has been incredibly enabling—for a business with a DNSP pedigree [Distributed Network Service Provider] to understand how communities can respond with competent, calm and aspirational approaches, and in reverse, how corporations can leverage a depth of expertise to action remarkable outcomes.[9] Mondo also extend this support to other communities. (TRY 2019, p. 3)

Here we see how TRY's efforts in creating congruence are having a flow-on effect beyond its locality by shaping how Mondo engages with citizens in other local communities.

## Limited congruence

Congruence between citizen spaces and relevant state, market, and civil society actors can also be less fully expressed. Citizens can be wary of being

---

[9] Distributed Network Service Providers are the companies that own and operate the hardware in the electricity distribution system, including the power poles, wires, transformers, and substations that move electricity around the grid (Solar Victoria 2024).

absorbed or co-opted by others but engage instrumentally to meet a regulatory or administrative requirement, to access funds, or to meet safety standards. Some citizen spaces may actively choose to limit congruence because they seek autonomy from the structures and actors involved in status quo public policy. In a situation like that, interaction and connectivity with other actors are minimized, and actors co-exist but do not actively collaborate. Limited congruence is akin to the kind of "parallel play" of early childhood; actors are present and aware of one another but there is little cooperation between them. Citizens might access necessary knowledge or resources from relevant actors, or seek to comply with regulations, but they are not buying into discourses or entering partnerships.

During the COVID-19 pandemic, limited congruence was common, as mutual aid efforts emerged and co-existed alongside the efforts of relevant local authorities. In Britain an estimated 4,000 mutual aid groups formed in the early stages of the pandemic, offering essentials such as food and shelter assistance, as well as emotional and social support (Thiery et al. 2022). These groups were highly diverse not only in terms of how they operated but also in terms of the relationships they formed or chose not to form with local authorities and relevant civil society organizations. Some mutual aid groups intentionally operated at arm's length from local authorities, co-existing but not collaborating. Some received funding from local authorities; others undertook necessary training but did not work closely, due to their different approaches to working with communities, particularly volunteers.

Limited congruence can also be a characteristic of how some citizen spaces interface with the market. For example, the Nundah Community Enterprises Cooperative (NCEC) is a member-owned cooperative in Queensland, Australia, that aims to provide employment opportunities for people with a mental illness, intellectual disability, or learning difficulty. This citizen-led initiative was formed in 1998 after a community organization, Community Living Association (CLA), facilitated a local meeting to address the issue of limited employment opportunities for individuals with mental illness and disabilities. Today NCEC has grown into three businesses—Espresso Train Café and Catering, The Good Food Project, and NCEC Parks & Property Maintenance—which provide regular employment for over 20 member-workers (NCEC 2019; 2024).

From the outset NCEC has engaged with relevant civil society and state organizations, but for the most part these have been transactional rather than collaborative connections. While NCEC was an initiative born out of a facilitated meeting convened by the CLA, it is run and governed as an autonomous member-led organization. NCEC also receives some state support, for example, it has a long-term contract with the Brisbane City Council to maintain local parks, which provides some secure funds and regular employment for NCEC member-workers (Hooper and Warner 2013, p. 28).

## Compromised congruence

Citizen spaces can also operate in a context where congruence is compromised, for example when their sense-making and practical work become absorbed into the state, market, or civil society. At worst the citizen space might be co-opted—a theme we will discuss further—but co-option is not inevitable when citizen spaces work with the state or are funded by it (see Craig et al. 2004). Even when congruence is compromised, citizens can exercise a degree of agency whereby they actively choose to hand their initiative over to a relevant state or market institution because these institutions might be better placed to expand the problem-solving work.

Compromised congruence was experienced in the citizen-led efforts to improve farming practices for sustainable land management across Australia. What began as local citizen-led spaces grew and evolved into the national Landcare movement. Landcare groups first emerged in the 1970s through the efforts of local landholders in north-east Victoria who self-organized to address the problem of dryland salinity on their properties (Landcare Australia 2019). After a community meeting, a group was formed, the Warrenbayne-Boho Land Protection Group (WBLPG). The group succeeded in receiving funding from a federal government program to employ a full-time coordinator to run a series of participatory and local engagement processes to empower local landowners in conservation and soil conservation practices—which became known as the "Landcare model" (Robins 2018).

From the start, this citizen space reached out for resources from the state, but on its own terms. As one founding member of the WBLPG group explained (Howell 2006, p. 121): "These gatherings of rural people announced to all tiers of government that, from here on, they would take the initiative in managing and combating land degradation issues inside and outside their property boundaries, and that they expected full government support for this work." At this point Landcare's interface with the state was congruent; the citizens driving the early local Landcare groups actively sought support and engagement from the state because they recognized that the state was better placed to develop their initiative.

By 1986 the WBLPG was so successful that it inspired the formal establishment of a state government program, the Victorian Landcare Program. This formal partnership between the state government and the Victorian Farmers Federation (an NGO) soon became a federal program, with the support of the Australian Conservation Foundation—the nation's largest nature conservation group—and the National Farmers' Federation. These organizations have traditionally been in opposition to one another (Landcare Australia 2019; Lockie 2004). Between 1997 and 2008 a process of regionalization occurred which was intended to address some of the limitations of local action in addressing landscape-scale ecological issues. The federal government established 56 Natural Resource Management (NRM) bodies responsible for distributing resources to specific target areas. This attempt to regionalize Landcare activities through state-driven funding and coordination processes undermined voluntary community Landcare efforts in many areas (Robins 2018). Since 2013, state support has shifted back to resourcing local-level Landcare groups through local grant schemes targeting "local community-based organisations."

Globally, Australia's Landcare movement is heralded as a success, and it has inspired similar schemes in more than 20 countries (Catacutan et al. 2009). In Australia there are now over 5,000 Landcare groups. Some local groups continue to thrive; others have died out or gone into hibernation. According to one commentator:

> In many instances it [the Landcare group] has simply vanished, perhaps died a natural death having done what it set out to do—or it has been strangled by bureaucratic strictures and transaction costs, starved through cost shifting between states and the Commonwealth, or confused by moving goalposts. (Munday 2017, p. 225, cited in Robins 2018)

As Landcare was progressively absorbed into the state, it appears that some groups struggled with the changing policy setting and funding schemes; these developments affected their citizen agency and the on-the-ground community activities from which the movement was born. In other words, Landcare's congruence has been compromised.

The congruence between a citizen space and other governance structures and actors can also be compromised in more subtle ways. Many community food-security initiatives in Canada are kept so "busy" trying to secure funding and donations, and providing food relief, that they have little or no time for advocacy to address the broader structural issues generating food insecurity (Wakefield et al. 2013). Moreover, they typically receive funding for service provision—namely, providing food—but not for advocacy. As one participant in a Canadian community health center explained:

> At this moment in time, for holistic reasons and given our role as a community centre, we don't do an excessive amount of advocacy work in terms of systems and policy. That is massive, it's time consuming, not that it's unimportant [but] … we don't get funding to do that. (Cited in Wakefield et al. 2013, p. 441)

In Canada, as in many other countries, there are rules governing the extent to which charitable organizations, which can accept private donations and offer tax receipts, can undertake advocacy. According to Wakefield et al., the broader challenge here—one faced by many community organizations—is that they can become increasingly "semi-autonomous"; closely connected to the goals of the state via funding arrangements and service contracts, yet enjoying few mechanisms of democratic governance (2013, p. 430).

## Avoided congruence

As discussed in the previous chapters, citizen spaces can push forward disruptive governance solutions and therefore they might actively choose to operate at a critical distance from state and market while working in a kind of mutual tension. There are also other reasons why citizen spaces might avoid congruence with relevant policy actors and systems of governance. Citizens might decide to undertake their governance work well separated from state services or NGO providers if they oppose those groups' governance approaches or question those groups' capacity or legitimacy. That was the case with the citizen spaces working on substance use—Vancouver Area Network of Drug Users (VANDU) and Serenity Café—discussed in previous chapters. In such cases, citizens' problem-solving work may violate laws, break conventional norms, and disrupt communities.

In turn, state agencies, local politicians, and other community advocates might avoid congruence by balking at the methods or actions of a particular citizen space. Consider how residents and some local authorities initially responded to the activities of OnPoint—the first quasi-sanctioned supervised injection center in the US—which opened two sites in New York City in 2022. While OnPoint performs several uncontroversial services, such as needle clean-ups in local parks, and food, clothing, medical, and psychological support for homeless residents, its commitment to harm reduction through safe injection remains at odds with majority public opinion and strict law enforcement. OnPoint's supervised injection site violates the federal "crack house" law that prohibits maintaining a space for the purposes of drug use. The site is only operating because of city officials' assurances that they will not prosecute. Residents, business owners, and local political representatives have objected to the project based on the possible community impacts of black-market activity: thefts and break-ins to provide money for drugs, drug dealing that could lead to street violence, and the encouragement of more substance using. Nevertheless, OnPoint delivers a solution to the problem of how to keep substance users alive, by offering a much less dangerous environment than the park or back alleyway. As the director notes, 100% of those using the safe injection site have tried to quit via traditional recovery programs and failed (Rivera 2022). There are no alternative state- or community-approved options.

Avoided congruence is not purely antagonistic; citizens might actively choose to undertake their problem-solving work alongside formal state actors, and thereby foster productive and critical dialogue and information sharing. By "just doing it," the needle-exchange programs that merged to form OnPoint generated knowledge about practices that were effective with substance users, and built credibility with the city's health professionals who had no better viable alternatives:

> New York City's safe consumption program began underground in the late 2000s when one syringe exchange known as the Washington Heights Corner Project began modifying its bathrooms so that people who shot heroin there could be monitored for signs of overdose. By 2016, enough groups were following suit that the State Department of Health published guidelines for the safe operation of such bathroom programs. And in 2017, the Washington Heights project began expanding its operation—to 13 bathrooms spread across two buildings and a mobile unit from just a few stalls in one location—and promoting it to people who use drugs. Technically speaking, the program was still unsanctioned. But its facilitators were sharing data with health officials. In 2018 the city's Department of Health and Mental Hygiene published a report suggesting that a citywide supervised consumption program could save some 130 lives every year and millions of dollars in health care costs alone. (Interlandi 2023)

As noted in Chapter 4, and previously, knowledge generation and information sharing from the ground-level can be an important form of influence.

Citizen spaces might avoid congruence, especially with state structures, to stay away from arduous administrative and regulatory procedures that can hinder their practical governance work. This is exactly what occurred during the COVID 19 pandemic in the UK when some mutual aid groups decided to work with communities, but significantly at arm's length from formal state responses such as those delivered by the local authority. By choosing to remain at a distance from state responses, these mutual aid groups—in contrast to those noted previously who chose a strategy of limited congruence—were able to retain their autonomy and informality, and had no need to meet complicated formal risk and safeguarding requirements (see Cook et al. 2020; Thiery et al. 2022).

Avoided congruence does not necessarily mean limited policy influence. In some cases, citizens might push along an initiative outside existing governance and legal structures, but over time its practical efforts gain momentum to a point where the state must get involved, either to regulate or to address the public problem the citizens are trying to solve. An example we discussed in Chapter 3 is the community-based Internet service networks that emerged across Indonesia in the early 2000s, offering low-cost, reliable Internet to poor and rural residents. The widespread growth of these non-compliant Internet services eventually attracted the policy attention of the Indonesian state and resulted in legislative change.

In rare cases a citizen space might be rejected by a particular state, market, or civil society actor. Here the interaction can at times be oppositional and even antagonistic. In the case of mutual aid groups during the pandemic lockdowns in the UK, qualitative research has found that a small minority of groups experienced:

> resistant, fractured and antagonistic relationships with local authorities and VCS [Voluntary and Community Sector] organisations. In many cases, organisations were unwilling to support or signpost to mutual aid groups. This became a source of frustration for groups, whose attempts to work with their council were rebuffed. Participants commented how this was a lost opportunity and that local authorities, while keen to "talk to the talk" of co-production and citizen-led action, were in reality risk-averse cultures that prevented collaboration. (Thiery et al. 2022, p. 20)

Similar tensions have been experienced in disaster contexts when community-led responses clash with "certified" or authorized civil society or state actors. For example, in the context of emergencies and disasters it is not uncommon for local residents to be the first responders, particularly in helping to set up and provide support at community recovery centers (McLennan 2020). Eventually, authorized organizations—such as formal community and charity organizations, state services, and the armed forces—begin to arrive in the disaster-affected area. Tensions can arise when the initiatives of informal community groups rub up against the "commissioned" work of professionalized civil society groups, who tend to view themselves as the experts when working with communities. In the immediate wake of the 2019–2020 "Black Summer" bushfires in Australia, many local communities self-organized and prepared food for disaster victims in community halls and recovery centers. Days later, however, charity organizations formally contracted by the NSW state government to provide emergency catering arrived, and their "trained" crews threw out the locally-cooked food because it was not prepared by following the "certified" catering protocols. This case of avoided congruence fueled community anger and distress at a time when people were traumatized from the fires and keen to assist and help.

## Challenges Citizens Face in Shared Governance

Working with or alongside state or non-state actors presents several complications and dilemmas for citizen spaces. Much has been written on the difficulties of collaboration in contemporary governance, particularly from the perspective of the state. Scholars of public policy and public administration have pointed out that government agencies find it challenging to collaborate with community-led initiatives because they do not align well with the strategies and operations of public-sector organizations: government agencies tend to be "risk-averse, sectoral organized and often unwilling to work beyond their functional tasks" (Duijn et al. 2019, p. 389).

Far less has been written on the challenges of collaborative governance from the perspective of citizens leading problem-solving efforts. Scholars of community development and community organizing stress that many attempts by the state to engage and collaborate with informal community initiatives fail because governments and communities have fundamentally different ways of governing (e.g., Eversole 2011). In the wake of "small government" and austerity measures, scholars have been especially concerned about the dangers of off-loading, where communities are "increasingly taking over from a supposedly discredited state" (Taylor 2018, p. 17).

Another danger for citizen spaces is co-option, whereby state or non-state actors use the ideas and programs from citizen-led governance efforts for their own strategic purposes. In one example, Dean Spade, drawing on his scholarship and activism on youth incarceration in Seattle, US, argues that the relevant local government, King County, has been "co-opting the message of the radical opposition, and showcasing grassroots, community-based programs to legitimize the expansion of racist infrastructure of state violence" (2020b, p. 53). Shared governance here is viewed as a trap; when citizen-led initiatives work with state and non-state actors they lose their independence and their capacity to resist, criticize, and change the system. Worse, their participation legitimates the very systems and structures that are the root-causes of the issues the community initiatives are trying to tackle (Spade 2020a, b).

Off-loading and co-option are real challenges facing citizen spaces, and they are not the only ones. Below we seek to draw attention to some equally important but less prominent challenges that citizens leading and participating in governance spaces have met when they interface with relevant state and non-state actors: 1) losing autonomy through increased dependence; 2) building, maintaining, and navigating complex governance networks; and 3) pressure to institutionalize, replicate, and scale-up.

## Challenge 1: Losing autonomy through increased dependence

Financial dependence can restrict autonomy and capacity of citizen spaces to work across sectors, innovatively and disruptively. In Australia's Landcare movement, from the outset, local groups have relied on some level of funding from various state and federal agencies. However, the funding came with significant administrative burdens and need for accountability, and these generated transaction costs for local groups and restricted their autonomy.

Funding programs from state or non-state actors also establish boundaries around an issue or a geographical area that may not match what the community seeks to do. In the Landcare case, when the state became actively involved in supporting and funding improved land-management practices it established various regional bodies. This regional focus made ecological sense, but it also meant there was then less funding available to local groups.

Some relationships create complex dependencies and can restrict the freedom of citizens to lead and make decisions. Narratives and ideas about dependencies can affect perceptions of community autonomy and delegitimize state regulation. According to Lockie, in the Landcare movement, the concept of "local action" reinforced a self-image of rural communities being autonomous and self-reliant, and this inadvertently framed state involvement and regulation in the community as interference (2004, p. 43). These existing narratives complicated subsequent state partnerships between Landcare and relevant local, state, and federal government organizations.

## Challenge 2: Building, maintaining, and navigating complex governance networks

For congruence, especially in the form of partnering, a citizen space needs citizens who are willing and able to advocate and negotiate with elites in state, market, and civil society organizations. This involves considerable expertise, as well as administrative and relational work for citizens—which becomes more complex with more numerous partners, in addition to their practical problem-solving work. Some interfaces take more energy and time from citizens than others, especially when the collaborations or relationships become complicated, counterproductive, or dysfunctional.

Consider, for example, the administrative and competitive processes that many citizen spaces engage in to secure funding. As scholars of community development have underscored, small grassroots initiatives are typically not well equipped with administrative capacities and resources to effectively compete for government tenders and grants. This can unfairly privilege large and more professionalized NGOs and charities (Onyx 2018). As Taylor argues:

> Governance is increasingly left to the mechanism of market competition, in which communities are at a considerable disadvantage and which also risks setting community organizations into competition with each other. There is of course the option of banding together or entering into a consortium with larger providers, but the first takes considerable resources while the second risks leaving community organizations at the mercy of larger contractors. (2018, p. 19)

Congruence involves hard work and "emotional labor" for community participants as they seek to form and sustain effective relationships across sectors (Larner and Craig 2005). It may also become gendered, where women find themselves taking on roles of brokering or maintaining a partnership.[10] Sustaining support for congruence can be difficult for a citizen space that is driving a problem-solving effort, especially over the long term. Related is the fragility of networks and shared governance. Considerable time and effort are required to learn, and operate within ever-changing governance landscapes.[11]

---

[10] On gender in community organizing, see Stall and Stoeker (1998); Mizrahi and Greenawalt (2017).

[11] In interviews with members of the citizen-led Goulburn Murray Resilience Taskforce (see Chapters 3 and 4), we were told that there is increasing churn within the public sector, so maintaining relationships with relevant actors is harder than ever (interviews conducted by Carolyn M. Hendriks between June and November 2023).

Effective collaboration also needs champions and support from actors based in other sectors. As Weir argues: "Unless those engaged in collaboration have the political power to defend the structures and resources that make collaboration possible, they can be scaled back or eliminated in the face of tightening budgets, unfavorable elections, or shifting fashions in public administration" (2010, p. 597). Advocates of co-production and collaborative ways of working between community and state and industry actors also point out that actors from various sectors are not homogenous. As Taylor puts it: "The state is not monolithic and there are allies within it" (2018, p. 21).

Citizen spaces also need to be sensitive to the roles and expertise of existing civil society groups. As Healey reflects: "There are always tensions between reaching out for a coordinated, collaborative and partnership way of working and the feelings of some other local groups and trusts that we are invading their turf. This means we have to tread carefully, respectfully and strategically" (2015b, pp. 22–23).

In summary, effectiveness in negotiating networks with these more formal and established actors comes with costs for citizens' governance spaces. Increased administrative work involved in collaboration and shared governance can force citizen spaces towards more professionalization, and reliance on highly skilled citizens with particular abilities and expertise.

## Challenge 3: Pressure to institutionalize, replicate, and scale-up

Partnerships with, and funding from, state and non-state actors such as corporate and philanthropic funding bodies often require citizen spaces to become institutionalized and grow. Highly successful spaces may experience pressure from sponsors and donors to scale-up via forms of reproduction, such as franchises. While at times useful, growth can also bring additional administration, which may undermine the capacity of the citizen space to rapidly adapt and operate nimbly.

When citizen spaces partner with other actors they have the increased burden of demonstrating accountability and impact. Yet citizen spaces often have difficulty measuring and demonstrating accountability and impact via the status quo "key performance indicators" (KPIs) common in public, corporate, and philanthropic sectors. Conventional measures of impact often overlook the broader contributions citizen spaces offer to contemporary governance and state and non-state actors. As Smith and Ely note in their study of grassroots citizen spaces innovating in the energy sector:

> the performance of a grassroots innovation may be associated narrowly with a particular artefact of the initiative and measured according to conventional policy criteria, such as a community energy initiative being assessed in terms of the quantity and costs of electricity provided. What these instrumental readings of grassroots innovation miss is some of the purposes and framings of the people involved in the initiative. In the case of community energy initiatives, this can include feelings of community identity, a sense of justice and claim over local renewable resources like the wind and sun, and promoting a degree of social and economic self-determination in matters of (electrical) power. (2015, p. 111)

Research on community-led environmental initiatives finds that "informal" community-led projects tend to be overlooked and even discounted relative to more state-led collaborative efforts (see Coffey et al. 2020). Thus, citizen spaces need to be savvy about how they can best assess, demonstrate, and communicate to state and non-state actors their performance, effectiveness, efficiency, and impact. The challenge is to find metrics and forms of knowledge that not only register their broader contributions but also are viewed by other actors as objective and well-grounded.

Amid pressures for citizen spaces to scale-up, we find evidence of citizens exercising autonomy and agency. There are good reasons why citizen spaces might intentionally decide not to scale-up. Being too large can stifle creativity and collaborative potential (Hanna and Park 2020). Growth can also undermine the participatory and inclusive ethos of a citizen space, and affect the manner in which it works with those in need. The Nundah cooperative (NCEC), discussed previously, decided not to scale-up after achieving success. Rather than engaging other citizens and expanding into other communities, NCEC decided to focus on making sure that its governance efforts could adequately support the people it is trying to serve. The driving idea for NCEC is growing at pace: "we have always chosen to grow at a pace which matches the gifts and needs of our workers" (Hooper and Warner 2013, p. 12). NCEC does not aim to recruit citizens to call for policy change, or lobby government to scale-up its model. By keeping its scope local and service-oriented, NCEC challenges a common idea—in the literature on social innovation and social enterprise—that groups should work towards large-scale change. NCEC offers a hard-won realism about the costs such growth could bring to the core service goals of the cooperative, as coordinator Richard Warner explains:

> People often ask us if we would like to scale NCEC to achieve a greater breadth of social impact, and the answer in short is "yes." However, we are also aware of a size beyond which depth of impact and, in particular, community ownership can be lost. This leads us back to the challenge that significant scaling of community owned models will only occur by proliferation and federative efforts to support that (i.e., "scaling across" as opposed to "scaling up"). (2016)

## Fostering Congruence

Throughout this book we have shown how citizen spaces emerge in response to failures or limitations of conventional state institutions, markets, and civil society organizations—such as energy infrastructure, courts and police, food distribution agencies, and NGOs—to address public problems. Yet our analysis in this chapter reveals that citizen spaces do not necessarily reject these institutions and organizations outright. Instead, they carve out pragmatic pathways and adopt well-thought-out strategies to connect on their own terms with relevant actors, and in ways that help the citizen spaces achieve their collective problem-solving goals. Citizens would find these spaces less appealing if they were part of a state agency or traditional civil society association, but also if they were completely detached. Success for citizen spaces, in other words, is not absorption into a department or institution, nor is it being removed from the system. Their hybrid or liminal nature seems essential to their identity and practice. As Wagenaar and van der Heijden argue, many citizen initiatives "do not seek to displace liberal democracy, but operate complementary to, and usually with the support of, private corporations, large-scale hierarchical government agencies and elected officials to provide more and better services with a higher level of control and agency by citizens" (2015, p. 132).

Today, citizens—like governments, NGOs, and firms—are part of a complex landscape of hybrid organizations, where power, accountability, resources, knowledge, and responsibilities are fragmented. The implications of this for citizen spaces and civil society more broadly is that there are new opportunities, openings, and expectations, especially in terms of who to partner with, when, and how (Jessop 2020). Sometimes citizens leading innovative problem-solving initiatives need administrative or legal authority to do their work. This can mean adopting advocacy or activist approaches to pressure officials to share this authority, but it can also mean insider negotiation, and highly pragmatic and non-ideological settlements. Over time, this kind of shared governance can build the respect of state and market actors, enabling citizens to use opportunities to incrementally shift cultural attitudes and practices within the system, as we illustrated with the case of FOG.

Under what conditions then does congruence flourish? A complex picture is emerging from some cross-national research on the capacity of communities to maintain their agency and independence in relation to the state (e.g., Edelenbos et al. 2018; Igalla et al 2021). At the country level, whether the citizen space should work with the state or against it depends on factors such as whether basic needs are met, the nature of democratic processes, and the political culture (see Kenny et al. 2016). However, such studies do not take into consideration the full complexity of contemporary governance where citizen spaces are navigating relationships with not just state actors but also actors from the market and civil society, and hybrid entities. This complexity makes it impossible to prescribe the exact conditions under which congruence will thrive alongside relevant state, market, or civil society organizations. Indeed in complex governance systems, change cannot be directed or controlled in a top-down fashion (Gilchrist and Taylor 2022, p. 75). What we see from the empirical cases presented in this chapter is how citizens can push along practical problem-solving efforts by making sense of a complex issue and its governance landscape, identifying people to work both within and outside the state, and then seizing opportunities for influence.

## Conclusion

Throughout this book we have argued that citizen spaces deserve more analytic attention by scholars and practitioners of democracy and governance. In this chapter we have demonstrated yet another reason why this is the case: citizen-led spaces are distinct from many social movements and community organizing projects because they adopt nuanced strategies when it comes to working across institutional and system boundaries. Importantly, we have shown that many citizen spaces view state and market actors not as opponents to be replaced or wallets to be emptied, but rather as resources, to be eyed warily and constructively as potential channels of support and expertise.

We have developed and applied the concept of congruence in this chapter to capture the self-styled ways that citizen spaces interact with relevant policy actors and systems of governance. When there is a high degree of congruence between citizens and relevant state and market actors, citizens leading governance work might actively initiate and engage in partnerships to leverage skills, knowledge, and capital to address a collective problem. We have avoided labeling such collaborations as co-production because that label is almost always applied to cases that involve outside influence and stage-setting. Congruence, we argue, is a term that better captures the pragmatic approaches taken by citizens leading governance efforts in relation to partnerships. They seek to strike a balance between their practical problem-solving work (goals) and their need to retain autonomy and agency (means).

Congruence between citizen spaces and existing actors and systems cannot always be fully expressed. When the goals and approaches of the citizen spaces diverge considerably from those of state and non-state actors, citizens might choose to work in parallel rather than in partnership. In circumstances where citizen spaces disrupt or undermine status quo policy approaches, citizens might actively work at a critical distance from relevant state, market, or conventional civil society actors. Occasionally state or non-state actors might seek to discredit or shun citizen-led efforts because their governance efforts fail to comply with standards or pose risks.

We hold that citizens leading their own spaces of governance are neither pawns—vulnerable to state or corporate co-option—nor hapless victims of neoliberal state off-loading. Instead, we have shown that citizens can and do exercise considerable agency in these spaces, especially when they have autonomy and resources to lead partnerships on their own terms, or scope for negotiation or to differ or retreat from state and market structures. Citizens are exercising agency not only in how they engage with others but also by actively choosing to keep their problem-solving efforts small rather than scaling-up, because being small affords them the agility needed to address local needs.

Citizen spaces, while valuing autonomy, are also modeling what other actors in public and private sector might do differently. In being good at what they do, where they do it, citizens' governance spaces can hope to contribute to large-scale change rather than solely local improvements.

# Chapter 6
# Risks and Opportunities of Citizens' Governance Spaces: Insights for Democratic Theory and Practice

## Democratic Opportunities Provided by Citizen Spaces

The previous chapters have identified distinct contributions citizen spaces make to democracy. They can foster a practical mode of agency in which citizens instigate, lead, and drive policy work. They offer a space for citizens to rethink and reframe issues, to push forward innovative experiments and solutions, and to work nimbly across sectors, networks, and boundaries. While small-scale they can have systemic reach by attracting the attention of relevant state, market, and civil society actors.

### Enabling civic agency

Unlike some modes of participation, such as voting and consumer choice, which may provide contemporary citizens little more than a "feeling of political agency" (Ci 2006), citizens in citizen-led spaces experience a practical and tangible form of political agency that is centered on collective problem solving, "doing" and "thinking." This kind of practical, bottom-up citizen agency is a refreshing departure from the "dumbing down" of participatory capacity found in some social movement strategies and participatory governance projects. For example, some activist leaders use slogans and simple narratives to mobilize dissent; and some participatory forums are designed to draw in prospective participants by reducing their time or knowledge commitments, or by offering financial incentives (Boyte 2004; OECD 2020). These participatory options, even when highly innovative, can leave citizens disappointed and cynical when procedures and agendas are highly scripted, issues foreclosed, or decisions predetermined.

By contrast, in citizens' governance spaces people expect each other to step up, meet challenges, be smart, and do something about problems too big for individuals to handle on their own. In Vancouver, Dean Wilson was stimulated to learn about practical action and about drug use by attending Vancouver Area Network of Drug Users (VANDU) meetings: "I started reading everything. I'd read an entire report, not just the executive summary.... So we knew how many people were dying and what they were dying of.... [It] turned us all into a bunch of epidemiologists" (Lupick 2017, pp. 183–184). In citizen-led spaces, citizens drive collective problem solving rather than wait for technocrats, government, the market or professionalized civil society organizations to invite or mobilize them. Indeed, by challenging conventional views of policy problems—addiction, energy, crime and punishment, among others—they disrupt settled policy expertise. By acting in constructive ways, they reveal citizen competencies often overlooked by those accustomed to mobilizing "the public" to protest, or to deliberate, or to vote.

## Enacting inclusion, voice, and outreach

Citizen spaces share power in their self-governance and in their problem-solving work, often in creative ways. Some, like Som Energia, have formal mechanisms of self-governance that provide opportunities for members to exercise their voice locally and nationally. Others, like VANDU, embrace informal norms to create a "community of everyone who arrives" (Zigon 2018, p. 80). The simplicity of their participatory processes allows for easy replication and adaptability. They provide a scaffolding upon which citizens elsewhere can make necessary procedural adjustments to suit their contexts and organize participatory processes on their own terms, without having to rely on external experts or consultants.

We have seen how citizen spaces bring in people who are not the well-resourced "usual suspects" of conventional civic engagement efforts. As exemplified by the outreach and connective activities of Orange Sky with its orange chairs, many citizens' governance spaces engage with some of the most marginalized members of society. Through their problem-solving work, and through outreach events, they also seek to make the concerns of marginalized people into public concerns by recruiting new members and volunteers, fund-raising, and sharing information.

## Rethinking and reframing

Throughout the book we have demonstrated the capacity of citizens to reframe policy debates and approaches through practical interventions in sectors as varied as substance addiction and recovery, renewable energy, criminal justice, elder care, funeral services, Internet services, and regional planning. In a citizens' governance space people engage with collective problems in practical and experimental ways. In the absence of prescribed recipes or agendas, they rethink and reframe policy problems, and sometimes in the process they offer new conceptual tools, norms, and practices. In Baltimore Community Conferences labels such as "crime," "offender," and "victims" are reconfigured as "conflicts" and "harms"—as in "the person who does harm," "the one responsible," "the person who experiences harm," "the survivor." Young people playing disruptive street football at night do not fit the label "offenders"; and the people who are affected—who are often relatives—are not easily understood as "victims" once a community conference that involves them gets underway. Indeed, such designations would hinder the creative problem solving that ultimately quiets the street (Abramson and Beck 2010).

The rethinking and reframing that citizens do in citizens' governance spaces can have broader flow-on effects in policy systems, often in highly dynamic and creative ways (Wagenaar 2007, p. 36). For example, the citizens in Tender Funerals are reframing how individuals and the state conceptualize funeral services in Australia: by offering more affordable and personalized funerals, they have initiated policy discussions about the need for more family involvement in the design and conduct of funerals, and greater pricing transparency. VANDU, in Vancouver, similarly reframed the public conversation about substance users: as members worked to make streets, public spaces, and low-cost dwellings safer they exemplified the ways harm-reduction concepts could take root. The citizens in the Goulburn Murray Resilience Taskforce are embedding resilience thinking into relevant arenas that govern land and waste management, water use, and development in their region, by using heuristics to promote long-term thinking. This capacity to trigger systemic rethinking of issues and solutions distinguishes citizen spaces from state-led participatory governance efforts where the boundaries of policy goals and approaches are typically fixed in advance and citizens have limited scope to reframe or rethink them, despite being crucial to their realization.

## Gaining experiential knowledge and practical reasoning

Citizens' governance spaces are conducive to the exercise, growth, and transmission of experiential knowledge and practical reason. Knowledge emerges through citizens' practical and participatory activities as they try to solve a collective problem, rather than via a strategic attempt to develop activist counter-expertise. As citizens work together, make mistakes, confront hurdles, and interact with those they are trying to assist or serve, they accumulate extensive experiential knowledge of techniques and practices that do, or do not, succeed. Some harness ground-level knowledge and provide insights that could not be generated otherwise.

Citizen spaces often encourage citizens, users, and practitioners to interact to share stories and experiences. This mixing of perspectives would be less likely to occur in more structured participatory spaces, where distinctions are often made between citizens, experts, and policy-makers (Elstub and Escobar 2019; Nabatchi et al. 2012). Citizen spaces show how lay people can work constructively with the experts and professionals from state or non-state entities—how new forms of social reason and epistemic reciprocity can develop such that lay citizens and experts learn together about the costs and consequences of policy choices. They are also typically ensconced in networks of citizen problem solvers, and some are engaged in unconventional epistemic policy communities that span regional and national boundaries. For example, like many restorative justice initiatives, the Baltimore Community Conferencing Center made use of practical knowledge drawn from similar efforts abroad; it tapped into the experience of restorative justice practitioners from New Zealand and Australia.

The situated knowledge generated in citizens' governance spaces enables them to adapt their problem-solving abilities to the tasks at hand, and can also inform long-term policy solutions, especially if that knowledge is recognized by, and uploaded to, policy institutions. The Savy Amira Women's Crisis Centre in Indonesia has amassed extensive experiential knowledge over 25 years of supporting women recover from gender-based violence (GBV). Today, volunteers at Savy Amira are regularly called upon as valued experiential experts by local and provincial governments seeking inputs on how to set up state-based GBV programs (e.g., Savy Amira 2019).

## Connecting across boundaries and sectors

Citizens' governance spaces often span formal boundaries to work congruently with public- and private-sector partners, interfacing with them to increase their effectiveness and influence. Some collaborate through partnerships that, while led and directed by citizens, involve ongoing communication and shared governance. Other citizen spaces seek out transactional relationships with better resourced partners, accepting funding and delivering outcomes without much ongoing mutual influence. More autonomous groups choose to work some distance away from traditional state, market, and civil society actors, yet still hope to influence conventional norms and policies by showing how a social problem can be addressed.

The connective work done by citizen spaces offers a different path to social change than social movements and community organizing. Private- and public-sector actors are not in the driver's seat in collaborations, but neither are they opponents to be replaced, or mere resource providers. Citizen spaces gain access to funding, expertise, and information, through their relationships with these other actors, but they are also able to increase their social problem-solving capacity and wider impact. This has been the experience of many community energy projects in Australia, where citizen spaces have established local projects to produce solar and wind energy in partnership with energy retail or distribution companies to assist them in selling and distributing renewable electricity (Curran 2021). Some are directly negotiating the engineering and financial arrangements as well as the terms of community engagement. In Totally Renewable Yackandandah, for example, citizens created a productive, much publicized partnership with a large multi-national energy company.

## Reflecting on Possible Risks Posed by Citizen Spaces

We have discussed distinct contributions citizen spaces make to contemporary democratic systems, but there is more empirical research to be done to better understand the people who become involved in these spaces, their short- and long-term impact on social problems, and how they connect citizens to one another and to state and market institutions. Scholars have raised six major overlapping concerns.

### Reproducing existing inequalities in civic capacity

Collective action rooted in civil society may favor individuals with more discretionary time and resources to contribute. Scholars note that conventional community groups are often highly exclusive and unrepresentative of the broader public (Schlozman et al. 2012; Skocpol 2003). Raising this concern with citizens' governance spaces, some worry that they are "for the most part founded by middle-class citizens in middle-class neighbourhoods" (Wagenaar and van der Heijden 2015, p. 132). If they rely on education, social networks, and social capital that are not distributed equally, then outcomes and benefits will be dispersed unequally:

> A growth of citizen self-organization implies that people become more dependent on the strength of their social network (its bridging and bonding capital). Self-organizing capacity is likely to be unequally dispersed among citizens, leading to issues of inequality. (Edelenbos and van Meerkerk 2016, p. 12)
>
> [I]t is often the highly educated and advantaged who participate most actively and who are best capable of organizing themselves. As such, self-organization may have the effect of perpetuating or increasing inequalities in society, both socio-economically and geographically. (Brandsen 2016, p. 347)

One risk here is that practices become skewed towards the interests of those social groups best able to network, leverage resources, and participate. This is especially so for the citizens who initiate and lead the collective effort. After all, turning an idea into something that is practically feasible, and then engaging other citizens, requires considerable skills, capacities, and resources. For example, citizens leading a governance space need to have a solid knowledge of how the relevant policy system works, and networks to draw on for resources and "know-how." They also need time and patience, and a willingness to experiment and move with fluidity between citizen and expert roles. A related risk is that those spaces organized by the privileged may be more successful at generating impact and sustaining themselves, via constructive interactions with public- and private-sector actors, than those operating by and for the marginalized.

There are broader democratic concerns here to consider, such as the capacity for citizens' governance spaces to fuel social divisions because they under-represent less-educated citizens (Newman and Tonkens 2011). The reasons why some people do not participate in citizen-led problem-solving initiatives extend well beyond resources such as time, money, social capital, skills, and knowledge. Emerging qualitative research finds that some people are not inclined to engage in citizen spaces because they do not feel socially entitled to participate, or because they have no taste for what they perceive as a time-consuming and inefficient form of engagement (Visser et al. 2023). While that is a significant issue, it must be noted that all forms of citizen action are affected by existing inequalities—from voting to volunteering through to a host of non-institutionalized forms of political engagement such as political consumerism, protesting, and Internet activism (Marien et al. 2010).

Attention must be paid to the demographic orientation of any initiative: namely, the people who are in the group, and the people whose interests are being advanced. On the demographics of participation, the evidence is mixed. Some studies indicate that many citizens' governance spaces do better than conventional organizations and institutions in engaging diverse citizens: "There ... appears to be a high latent willingness of citizens to become even more involved—but only if they feel they can play a worthwhile role, which usually means in a relatively narrow range of activities that are genuinely important to them" (Bovaird and Loeffler 2016, p. 273). Civic capacity is not a fixed quantity but can be encouraged and grown.

Also, the critique that citizen spaces reproduce inequality lacks a nuanced understanding of the varied modes of participation within a citizen space. As noted in Chapter 2, those leading and driving the space are likely to need considerable knowledge of the governance system and resources to be able to engage and reshape it. But citizen spaces also organize and involve other citizens who might participate in an informal capacity, volunteering their time, and "stepping up" when and how they can. Evidence from studies of informal volunteering—defined as activity that "occurs directly between individuals and communities without being mediated by an organization" (UNV 2021, p. 33)—finds that its sporadic and informal nature is especially attractive to more marginalized citizens, such as working-class communities and ethnic and racial minorities, because they do not feel comfortable or included in more professionalized charities and civil society organizations (Dean 2021). Studies in Australia, for example, find that people from Culturally and Linguistically Diverse (CALD) backgrounds, recent migrants, and First Nations people are more likely to volunteer informally than formally (CIRCA 2016).

Further evidence of the kinds of people who participate in citizen spaces can be found in studies of the various mutual aid groups and community-led projects that emerged around the globe during the COVID-19 pandemic (UNV 2021). Reflecting on the hyper-local, spontaneous efforts that surfaced in the UK during lockdowns, Tiratelli and Kaye found that:

> These efforts do not reflect the traditional "helper and helped" relationship, which prevails in public services and the formal charity sector. They obey the deeper obligations of mutualism: free citizens combining to protect their communities, and the most vulnerable, against a threat to all ... "Ordinary" people, not just those usually active in their town and village life, have stepped forward in astonishing numbers. Neighbourhoods have become more than geographies, but active social webs, linked by new connections and reciprocal dependencies. (2020, p. 5)

Further research is needed to examine the citizens who choose to participate in citizen governance. What separates the more from the less active members, for example? Are there gender differences? Some studies find that women appear to be more attracted to non-institutionalized forms of political participation compared to institutionalized channels (Marien et al. 2010). While this might be viewed positively, some scholars worry about the gendered nature of citizen governance work.[1]

## State off-loading onto citizens and markets (DIY democracy)

A second major risk is that citizen governance may contribute to a form of do-it-yourself (DIY) democracy that legitimates state withdrawal from social welfare commitments. A shelter for domestic violence victims funded and staffed by a local citizen space may do good work while also providing cover for state agencies to cut funding for similar state-led programs. "While the rhetoric continues to be one of 'empowerment', 'participation', 'localism' and 'democratic renewal,'" note Aiken and Taylor, "the reality is often one of shifting responsibility for services to citizens and employees in pursuit of efficiency savings and, ultimately, a shrinking state." Rather than "engaging with the state," citizen spaces are "taking over the libraries and parks that used to be run by the state" (2019, pp. 22, 24). Marginalized people and those with fewer resources should not have to rely on these to "have the same claim on service quality and provision as other members of society have" (Taylor 2011, p. 217).

This argument implies that the state is creating the structural conditions for citizens' governance spaces to emerge; they would not exist without the state withdrawing and valorizing "ethical citizens" who fit well into neoliberal institutional arrangements (Eliasoph 2013; Parsell et al. 2021). As some scholars put it, the state is trying to manufacture civil society (Brandsen et al. 2017). Thus, if a citizen space does a good job solving a problem, critics argue that this creates a downward spiral because the state has more reason to further withdraw by claiming that "civil society does this better than we can."

It is evident that state withdrawal or absence in some sectors is a motivating factor for some citizen spaces. Yet it is a mistake to describe the state

---

[1] Consider, for example, Newman and Tonkens critique of the active citizenship and responsibilization agenda in the UK: "The implicit coupling of participation and responsibility ...tends to privatise active citizenship and allocate responsibility for people's (often women's) daily, seemingly private, acts" (2011, p.196).

as the active agent that "produces" them, or to insist that the citizens initiating or participating in them would be less likely to do so if not valorized by the state. Off-loading and state inducement arguments miss how much self-driven energy and motivation are present in citizen governance; people find it more desirable to do citizen governance work than formal political and conventional civil society work:

> Today, and this differs from traditional forms of citizen engagement, citizens want to engage in informal and loosely structured organizations and keep aloof from existing political and governmental structures and procedures, which they consider no longer legitimate and/or effective. (Edelenbos and van Meerkerk 2016, p. 3)

"Off-loading" thus mischaracterizes the forms of political dysfunction impacting many contemporary political systems, which prompt citizens to organize and join governance spaces—from polarization and hyper-partisanship to the heavy influence of corporate power, effective policy solutions often fail to emerge from formal institutions and agencies. Participating in citizen spaces is a conscious choice to make an impact in political contexts that offer citizens few other viable options (Levine 2022; Macy 2022).

Studies from different disciplines indicate that people want to engage in local issues if they can participate in everyday practical ways. Jupp's in-depth study of how people participated in small community groups in disadvantaged neighborhoods in the UK found that "helping out" was a strong enabler for community action. "Collective activities drew people in a shared 'taskscape' … although small-scale, and temporary, such moments could be powerful with participants going away feeling energised and positive about involvement in further activities." Her participants note "feeling comfortable" and "feeling at home" and described the "buzz" they experience when they get together as a group of residents to lead a project on their housing estate, such as youth clubs, or new playgrounds … rather than "have things done to them" (2008).

## Accountability and regulation

A third major risk is a side effect of the ways citizens' governance spaces operate with relative autonomy from state and market actors. Groups bypassing administrative, legal, and accountability processes may be able to be more experimental in their approaches to social problems, but this can lead to disparate outcomes. A citizen space operating a community justice center in one neighborhood may handle vandalism cases differently from one in a similar neighborhood some distance away if neither organization is held to common oversight standards (Tiarks 2019). Relatedly, in this case state justice agencies are the court of last resort to which parties dissatisfied with citizen governance turn, raising questions about the efficacy and desirability of problem solving in the absence of state backstops.

An underlying question is not only "who the authorizing actors are but also if they are recognized as being sufficiently legitimate to foster the creation of a governance site. In other words, are they authorized to authorize" (Papadopoulos 2016, p. 149)? Stakeholder accountability is not the same as public accountability: "even if accountability to stakeholders is safeguarded, this does not guarantee accountability to the demos at large" (Papadopoulos 2016, p. 157). Moreover, there may be "multiple accountability disorders": "the requirements of peer accountability may collide with those of accountability to principals or affected populations, whose preferences may diverge from those of the network members" (Papadopoulos 2016, p. 158). Indeed, some scholars question whether citizen spaces are, in fact, delivering the kinds of effective services their stakeholders need and want. For example, as mentioned in Chapter 4 and as we will soon see, some critics have suggested that Orange Sky is focusing on the wrong services, since homeless people need housing above all else, rather than showers and clean washing (Parsell et al. 2021).

This concern is often raised regarding informal organization and citizen action. One response is to say that citizens' governance spaces are not like state bureaucracies so should not be judged on standards that emerged inside them. Moreover, accountability is a function of the ability of citizen spaces to operate publicly and transparently. There is no reason to think they are worse at doing this than conventional civil society groups or even formal government agencies. As with the issue of effectiveness (which we will discuss), accountability can be enhanced by "boundary spanners" in citizen spaces and in state agencies willing to work with them (Igalla et al. 2020).

With respect to accountability to stakeholders and clients, our cases suggest that citizens' governance spaces are highly sensitive to their needs; if there is no ongoing demand for the solutions or services they generate, then they will fold. They thrive in those contexts where members, clients, and the broader public support the solutions being generated, whether that be clean showers, renewable energy, or social spaces for those recovering from substances or wanting to use them safely. Our findings concur with other studies that have also found that citizens leading governance initiatives are keen to be accountable to non-involved citizens, for example by trying to gain their support (Bakker et al. 2012; Dekker 2019).

## Ineffective and piecemeal governance ("small potatoes")

A fourth risk is the potentially limited impact of the activities of citizens' governance spaces. Some critics point out that too often a citizen space offers only temporary, small-bore solutions while failing to address the larger public policy issues (Eliasoph 2013). They say that the contributions of citizen spaces' are too little—"small potatoes"—such as community gardens and food banks that feed merely thousands, rather than a government food policy that could feed millions. Other scholars worry that citizens' governance spaces can myopically focus on the narrow range of problems that interest them but neglect important non-salient issues (Bovaird and Loeffler 2012). Some have pointed out that while they might demonstrate alternative ways of doing things, they are not equipped to produce public goods that require resources to be pooled (F. Hendriks 2019). A broader concern is that many micro community projects are not only inefficient but can undermine the functioning and capacity of pooled infrastructure. Decentralized community energy initiatives, for example, can cause coordination, planning, and regulatory challenges for centralized electricity networks (CEER 2019; Terzon 2021).

While a relevant concern, the issue of effectiveness is context-dependent and highly perspectival. Most citizen spaces are short-lived, but that does not mean they are ineffective: they communicate important ideas and practices if others are willing to listen and learn. Indeed, effectiveness is often a register of how well outside agents understand a problem and accept what citizens are doing about it: do state agencies and private actors understand the experiential aspects of those most impacted by the collective problem, and do they seek to work with, or block, citizen governance?[2]

Questions of effectiveness typically focus on ensuring that governance interventions generate substantive outcomes. But for many citizens working on community solutions there are important procedural aspects to ensuring

---

[2] It is also worth noting the elitism behind the effectiveness critique, as Wagenaar argues: "Perceiving such initiatives as alternatives—interesting but in the end rather ineffective local experiments—to the reigning democratic order would amount to a shallow and misguided understanding of informal, civic sphere practices and their role in a deeper, more inclusive conception of democracy. Such a perception is informed by the democratic elitism that affects so much of our understanding of governance and democracy" (2016, p. 112).

that an initiative is effective. Outside agents often fail to recognize the importance of procedural issues for citizens driving forward solutions to particular problems. Consider, for example, the view of one state official in Jupp's study who was critical of how the local citizens were organizing:

> one paid community worker I met was extremely critical of resident-led initiatives, which she said did not represent "the community" and were dominated by small numbers of individuals. Furthermore, she said that they had too narrow a focus: …. They're only interested in their own neighbourhoods, there's too much competition between them. They don't realise it's important for people to work together. (Jupp 2008, p. 340)

Jupp argues that in this instance the public official failed to recognize not only that government-led initiatives were disempowering local people, but that residents preferred to meet and discuss issues in more informal "everyday" ways. They created their own participatory spaces through which they were able to identify and organize projects and develop their own local solutions.[3]

The "small potatoes" critique reflects the marginalization of citizen spaces in disciplinary frameworks about governance. As Brandsen notes, "public administration and management research logically tend to focus on issues of governance and policymaking, in which citizens tend to be only minor players (or an unseen force such as 'the public')" (Brandsen 2016, p. 340). The same can be said for social movements when their approaches to change privilege large-scale mobilization for effective pressure on state actors. Yet, it is a mistake to place citizens' governance spaces at the margins of this historical narrative: effective social welfare practices were built up, over time, drawing from the experiences of small-scale experiments like those we see in citizen spaces:

> This state-centred concept of change and reform is historically untrue, as many social innovations *avant la lettre* were incorporated into state-sponsored schemes and reality is more hybrid than often acknowledged. The focus on welfare regimes in academic debate has all but written bottom–up innovation out of a welfare state and presents the history of social reform history as top–down process of large-scale institutions and regulations. It ignores the basic role of experimentation and bottom–up innovation in nudging and realising successful reforms. (Brandsen et al. 2016b, p. 309)

---

[3] Taylor makes a similar point in response to the claim that communitarian approaches to community development struggle to address underlying structural issues. While she concedes that this can be the case, she points out that "it has also been possible … for communities to invite external actors into spaces for changes that they create, increasing the chances that co-production can work for communities in ways that allow them to draw on additional resources of knowledge and skills" (2018, p. 20).

## Depoliticization of deep underlying structural issues

A fifth hazard is that citizens' governance spaces perpetuate a pragmatic approach to politics that fails to provide people with enough room to engage in deeper or broader political struggles. As we have shown, citizens' governance spaces are not activist spaces in the conventional sense; they do not typically make claims to new rights, or challenge the state or market to protect existing rights (Aiken and Taylor 2019). The risk here is that citizens busy themselves with self-organizing and problem solving, while deeper underlying structural issues are depoliticized (Forkert 2016; Dekker 2019). By focusing on the practical work of "fixing" social problems in any way they can, the danger is that citizen spaces fail to socialize citizens to stand up for their rights, and challenge social, political, and economic institutions to work for the broad public rather than the well-resourced few (Taylor 2017, p. 20). Even while benefiting "their participants and communities," citizen spaces may "reconcile, rather than contest, the inequities produced by markets and states" when they provide a bridge to these sectors (Barraket and Archer 2010, p. 26).

This critique is perhaps more aptly addressed to the academic discourse about citizens' governance spaces, which tends to be brightly optimistic, rather than their actual work, which is often hands-on and not easily characterized as political or non-political. Moreover, like the concerns regarding state off-loading, inequality, and ineffectiveness, it implicitly judges citizen spaces on universal standards that do not fit the contingent and contextual nature of their work. Many citizen spaces emerge because citizens form connections and relationships in their oppositional work, for example contesting a political decision, or opposing a status quo solution, or harmful infrastructure. Consider, for example, the hundreds of community-led renewable energy initiatives that have emerged in Australia. Many of these citizen spaces were seeded when diverse people mobilized in opposition to the expansion of coal seam gas mining in regions around the country (Curran 2021, p. 214). On the other side of the planet, a similar story can be told about the hundreds of community-led social enterprises that have emerged in the UK to run local libraries in the wake of austerity measures. While academics might view these as spaces of depoliticization and responsibilization, as Forkert does, even she concedes that practical citizen-led efforts often evolve out of experimental oppositional campaigns that "prefigure alternative futures" (2016, p. 27). Moreover, Forkert points out that for some citizens now volunteering to help run the libraries, they value their governance work because it represents a break from dogmatic political party organizations, and a chance to engage in something positive and productive (2016, p. 27). Thus, to read them simply as spaces of "depoliticization" is to ignore the political contestation through which citizen governance often emerges, and to overlook the kind of action-focused and constructive form of political participation they offer people.

As with the other critical stances, the charge of depoliticization is typically grounded in a state-centric understanding of how innovative social change occurs; it ignores conceptions of systemic change that rely less on big state-led policy interventions and more on incremental groundswell delivery. It also consistently undervalues the role of alternative providers, such as voluntary organizations and informal initiatives, as they tend to produce the types of locally-embedded social innovations that remain under the radar (Larsson and Brandsen 2016, p. 295).

The way citizen spaces work can seem non-political, but this is because they follow a "connective" logic rather than the "individualist" and "collectivist" logics of state, market, and social movements (Bang 2016, p. 80). Yet it is worth conceding that such connective work runs many attendant risks that befall any political action: "In the happy positive discourse of self-organization and participation, it is often forgotten that citizens' initiatives are (micro-) political choices on how to organize society. Political choices rarely have unanimous support and nearly always have losers as well as winners" (Brandsen 2016, p. 346).

## Increasing rather than decreasing social fragmentation

A sixth hazard is that citizens' governance spaces fail to build generalized support for the vulnerable and marginalized because of the local and piecemeal nature of their efforts. Citizen governance teaches people to "fend for themselves" and connect to those in proximity to them, rather than recognize the needs and values of others who may be different in some respects. This risk is a product of the issues raised by the previous five concerns and points to the way citizen spaces fail as a form of collective action even when they might succeed to deliver goods and services to disparate groups.

The cases we discuss are not immune from any of these concerns. As raised previously and in Chapter 4, scholars with significant criticisms of Orange Sky Australia (see Parsell and Watts 2017; Parsell et al. 2021) view it as tinkering around the edges of problems caused by the failure of the neoliberal welfare state to provide shelter for the highly marginalized. Orange Sky, they argue, is simply a "feel good" charity that valorizes volunteers, and distracts important public and policymaker attention and funding away from improving housing options for the homeless:

> Those intending only to ameliorate the suffering of those on the street should face legitimate questions about their poverty of ambition, not uncritical praise. Providing mobile washing facilities to people who are homeless risks shifting the debate away from different forms and models of housing, and other evidence-informed responses. When we provide people who are poor with the means to temporarily wash themselves and their clothes in public spaces we are not thinking through, much less lobbying for, the necessity of housing as part of the solution.
>
> Rather than mobile washing facilities, people experiencing homelessness require housing in which they can decide when and how to wash themselves and their clothes. (Parsell and Watts 2017, pp. 68, 71)

We concede that Orange Sky Australia is not doing the "heavy lifting" on homelessness, in terms of providing shelter and addressing chronic poverty on the street. However, we dispute the idea that it is simply a charity. It is a citizens' governance space, driven and led by people through their agency and resourcefulness, and not an institutionalized effort to deliver something to the poor. We also do not see a zero-sum game between people assisting in citizens' governance space activities, on the one hand, and more conventional activist and formal political efforts to strengthen social welfare policy and state agencies, on the other. One mode of action does not have to come at the expense of another. Indeed, several of the case examples we have discussed throughout the book show that activism and citizen problem-solving can each lead to or enrich the work of the other. In other cases, such as Savy Amira Women's Crisis Centre, the work of citizen spaces can expand from discrete problem solving into other modes of political engagement such as advocacy, mobilization, or oppositional protests.

Moreover, many of the concerns raised about citizen spaces reflect an antiquated picture of the welfare state whereby the state can develop and implement expert-led social work programs or technocratic solutions. Such practices might have had enough elite and popular support at the height of the modern welfare state, but their legitimacy has significantly eroded in the last generation. Any solution to homelessness is going to rely on state agencies connecting up with various non-state programs involving both corporate and civil society actors. Citizen spaces are now an important bottom-up partner in the mix.

## How Citizens' Governance Spaces Fit into the Broader Democratic Ecosystem

As the critiques suggest, the forms of citizen agency evident in citizens' governance spaces diverge from voting-centered and protest-centered action; they are also different from deliberation-oriented approaches that stress lay citizen or representative group dialogue. Theories of democracy in which voting, protest, and deliberation take center stage do not typically have much to say about the place and importance of citizen spaces or the value of what members are doing in them. The problem-solving work of citizen spaces is partly reflected, however, in democratic theory influenced by Dewey and the tradition of pragmatism. This theory helps place citizen spaces into the broader democratic ecosystem; yet care must be taken with core concepts developed by contemporary pragmatists such as "democratic experimentalism" in doing so.

### Democratic pragmatism and experimentalism

Pragmatism in democratic theory is rooted in the way Progressive-era intellectuals and activists responded to the failures of conventional institutions to adequately address issues of social integration, workplace safety, public health, and housing. In the late 19th and early 20th centuries in the US, Dewey, Addams, Follette, and others developed a democratic framework emphasizing problem solving; reflexivity; the production, use, and sharing of knowledge; the testing of inherited conventions; and broad civic empowerment (Gross 2009). In their view, political institutions and the public had not yet formed the tools needed to solve the kinds of problems they faced in the modern era where broad socio-economic shifts were underway, such as those related to industrialization, urbanization, and immigration. Moreover, traditional social norms and habits of thought—regarding education, for example, or property rights—were preventing innovative experimentation. Opening up laboratory schools, settlement houses, neighborhood workshops and other sites that were quasi-autonomous from established institutions (like universities and government agencies) they showed how collective problem solving could lead to growth in capacity for individuals and communities.

Contemporary pragmatic democratic theory that draws from these early examples places formal representative bodies and state agencies in a broad problem-solving ecosystem—one that nurtures intellectual and practical capacity across numerous local sites, and thrives on a widespread and diverse network of discussion and knowledge testing. Social problems are "deliberate opportunities for learning," in this framework: "Problems generate reflection, which generates deliberation, which may produce a refined definition of the problem. When individuals or collectivities take control of this learning cycle, scholars refer to it as 'experimentalism'" (Ansell 2011, p. 12). Which individuals and collectivities are taking control, however, is an open question (Ansell 2012).

Some contemporary pragmatists see state agencies as steering the experimentation process, albeit in a highly collaborative way:

> The point is to complement traditional channels of representation with more direct and deliberative forms of consent building focused on problem solving. Although public agencies are not the sole site of deliberation, participation, expertise, or problem solving, they comprise a relatively unique place where these values can be brought together. They are the linchpin between popular sovereignty expressed through elections and local problem-solving efforts.
>
> Public agencies can serve as a linchpin of democracy because they can build up societal consent for policies through effective local problem solving and institutional revision.
>
> Public organizations working on solving specific public problems ... create opportunities for focused and organized civic engagement. They are focal points for the creation of problem-solving publics. (Ansell 2011, p. 18)

Consider the role of the state in steering experiments in "problem-solving" courts and "problem-solving" policing in the criminal justice field. Recognizing the complexity of the situations in which people commit offenses, court systems and police departments have formed specialized units that deal with specific issues, such as substance use, or domestic violence, or mental health. These units adjudicate and enforce the law on the books, but to do these tasks effectively they draw knowledge from people active in allied fields, such as social work, drug treatment, or counselling, in working out strategies for sentencing, probation, and law enforcement. Knowledge generation and communication across traditional barriers are central to their operation:

> [C]entral authority and decentralized actors can together explore and evaluate solutions to complex problems that neither alone would have been likely to identify, much less investigate or address, without the exchanges with the others. The same exchanges of information, moreover, enable the institutions continually to adjust their means and ends in the light of experience. (Dorf and Sabel 2000, p. 834)

Benchmarks and standards are set at the state and national level, then revised as new information emerges from the local level.

Community policing innovations steered by municipal departments are extensions of this problem-centered pragmatic approach to governance that aim to engage with the public more explicitly. In Chicago, the police department shifted away from a traditional top-down structure to begin facilitating regular meetings with residents in 280 neighborhood "beats" to bring community problems to light, identify what is working and not working with police responses, and to welcome citizen ideas. These "beat meetings," and the subsequent citizen networks and interactions that fed back into future meetings, pressed the department and its officers to think and work differently:

> [They have] forced officers to look beyond standard, comfortable, but ineffective approaches such as preventative patrolling, emergency response, and retrospective investigation of crimes. Relatedly, when citizens engage in searching deliberation with police officers, they often develop different priorities and approaches than professional police officers would have developed on their own. Third, neighborhood residents provide distinctive capabilities and resources that make different kinds of public safety strategies possible. For example, residents can monitor "hot spots" such as parks, liquor stores, or residential drug houses with more scrutiny and constancy than a handful of thinly spread police officers. (Fung 2012, pp. 621–622)

The democratic experimentalism in this case leads to civic empowerment regarding social order and related issues. The Chicago police department catalyzed problem-solving public action: "creating institutions in which a core of active residents who have taken a deep interest in public safety in each neighborhood constitute 'lay stakeholders' who deliberate with one another and co-govern the use of policing and other city resources" (Fung 2012, p. 622).

> By inviting direct resident participation in the identification of problems, formulation of strategies, and evaluation of results, the plain intent of the reform was to ensure that the choice of experimental projects and their evaluation would immediately reflect the judgment and preferences of those who, as the primary consumers of police services, must bear the brunt of police failure. (Dorf and Sabel 1998, p. 330)

## Civic agency and the decentering of democratic experiments

The question is: who is running the experiment? In the early Progressive-era vision that has matured into today's contemporary neo-pragmatism, educated experts and open-minded state agents run the experiments; the citizens, whose level of agency varies between "consumer" and "stakeholder," benefit. This is not a technocratic vision, since pragmatists believe that as experiments proliferate, scientific norms of fallibility, empirical testing, peer review, and critical discourse become more common; these in turn encourage a more reflective public, better able to respond to social problems in daily life and via electoral choices. As Ansell puts it, "a Pragmatist model is not content with building problem-solving capacity in agencies alone. It would also build capacity in the wider public" (2011, p. 97).

A decentralized approach to experimentation that taps into citizens' governance spaces may better express the pragmatic commitment to reflexivity, to forming institutions that can learn and grow in tandem with the evolution of public knowledge.[4] According to Loader and Sparks:

> Any experimental approach to finding better solutions to crime questions ... requires reconstruction of the institutional preconditions for the full application of social intelligence to these issues ... [and] ... institutional arrangements that foster and sustain extended democratic participation in determining how crime and security questions are addressed and resolved. (2019, p. 116)

As long as problem solving and community policing are steered by state agencies, they will inevitably bear conventional habits of thought and practice, which reinforce the norms of police as the legitimate provider of public security services that require active and alert responses to discrete crimes, reinforced by threats of punishment and incarceration. Public involvement, even if encouraged by departments, will still be no more than community service—helping the police with *their* work. Community and problem-solving policing programs may encourage citizen voice and even agency,

---

[4] The concept of "public arenas" in recent sociological theory influenced by pragmatism is similarly decentralized: "public arenas can be seen as 'political laboratories' composed of individual, organizational and institutional actors who commit themselves to a collective effort to identify and manage public problems. So it is not a place of consensus, but a patchwork of ways to judge, to see the world, and to exist" (Andion et al. 2017; cf. Cefaï 2022).

but unlike citizens' governance spaces focused on social order, these programs are cabined within terms set by police departments, and thus standard assumptions about crime and punishment are not radically questioned.

The citizen-led Peace Committees active in Zwelethemba, South Africa from 1997 to 2009 offer a very different model of experimentation in problem-solving and community policing. In discussing community problems, citizens came to see that "crime" was a fluid process that often started with small breaches in norms, "disputes in which victims and offenders oscillated—today's victim was tomorrow's offender and vice versa. For a crime to be constituted, so that a harm could be responded to by the institutions of criminal justice, this fluidity had to be frozen to constitute a victim-offender dyad" (Berg and Shearing 2018, p. 81). "Experimentation ensued" and the committee decided that it wanted to respond to disputes "before they escalated to a point where they became crimes, and victim and offender roles could be solidified":

> [It] ... enabled a harm-reduction process in which the aim was not to identify wrongdoers who could be blamed and punished or to deter wrongdoers. Rather, the focus was on understanding and resolving disputes to create a "better tomorrow." Instead of assigning blame, the processes drew on the wisdom of community members to identify and resolve the sources of disputes. (Berg and Shearing 2018, pp. 81–82)

As with the cases of the Baltimore Community Conferencing Center and Crisis Assistance Helping Out On The Streets (CAHOOTS) discussed in earlier chapters, this South African citizen-led space sought solutions to a criminal justice problem while also reconceiving the problem and in doing so legitimating citizen knowledge and action. What is essential here is not that the citizens involved in the Peace Committee decided to adopt harm reduction ideas and dispute resolution practices, it is that they took up the task of providing social order: citizens were both producers and consumers of this crucial public service. As Berg and Shearing note, "Public goods provision need not be restricted to the activities of any single node or institution. Under the appropriate conditions, many nodes can provide policing for the public good" (2018, p. 83). Reflecting Dewey's pragmatic dictum of knowing by doing, the organized citizens in Zwelethemba began to know more about crime because they began to do more about it, and as they did more about it their concepts shifted, and as their concepts shifted what they did shifted in turn.

Citizens' governance spaces like these are generating democratic experiments all over the world (see Evers and Brandsen 2016). Certainly, they are reacting to what state, private sector, and civil society actors do and fail to do, but they are not the products of these other agents, and they are enacting their own forms of knowledge gathering, problem formulation, norm creation, and reflexivity. No mere "government helpers," in furthering the growth of healthy policy in the contemporary political ecosystem, they are finding the seeds, nurturing the plants, and harvesting the produce. They are not averse to educated experts and open-minded state and corporate agents, but they wish to do their own thinking and acting.

## An Expanded Notion of Citizen Agency

As noted at the outset, one of the democratic opportunities offered by citizens' governance spaces is to enable citizen agency by expanding the range of options beyond activism and voting. In doing so, they are facilitating what Boyte (2004) calls "public work" and Bang and Sørensen (1999) call "everyday making." Scholars developed these related concepts to show how people do not have to be elected or part of movements or even part of community organizing efforts to work on social problems. They also wanted to indicate that what scholars and practitioners alike typically define as "politics" and "political" mistakenly amplifies the work of politicians and officials while ignoring the routine, smaller scale activities of citizens. Such concepts are useful, too, to express the motivations and interests, indeed excitement, displayed by people taking their own time to *make* something others can also use—to be part of a public that *works* rather than one in which the options extend from voting to agitating. In an era of generalized distrust of "politics," it is important to show how many people are already doing a different kind of "politics."

We have extended these insights by insisting that in addition to doing public work and everyday making, citizen spaces are doing *governance* work. The kinds of agency they express are:

- directed to real-world social problems via action-oriented experiments;
- even when their experiments are local, citizens are often learning from and communicating with others in different locations, regions, and countries;

- while semi-autonomous, the governance work of citizen spaces is congruent with, and not hostile to norms, knowledge, and the advice of public- and private-sector actors; and,
- the work of citizen spaces is interconnected with the public and private spheres, drawing resources and authority on the one hand, and modeling innovation and change on the other.

Yet if citizen spaces are doing more governance than "public work" and "everyday making" they are also doing less than states do. Citizen spaces take up some, but not all, of the problems citizens face; they are therefore decidedly not governments. Their work decenters governance, but it is not appropriate to characterize it as fostering "nodal" or "polycentric" governance (cf. Ostrom 2010; Shearing and Wood 2003). Members of citizen spaces do not want to exercise all forms of self-governance in every part of their lives, and they want government agencies and private firms to do things differently because of what they learn from the practical problem-solving work citizen spaces do. The democratic experiments that citizen spaces conduct are not just for those immediately affected and their neighborhoods; they provide lessons, practices, insights for similarly situated citizen spaces as well as for governments and markets. Citizen spaces do not imply small or fractured governance; they imply governance led by citizens.

Capturing the agency of citizen spaces aligns with an emergent "civic studies" paradigm which puts the work that citizens are doing to shape their surroundings—and to influence and shift how others are acting—as central to our understandings of democracy. This paradigm confronts "dominant ways of thinking about human action and human agency, about power and politics" by reconceptualizing citizens "[a]s co-creators of the structures of power (large and small) that govern us and the systems of culture that give meanings to our lives" (Boyte et al. 2014). In his discussion of the emerging field of "a new civics," Sołtan explains:

> Our subject is human beings as co-creators, agents who help improve their worlds. It is not human beings as spectators, or as victims or puppets of forces beyond their control, or as very complex machines. The human mind is creative. We act. We take initiatives. And the greatest products of this creative activity require us to create together with others, to co-create. (2014, p. 10)

This is to revalue the place of citizen agency in democratic systems, to acknowledge conflicting interests and power disparities and entrenched biases and inequalities, but also to see self-organized citizen groups as essential political resources—akin to the way that journalists are often referred to as the "fourth branch of government."

Such a revaluation of citizen agency is captured by Kay Pranis, a longtime restorative justice practitioner in Minnesota who has pioneered the use of community sentencing circles. For Pranis, even serious criminal offences are opportunities for citizens to come together, share their feelings, and decide what to do. She explains in an interview:

> When we did the first sentencing circle projects here, I felt that it had to be driven by community. In partnership with the system, to be sure, but it had to be driven by community. We had to community organize first, to find a group of citizens who would be willing to commit volunteer time to help implement these processes, very much in partnership with the system. In so doing, we would actually be strengthening community.
>
> I always argue that there is energy around crime. If there is a robbery in your neighborhood, there is a whole bunch of energy around that. This is initially negative energy. The restorative processes—particularly circles because they can engage more people—give you a way to transform the negative energy that arises naturally into positive community-building energy. (Dzur 2016, p. 261)

Pranis's default presumption is that there are some problems for which there is no substitute for citizens thinking, and talking, and acting on their own accord, albeit "in partnership with the system." As this book has shown, these are not minor problems, but indeed some of the most serious, headline-catching problems societies face: elder care, crime, homelessness, substance use, renewable energy, and environmental protection. Pranis, through long experience, has come to see organized citizens as a fifth branch of government. How can this perspective be shared with other citizens and public- and private-sector actors who lack her experience?

## Lessons for Democratic Practice

To draw out lessons for democratic practice from our analysis, we begin by reflecting on what our empirical research says about why people might choose to participate in a citizens' governance space over other forms of collective action and democratic participation. We then question how these might become more democratic, and how people in well-resourced positions in the public and private sectors can improve their relations with them.

## On the appeal of citizens' governance spaces

For the most part the citizens that feature in the various cases we have discussed throughout the book are "doers," focused on practical action; they are not activists, advocates, or deliberators. As discussed in Chapter 3, citizens are motivated to start a governance space to do something about a pressing collective problem. Why, exactly, might this kind of practically oriented form of political engagement be appealing for citizens?

### Agency and autonomy
Unlike many spaces of democratic engagement, citizens in governance spaces self-organize, choose the problems they will work on, and determine how they will proceed. Their participation is thus not beholden to elites crafting how they engage and what topics they take on. This means they can engage in flexible approaches and shape the form and nature of the participation in ways that work for them.

### Informality
Citizen spaces offer relatively informal opportunities to participate, compared to institutionalized forms of political participation such as voting, standing for office, or party membership. Although informal, they are not necessarily unstructured; informality is more a characteristic of the way citizens engage, and the kinds of expectations placed on them. Citizens are typically not bound by formal rules, moral expectations, and legacies, that can be attached to traditional civic associations, such as charities. Being informal also provides people with greater flexibility; they can contribute in ways that they best can and pull back when they need to. Participation in governance spaces is potentially more accommodating of life's chaos and unpredictability, enabling people to contribute in the midst of work pressures, parenting, care, illness, or fatigue.

### Efficacious and rewarding
Citizens participate in these spaces because they can see the tangible and immediate impact of their practical efforts. In the cases we have discussed in this book, citizens often work nimbly across sectors as well as across siloed bureaucracies. Their agency, autonomy, and informality afford these citizens greater capacity to find cross-cutting solutions that evade governments and civil society organizations that are locked into administrative protocols and institutional silos. For some, the rewards might be less about the policy impacts, and more about the social connections they form, such as with other

volunteers, or with people on the fringes of society such as the homeless, former offenders, or substance users.

### Generative
When citizens participate in a governance space they learn, question, and create solutions as they go. They are not "instructed" to recite a slogan or hold a placard, or to use a particular approach or method. Instead, what we observe in our research is a form of political participation that is highly iterative: they self-organize and work together on aspects of a collective problem; they "give things a go," experiment, make mistakes, and try again. This kind of participation not only involves taking risks; it also requires having faith in a generative way of working with others.

### Being backstage
Much of the work citizens do in governance spaces is "backstage" governance work that often goes unnoticed by policy makers and the media. Citizens who may not have the capacity or inclination to be involved in contentious protests or public advocacy campaigns may be attracted to this kind of practically oriented form of citizen engagement. Unlike a protest or an advocacy campaign, citizen governance work is not about attracting attention. Practical collective problem-solving acts are not designed to circulate on Instagram.

## Democratizing citizens' governance spaces

Our research offers insights for citizens on how they can best undertake collective problem solving in democratically enhancing ways. There is much to say here. For brevity, we focus on three key elements we observe across the majority of our empirical cases, which reflect the principles of good citizen governance practice we noted in Chapter 1, namely that these spaces:

- identify and respond to basic needs (including self-realization and recognition),
- increase democratic governance,
- empower people,
- improve governance processes,
- reproduce and spread to other locales,
- create and transmit knowledge.

### Openness and inclusion

Citizen spaces that are democratically enhancing are open to learning, and to rethinking problem frames and possible solutions. They also include people at the center of the collective problem and people affected by any proposed solutions. Inclusion can be enacted in relatively informal and unstructured ways: an orange chair; a café table; a community of all who show up.

### Networking and sharing

Democratically enhancing citizen spaces pool knowledge and resources with state and non-state actors. They thrive when they utilize existing networks and expand into new ones. They also do well when they find champions and mentors within other sectors, and when they are discerning about the opportunities and risks of external funding, sponsorship, and partnerships. We learned how sometimes citizens need to resist an opportunity to grow or form partnerships. Staying small and independent can have advantages, especially in terms of being nimble and responsive.

### Span boundaries

Democratically enhancing citizen spaces work across administrative, jurisdictional, geographic, and policy-domain boundaries. In our research we find that, for complex policy problems, citizens often are better placed to work across administrative silos and governance boundaries than are governments and large corporate or civil society organizations, because the citizens understand the local context and have to live with the consequences of action or inaction.

## Supporting citizen-led governance

How can practitioners of public governance who are located in government agencies and in the not-for-profit and private sectors support and work with citizens' governance spaces? There is no magic formula. As we saw in Chapter 5, citizens' governance spaces vary considerably in their willingness and capacity to partner with state and non-state actors, and in the various types of support they might need from partners. Some citizen spaces need funding; others require access to knowledge and networks, administrative flexibility, or capacity building. We suggest that when it comes to supporting citizen spaces, well-resourced state and non-state actors can be guided by the following principles.

**Recognize what citizens' governance spaces do and the value they bring**
Citizen spaces need to be noticed and valued by those involved in public governance. Policy practitioners must learn to recognize the distinct problem-solving work that citizens are undertaking, and appreciate the value of their more informal, iterative ways of working, particularly in an era when there is low trust in formal institutions and fatigue with consultation. In contrast to conventional state-led participatory projects, citizen spaces provide opportunities for policy practitioners to connect with, and learn from, informal groups and networks within the community. As one local authority, reflecting on the various mutual aid efforts that emerged during the COVID-19 pandemic in the UK, explained:

> Just recognising the amount of strength, the number of strengths that there are in the community, and really having that hands-off, facilitating approach … and recognising that the communities do have the gift and the skills and the experiences to solve some of their own problems, through local solutions, and support each other locally, without access to services. (Cook et al. 2020, p. 5)

**Support but not control**
Although public governance actors often want to assist community-led approaches, their support often "goes wrong": it can be ill-timed, ill-purposed, and paternalistic. Any policy settings or programs of support need to ensure that they do not unintentionally stifle informality, responsiveness, creativity, and agency of citizens. Support also needs to look well beyond financial matters, to thinking about how to build capacities in the governance system for citizen-led governance. This requires rethinking conventional approaches, both in the community and in the public sector. Public agencies often run programs with community groups to build their capacity to engage with government; and hold workshops with citizens on how to prepare grant applications for public funds. More consideration needs to be given to finding better ways to support both citizens and the public sector to enable citizen-led governance. This could be about building capacity in the community for partnering with a variety of actors from government, market, and professionalized civil society; and on building capacity in the public sector and in civil society to facilitate and nurture community-led problem solving.

For many citizen-led groups, working effectively with market players is the "new frontier." In cases discussed in this book, citizens recognize that the state has limited financial and knowledge resources to address the complex issues the citizens want addressed. As one community member of the citizen-led Goulburn Murray Resilience Taskforce explained:

> Industry will be driving most of the resilience work into the future and so the Taskforce has to learn how to offer itself to industry. The Taskforce will always be compromised with government involved particularly as budgets are tight. The new game is about communities working with industry …. but we need to build capacity in the community on how to do this well.[5]

### Trust and respect citizen autonomy and agency

Community-led problem solving thrives when relevant state and civil society organizations are willing and able to "get out of the way" or, at most, take on a role as funder, facilitator, or coordinator. When formal state, market, and civil society institutions let communities get on with solving collective problems, they support citizen autonomy and agency, and enable citizens to work nimbly across sectors to find cross-cutting solutions. Supporting or partnering with a citizens' governance space entails trusting that communities themselves can lead solutions. According to Carl Walters, a public manager who has spent the past two decades supporting effective community-led projects in land management:[6] "If you trust the community, they won't let you down." Most successful collaborations between citizen-led efforts and others occur when relevant actors respect the autonomy of citizen-led efforts, and there is limited expectation to institutionalize or formalize community-led action. Research on mutual aid groups during the COVID-19 pandemic found that: "De-bureaucratization was key to the collaborative processes" (Cook et al. 2023, p. 16). Trust means accepting that communities work in ways that are more informal, relational, and networked than formal organizations of the state and market. It also means enabling groups to work at small scales, resisting the temptation to encourage them to grow. It is often unhelpful to view citizen spaces as embryonic civil society associations, or as local groups needing assistance to formalize, grow and scale up. Indeed, their informality, and local or small scale are central to their problem-solving capabilities.

---

[5] Interview, John Ginnivan, community representative member on the Goulburn Murray Resilience Taskforce with Carolyn M. Hendriks, September 5, 2023.
[6] Interview, government representative member on the Goulburn Murray Resilience Taskforce with Carolyn M. Hendriks, November 8, 2023.

## Rethinking how to assess and value citizens' governance spaces

As our discussion of risks in this chapter and throughout the book has indicated, not everything attempted by citizens' governance spaces warrants public support; along with the "good" are many instances of "bad" and "ugly" citizen governance. Support should not be unthinking and uncritical, but indeed tailored to favor those spaces that are open to constructive critique and feedback from non-members, foster respect and inclusivity, generate reflexive knowledge, and make meaningful contributions.

### Organic transparency and accountability

Actors in more formal organizations, whether located in the state, market, or civil society, want to know that citizen spaces are transparent about their activities and held to account for any public funds they have spent. But to apply conventional standards of transparency and accountability onto small grassroots groups places considerable administrative burden and strain onto citizens. Rather than try and formalize the informal, we suggest that the conventions and practices of accountability in public governance be rethought, particularly with respect to funding and reporting requirements. We saw glimpses of this kind of rethinking during the height of the COVID-19 pandemic where access to funds was made easier; for example, by offering flexible ways to fund local mutual aid groups via existing community organizations. Research in the UK on mutual aid groups in the pandemic revealed that: "In the face of unprecedented pressures, barriers that once seemed immovable (notably around risk, data sharing and funding) were circumvented at speed" (Cook et al. 2023, p. 16).

### Openness to critique

As noted previously, core goals of citizens' governance spaces include identifying and responding to basic needs, improving democratic governance, empowerment, and the creation and transmission of knowledge. Healthy citizen spaces are open to ongoing discussion about how well they are accomplishing these goals. They also have ways of addressing questions raised about their organizational process or work to make sure they are free of coercion, deception, and bias.

### Knowledge and collective impact

Our research has shown that some of the more efficacious governance spaces have engaged in systematic knowledge-gathering, sometimes in partnership with universities and state agencies, to monitor the progress of their work. To address the valid concerns of academics and practitioners, attention needs to be paid to not only whether governance spaces are "doing no harm," but are also actually accomplishing their core social problem-solving aims.

## Conclusion

At a time when trust in formal democratic institutions is in decline, reformers are turning increasingly to the potential of novel participatory designs to fill legitimacy gaps, to boost deliberation, and to promote listening. Designed participatory forums might help to supplement ailing democratic institutions, but they typically offer citizens limited opportunity for agency and action. We have shown that practical action is an important motivator for citizens to engage in democracy. Many citizens want collective problems solved; some are willing to initiate and lead collective efforts to tackle these problems, often with assistance from state and non-state actors. In these problem-solving spaces the emphasis is less on talking and listening and more on getting things done.

In this book we have conceptualized and analyzed citizens' governance spaces; arenas of citizen-led problem solving that have been largely overlooked in contemporary debates on democracy and democratic renewal. In thinking through the contributions of civil society for modern democracy, Mark Warren argues that different kinds of associations can contribute to deepening democracy in different ways (2011). But to understand fully the "democratic associational ecology," we need to take a closer look at a wide variety of associational types and what they do (Warren 2011, pp. 385–386). Like Warren we do not think that one associational type alone can deepen democracy. But knowing more about the kinds of spaces in civil society that we have explored in this book helps us better understand the kinds of initiatives that citizens are self-organizing and leading to address public problems in contemporary democratic governance. Importantly, we have shown that these citizen spaces are not social movements, nor are they conventional associations with formal or paid members. Instead, they are relatively informal, problem-focused initiatives that citizens form and drive on their own terms. These spaces are not anti-state or anti-market, and many seek out productive partnerships with governments and private corporations.

Drawing on over 30 empirical studies across a wide variety of policy areas from different corners of the globe, we have uncovered citizens motivated by a range of reasons, doing problem-solving work on diverse collective issues.

We have identified a number of governance activities that citizen spaces undertake. In exploring how they interact with state and non-state actors, we have moved beyond the narratives of off-loading and co-option and have developed the idea of congruence.

We contend that citizens' governance spaces represent a form of democratic experimentalism in which citizens work on social problems they care about, generate knowledge, build civic capacity, and interface with public- and private-sector actors. They are a form of political participation that is not well recognized or understood. In labeling and studying citizens' governance spaces we have sought to draw attention to the governance work they do in all their complicated reality, and to explore both their democratic contributions and their risks.

Our book has drawn from our own research as well as from other empirical studies that have tried to tease out how citizens can retain their autonomy and agency in community-led collaborations with other actors. There is much more to learn empirically about what goes on inside these overlooked spaces of civil society in contemporary democracies, and the nuanced ways they work alongside, and sometimes in tension with, other modes of democratic participation. Just how well citizen spaces can deliver democratic benefits while minimizing attendant risks should be at the core of future research.

Studies are needed to probe deeper into the inclusivity and participatory nature of these spaces; how they negotiate state and market power; and the risks they pose to accountability and regulation. For example, survey research and ethnographic studies could examine aspects of power as citizen spaces navigate partnerships with state and non-state actors. We also need to better understand how informal citizen-led initiatives interface with more professionalized civil society groups. Future research should consider the form, function, and democratic implications of citizen governance marked by traditional or conservative goals. In addition, there needs to be more research based in the Global South, and more studies using Indigenous-led approaches.

Under conditions where democratic opportunities are realized in practice and risks are minimized, citizen spaces offer important lessons on how to engage citizens in processes of collective decision-making and problem solving in this era of low trust in institutions and popular perceptions of ineffective governance. Most significantly, citizens' governance spaces demonstrate that, when it comes to informal political participation, there may be more than meets the eye in contemporary societies: citizens are engaging informally far beyond ground-level protest and top-down participatory governance. As our diverse cases reveal, citizens are working in a range of innovative ways to govern complex policy issues on their own terms. In these experimental—sometimes challenging and disruptive—governance efforts, citizens are willing to work with, and at a distance from, relevant state and market structures or traditional civil society associations. As they navigate complex relationships with both state and non-state entities, they are generating practical lessons in "doing democracy" that could provide essential guidance for reformers in the coming decades. Some citizens' governance spaces may offer more useful lessons than others, of course, but the first step towards learning is to start noticing them.

APPENDIX:

# List of Empirical Cases

|   | Case | Collective problem | Chapter(s) |
|---|---|---|---|
| 1 | Baltimore Community Conferencing Center, US | Criminal justice | 1, 3, 4, 6 |
| 2 | Border patrols, US | Civilian Border protection | 1, 3 |
| 3 | Bourke Tribal Council (BTC), Australia | Indigenous criminal justice | 5 |
| 4 | CAHOOTS, US | Crisis support and social order | 3, 4, 6 |
| 5 | COVID-19 response groups, UK | Health and community support | 2, 5, 6 |
| 6 | Common Unity Project Aotearoa (CUPA), New Zealand | Adaptation to climate change | 3 |
| 7 | Community-based internet providers, Indonesia | Accessible and affordable internet services | 3, 5 |
| 8 | Elevated Access, US | Pre-natal support | 4 |
| 9 | Food relief, Canada | Food security | 5 |
| 10 | Friends of Canberra Grasslands (FOG), Australia | Conservation and land use | 5 |
| 11 | Glendale Gateway Trust, UK | Local planning and welfare services | 3, 4 |
| 12 | Goulburn Murray Resilience Taskforce, Australia | Regional planning and climate change adaptation | 3, 4, 5, 6 |
| 13 | Health cooperatives, Japan | Health care | 2, 3 |
| 14 | Heart of Dinner (HoD), US | Food security and elder care | 3 |
| 15 | Landcare, Australia | Land use and environmental protection | 5 |
| 16 | Nundah Community Enterprises Cooperative (NCEC), Australia | Disability employment | 5 |
| 17 | OnPoint, Safe Injection, New York City, US | Safe drug usage | 5 |
| 18 | Orange Sky Australia | Support services for homeless people | 2, 3, 4, 6 |
| 19 | Oregon fires, US | Local security | 4 |
| 20 | Restorative Justice for Oakland Youth, US | Criminal justice | 3, 4 |

*Continued*

|    | Case | Collective problem | Chapter(s) |
|----|------|-------------------|------------|
| 21 | Savy Amira, Indonesia | Support for gender-based violence | 3, 6 |
| 22 | Serenity Café, UK | Substance recovery | 2, 3, 4, 5 |
| 23 | Som Energia, Spain | Renewable energy | 1, 3, 6 |
| 24 | Squatters in Lingewaard, The Netherlands | Housing | 3 |
| 25 | Strathewen Community Renewal Association, Australia | Disaster recovery | 4 |
| 26 | Tender Funerals Australia | Affordable and personalized funeral services | 1, 3, 4, 6 |
| 27 | Totally Renewable Yackandandah (TRY), Australia | Renewable energy | 3, 4, 5, 6 |
| 28 | Vancouver Area Network of Drug Users (VANDU), Canada | Safe drug usage | 3, 4, 5, 6 |
| 29 | Wabash Valley Crisis Pregnancy Center, US | Pre-natal support | 1 |
| 30 | Yackandandah Community Development Company (YCDCo), Australia | Local fuel service | 3 |
| 31 | Zwelethemba, South Africa | Criminal justice | 6 |

# References

ABC. 2020. "Grass-roots Project to Address Indigenous Incarceration in Regional NSW Leads to Reduction in Crime." *Australian Broadcast Corporation (ABC) NewsRadio* posted June 11, 2020. https://www.abc.net.au/news/2020-06-11/grass-roots-project-to-address-indigenous/12343390

ABC. 2022. "A Community Undertaking", *Australian Story*, Australian Broadcast Corporation (ABC) aired June 20, 2022. https://www.abc.net.au/news/2022-06-16/a-community-undertaking/13932294

Abramson, Lauren and Elizabeth Beck. 2010. "Using Conflict to Build Community: Community Conferencing." In *Social Work and Restorative Justice: Skills for Dialogue, Peacemaking, and Reconciliation*, edited by Elizabeth Beck, Nancy P. Kropf, and Pamela Blume Leonard, pp. 149–174. New York: Oxford University Press.

Abramson, Lauren and David B. Moore. 2001. "Transforming Conflict in the Inner City: Community Conferencing in Baltimore." *Contemporary Justice Review* 4 (3, 4): 321–340.

Adams, David. 2004. "Usable Knowledge in Public Policy." *Australian Journal of Public Administration* 63 (1): 29–42.

Adams, James (Ike) and Erin Payseur Oeth. 2020. "Leaderful Communities: Exploring Citizen-Leaders." *Connections*, pp. 15–20. Dayton: Kettering Foundation.

Aertsen, Ivo. 2015. "Belgium." In *Restorative Justice and Mediation in Penal Matters: A Stock-Taking of Legal Issues, Implementation Strategies and Outcomes in 36 European Countries*, edited by Frieder Dünkel, Joanna Grzywa-Holten, and Philip Horsfield, Vol. 1, pp. 45–87. Mönchengladbach: Forum Verlag Godesberg GmbH.

Aiken, Mike and Marilyn Taylor. 2019. "Civic Action and Volunteering: The Changing Space for Popular Engagement in England." *VOLUNTAS: International Journal of Voluntary and Nonprofit Organizations* 30 (1): 15–28. DOI: https://doi.org/10.1007/s11266-019-00090-y

Alinsky, Saul D. 1971. *Rules for Radicals: A Practical Primer for Realistic Radicals*. New York: Random House.

Alinsky, Saul D. 1989. *Reveille for Radicals*. New York: Vintage Books.

Alkon, Alison Hope and Julie Guthman (eds). 2017. *The New Food Activism: Opposition, Cooperation, and Collective Action*. Berkeley: University of California Press.

Allen, Peter. 2018. *The Political Class: Why it Matters Who Our Politicians Are*. Oxford: Oxford University Press.

Amnå, Erik and Joakim Ekman. 2014. "Standby Citizens: Diverse Faces of Political Passivity." *European Political Science Review* 6 (2): 261–281. https://doi.org/10.1017/S175577391300009X

Andion, Carolina, Luciana Ronconi, Rubens Lima Moraes, Aghata Karoliny Ribeiro Gonsalves, and Lilian Brum Duarte Serafim. 2017. "Civil Society and Social Innovation in the Public Sphere: A Pragmatic Perspective." *Revista de Administração Pública* 51 (3): 369–387. DOI: 10.1590/0034-7612143195

Ansell, Christopher K. 2011. *Pragmatist Democracy: Evolutionary Learning as Public Philosophy*. New York: Oxford University Press.

Ansell, Christopher K. 2012. "What is a 'Democratic Experiment'?" *Contemporary Pragmatism* 9 (2): 159–180. https://doi.org/10.1163/18758185-90000235

# References

Ansell, Christopher and Jacob Torfing. 2021. *Public Governance as Co-creation: A Strategy for Revitalizing the Public Sector and Rejuvenating Democracy*. Cambridge: Cambridge University Press.

Ansell, Christopher, Eva Sørensen, and Jacob Torfing. 2021. "When Governance Theory Meets Democratic Theory: The Potential Contribution of Cocreation to Democratic Governance." *Perspectives on Public Management and Governance* 4 (4): 346–362. DOI: 10.1093/ppmgov/gvab024

AusNet. 2017. "Australia's First Community Mini Grid Launched in Yackandandah." *AusNet News*, December 1, 2017. https://www.ausnetservices.com.au/news/australias-first-community-mini-grid-launched-in-yackandandah

Bacchi, Carol. 2009. *Analysing Policy: What's the Problem Represented to Be?* Frenchs Forest: Pearson Education Australia.

Bail, Christopher A., Lisa P. Argyle, Taylor W. Brown, John P. Bumpus, Haohan Chen, M.B. Fallin Hunzaker, et al. 2018. "Exposure to Opposing Views on Social Media Can Increase Political Polarization." *Proceedings of the National Academy of Sciences* 115 (37): 9216–9221. https://doi.org/10.1073/pnas.1804840115

Bakker, Judith, Bas Denters, Mirjan Oude Vrielink, and Pieter-Jan Klok. 2012. "Citizens' Initiatives: How Local Governments Fill Their Facilitative Role." *Local Government Studies* 38 (4): 395–414. http://dx.doi.org/10.1080/03003930.2012.698240

Bang, Henrik. 2005. "Among Everyday Makers and Expert Citizens." In *Remaking Governance: Peoples, Politics and the Public Sphere*, edited by Janet Newman, pp. 159–178. Bristol: Policy Press.

Bang, Henrik. 2016. "Interactive Governance: A Challenge to Institutionalism." In *Critical Reflections on Interactive Governance: Self-organization and Participation in Public Governance*, edited by Jurian Edelenbos and Ingmar van Meerkerk, pp. 66–92. Cheltenham: Edward Elgar Publishing.

Bang, Henrik and Eva Sørensen. 1999. "The Everyday Maker: A New Challenge to Democratic Governance." *Administrative Theory & Praxis*, 21 (3): 325–341. https://doi.org/10.1080/10841806.1999.11643381

Baptista, Nuno, Helena Alves, and Nelson Matos. 2020. "Public Sector Organizations and Cocreation With Citizens: A Literature Review on Benefits, Drivers, and Barriers." *Journal of Nonprofit & Public Sector Marketing* 32 (3): 217–241. DOI: 10.1080/10495142.2019.1589623

Barraket, Jo and Verity Archer. 2010. "Social Inclusion Through Community Enterprise? Examining the Available Evidence." *Third Sector Review* 16 (1): 13–28.

Barraket, Jo, Robyn Eversole, Belinda Luke, and Sharine Barth. 2019. "Resourcefulness of Locally-Oriented Social Enterprises: Implications for Rural Community Development." *Journal of Rural Studies* 70: 188–197. https://doi.org/10.1016/j.jrurstud.2017.12.031

Bayat, Asef. 2013. *Life as Politics: How Ordinary People Change the Middle East*. 2nd ed. Stanford: Stanford University Press.

Beckwith, Melinda, Ana-Maria Bliuc, and David Best. 2016. "What the Recovery Movement Tells Us About Prefigurative Politics." *Journal of Social and Political Psychology* 4 (1): 238–251. https://doi.org/10.5964/jspp.v4i1.548

Beito, David T. 2000. *From Mutual Aid to the Welfare State: Fraternal Societies and Social Services, 1890–1967*. Chapel Hill: The University of North Carolina Press.

Berberoglu, Berch (ed.). 2019. *The Palgrave Handbook of Social Movements, Revolution, and Social Transformation*. Cham: Palgrave Macmillan.

Berg, Julie and Clifford Shearing. 2018. "Governing-through-Harm and Public Goods Policing." *Annals of the American Academy of Political and Social Science* 679 (1): 72–85. https://doi.org/10.1177/0002716218778540

Bergheim, Berit. 2021. "Accessing Tacit Knowledge: A Street-Level Method." *Journal of Social Work Practice* 35 (1): 51–61. https://doi.org/10.1080/02650533.2019.1700491

Bevir, Mark. 2013. *A Theory of Governance*. Berkeley: University of California Press.

Bherer, Laurence, Pascale Dufour, and Françoise Montambeault. 2024. "Creating Local 'Citizen's Governance Spaces' in Austerity Contexts: Food Recuperation and Urban Gardening in Montréal (Canada) as Ways to Pragmatically Invent Alternatives." *Urban Affairs Review* 60(5): 1507–1539. https://doi.org/10.1177/10780874231224359

Blad, John R. 1996. "Neighbourhood-Centred Conflict Mediation: The San Francisco Example." *European Journal on Criminal Policy and Research* 4 (1): 90–107.

Borzaga, Carlo, Luca Fazzi, and Giulia Galera. 2016a. "Social Enterprise as a Bottom-up Dynamic: Part 1. The Reaction of Civil Society to Unmet Social Needs in Italy, Sweden and Japan." *International Review of Sociology* 26 (1): 1–18. https://doi.org/10.1080/03906701.2016.1148332

Borzaga, Carlo, Luca Fazzi, and Giulia Galera. 2016b. "Social Enterprise as a Bottom-up Dynamic. Part 2: The Reaction of Civil Society to Unmet Social Needs in England, Scotland, Ireland, France and Romania." *International Review of Sociology* 26 (2): 201–204. DOI: 10.1080/03906701.2016.1181387

Boswell, John, Jack Corbett, Kate Dommett, Will Jennings, Matthew Flinders, R. A. W. Rhodes, and Matthew Wood. 2019. "State of the Field: What Can Political Ethnography Tell Us about Anti-politics and Democratic Disaffection?". *European Journal of Political Research* 58 (1): 56–71. https://doi.org/10.1111/1475-6765.12270

Bovaird, Tony. 2007. "Beyond Engagement and Participation: User and Community Coproduction of Public Services." *Public Administration Review* 67 (5): 846–860. https://doi.org/10.1111/j.1540-6210.2007.00773.x

Bovaird, Tony and Elke Loeffler. 2012. "From Engagement to Co-production: The Contribution of Users and Communities to Outcomes and Public Value." *VOLUNTAS: International Journal of Voluntary and Nonprofit Organizations* 23 (4): 1119–1138. https://doi.org/10.1007/s11266-012-9309-6

Bovaird, Tony and Elke Loeffler. 2016. "What Has Co-Production Ever Done for Interactive Governance." In *Critical Reflections on Interactive Governance: Self-organization and Participation in Public Governance*, edited by Jurian Edelenbos and Ingmar van Meerkerk, pp. 254–277. Cheltenham: Edward Elgar Publishing.

Boyd, Susan C., Donald MacPherson, and Bud Osborn. 2009. *Raise Shit!: Social Action Saving Lives*. Halifax: Fernwood Publishing.

Boyte, Harry, Stephen Elkin, Peter Levine, Jane Mansbridge, Elinor Ostrom, Karol Soltan, et al. 2014. "The New Civic Politics: Civic Theory and Practice for the Future." *The Good Society* 23 (2): 206–211. https://doi.org/10.5325/goodsociety.23.2.0206

Boyte, Harry C. 2004. *Everyday Politics: Reconnecting Citizens and Public Life*. Philadelphia: University of Pennsylvania Press.

Brabham, Daren C. 2015. *Crowdsourcing in the Public Sector*. Washington, DC: Georgetown University Press.

Brandsen, Taco. 2016. "Governments and Self-Organization: A Hedgehog's Dilemma." In *Critical Reflections on Interactive Governance: Self-organization and Participation in Public Governance*, edited by Jurian Edelenbos and Ingmar van Meerkerk, pp. 337–351. Cheltenham: Edward Elgar Publishing.

Brandsen, Taco, Sandro Cattacin, Adalbert Evers, and Annette Zimmer (eds). 2016a. *Social Innovations in the Urban Context*. Cham: Springer.

Brandsen, Taco, Adalbert Evers, Sandro Cattacin, and Annette Zimmer. 2016b. "The Good, the Bad and the Ugly in Social Innovation." In *Social Innovations in the Urban Context*, edited by Taco Brandsen, Sandro Cattacin, Adalbert Evers, and Annette Zimmer, pp. 303–310. Cham: Springer.

# References

Brandsen, Taco, Willem Trommel, and Bram Verschuere. 2017. "The State and the Reconstruction of Civil Society." *International Review of Administrative Sciences* 83 (4): 676–693. https://doi.org/10.1177/0020852315592467

Brenna, Owen. 2020. "Growing Calls for Police Reform Shine Spotlight on Oregon: City Group's Model for Crisis Intervention Focuses on Mental Health-Based Approach." *The Vancouver Sun* (July 11): A.8.

Bridge, Simon, Brendan Murtagh, and Ken O'Neill. 2014. *Understanding the Social Economy and the Third Sector*, second edition. London: Palgrave Macmillan.

Brown, Richard Maxwell. 1975. *Strain of Violence: Historical Studies of American Violence and Vigilantism*. New York: Oxford University Press.

Brummer, Vasco. 2018. "Community Energy—Benefits and Barriers: A Comparative Literature Review of Community Energy in the UK, Germany and the USA, the Benefits It Provides for Society and the Barriers It Faces." *Renewable and Sustainable Energy Reviews* 94: 187–196. https://doi.org/10.1016/j.rser.2018.06.013

Bryant, Gareth and Ben Spies-Butcher. 2022. "From Marketisation to Self-determination: Contesting State and Market Through 'Justice Reinvestment.'" *Environment and Planning A: Economy and Space* 56 (1): 216–234. https://doi.org/10.1177/0308518X221125797

Bua, Adrian and Sonia Bussu. 2020. "Between Governance-Driven Democratisation and Democracy-Driven Governance: Explaining Changes in Participatory Governance in the Case of Barcelona." *European Journal of Political Research* 60 (3): 716–737. https://doi.org/10.1111/1475-6765.12421

Bua, Adrian and Sonia Bussu (eds). 2023. *Reclaiming Participatory Governance: Social Movements and the Reinvention of Democratic Innovation*. Abingdon, UK: Routledge.

Burkett, Ingrid. 2011. "Organizing in the New Marketplace: Contradictions and Opportunities for Community Development Organizations in the Ashes of Neoliberalism." *Community Development Journal* 46 (suppl_2): ii111–ii127. https://doi.org/10.1093/cdj/bsr002

Caldwell, Alicia A. 2019. "Civilian Militia Group Stops Migrants at the U.S.-Mexico Border: New Mexico Attorney General Faults Exercise of 'Authority Reserved for Law Enforcement.'" *Wall Street Journal* (April 19). https://www.wsj.com/articles/civilian-militia-group-stops-migrants-at-the-u-s-mexico-border-11555703831

Cameron, Sarah. 2020. "Government Performance and Dissatisfaction with Democracy in Australia." *Australian Journal of Political Science* 55 (2): 170–190. https://doi.org/10.1080/10361146.2020.1755221

Campbell, Ruth, Kane Duffy, Michael Gaughan, and Michael Mochrie. 2011. "Serenity Café—on the Road to Recovery Capital." *Journal of Groups in Addiction & Recovery* 6 (1–2): 132–163. https://doi.org/10.1080/1556035X.2011.571129

Caramizaru, Elena and A. Uihlein. 2020. *Energy Communities: An Overview of Energy and Social Innovation*. Joint Research Centre Science for Policy Report, European Commission. Luxembourg: Publications Office of the European Union.

Carson, Lyn. 2007. "Creating Democratic Surplus through Citizens' Assemblies." *Journal of Public Deliberation* 4 (1): Article 5. https://delibdemjournal.org/article/336/galley/4730/view/

Catacutan, Delia, Constance Neely, Mary Johnson, Horrie Poussard, and Rob Youl (eds). 2009. *Landcare: Local Action—Global Progress*. Nairobi, Kenya: World Agroforestry Centre.

CEER (Council of European Energy Regulators). 2019. *Regulatory Aspects of Self-Consumption and Energy Communities*. CEER Report C18-CRM9_DS7-05-03, June 25, 2019. Council of European Energy Regulators. Available at: https://jalon-ce.eu/wp-content/uploads/2024/04/Regulatory-Aspects-of-Self-Consumption-and-Energy-Communities-EN.pdf Accessed September 28, 2024.

# References

Cefaï, Daniel. 2022. "The Public Arena A Pragmatist Concept of the Public Sphere." In *The New Pragmatist Sociology: Inquiry, Agency, and Democracy*, edited by Neil L. Gross, Isaac Ariail Reed, and Christopher Winship, pp. 377–405. New York: Columbia University Press. https://doi.org/10.7312/gros20378-015

Chambers, Simone and Jeffrey Kopstein. 2001. "Bad Civil Society." *Political Theory* 29 (6): 837–865. https://doi.org/10.1177/0090591701029006

Chenery, Susan and Olivia Rousset. 2022. "A Community Undertaking: Step Inside the Not-For-Profit Funeral Home That's Doing Death Differently." *Australian Broadcasting Corporation ABC News*, June 21. https://www.abc.net.au/news/2022-06-21/tender-funerals-doing-death-differently/100631330.

Christens, Brian D. and Paul W. Speer. 2015. "Community Organizing: Practice, Research, and Policy Implications." *Social Issues and Policy Review* 9 (1): 193–222. https://doi.org/10.1111/sipr.12014

Christens, Brian D., Jyoti Gupta, and Paul W. Speer. 2021. "Community Organizing: Studying the Development and Exercise of Grassroots Power." *Journal of Community Psychology* 49 (8): 3001–3016. https://doi.org/10.1002/jcop.22700

Ci, Jiwei. 2006. "Political Agency in Liberal Democracy." *Journal of Political Philosophy* 14 (2): 144–162. https://doi.org/10.1111/j.1467-9760.2006.00236.x

CIRCA (Cultural & Indigenous Research Centre Australia). 2016. *Giving and Volunteering in Culturally and Linguistically Diverse and Indigenous Communities*. Australia: Commonwealth of Australia. https://volunteeringhub.org.au/wp-content/uploads/2021/02/Giving%20and%20Volunteering%20in%20Cultural%20and%20Linguistically%20Diverse%20and%20Indigenous%20Communities.pdf

Cissner, Amanda, Erika Sasson, Rebecca Thomforde Hauser, Hillary Packer, Joan Pennell, Emily L. Smith, et al. 2019. *A National Portrait of Restorative Approaches to Intimate Partner Violence: Pathways to Safety, Accountability, Healing, and Well-Being*. New York: Center for Court Innovation.

Citrin, Jack and Laura Stoker. 2018. "Political Trust in a Cynical Age." *Annual Review of Political Science* 21: 49–70. https://doi.org/10.1146/annurev-polsci-050316-092550

Coade, Melissa. 2023. "Chief Mandarin's Direction to APS: Learn to Follow Community." *The Mandarin* December 7, 2023. https://www.themandarin.com.au/236070-chief-mandarins-direction-to-aps-learn-to-follow-community/

Coffey, Brian, Judy Bush, Laura Mumaw, Lisa de Kleyn, Casey Furlong, and Raven Cretney. 2020. "Towards Good Governance of Urban Greening: Insights from Four Initiatives in Melbourne, Australia." *Australian Geographer* 51 (2): 189–204. DOI: 10.1080/00049182.2019.1708552

Connelly, Steve. 2011. "Constructing Legitimacy in the New Community Governance." *Urban Studies* 48 (5): 929–946. https://doi.org/10.1177/0042098010366744

Cook, Joanne, Harriet Thiery, and Jon Burchell. 2023. "No Longer 'Waiting for the Great Leap Forwards'? Advances in Local State-Voluntary and Community Sector Relationships During Covid-19." *Journal of Social Policy* 1–20. https://doi.org/10.1017/S0047279422000939

Cook, Joe, Harriet Thiery, Jon Burchell, Fiona Walkley, Erica Ballantyne, and Jenny McNeill. 2020. *Report #1 Lessons from Lockdown*. Research Report from MoVE: Mobilising Volunteers Effectively. Sheffield, Hull, and Leeds: Universities of Sheffield, Hull, and Leeds. https://doit.life/channels/11997/move-findings/file/md/139216/report-1-lessons-from-lockdown

Cornwall, Andrea. 2004. "Introduction: New Democratic Spaces? The Politics and Dynamics of Institutionalised Participation." *IDS Bulletin* 35 (2): 1–10. https://doi.org/10.1111/j.1759-5436.2004.tb00115.x

Cox, Laurence. 2014. "Movements Making Knowledge: A New Wave of Inspiration for Sociology?" *Sociology* 48 (5): 954–971. https://doi.org/10.1177/0038038514539063

Craig, Gary, Marilyn Taylor, and Tessa Parkes. 2004. "Protest or Partnership? The Voluntary and Community Sectors in the Policy Process." *Social Policy and Administration* 38 (3): 221–239. https://doi.org/10.1111/j.1467-9515.2004.00387.x

Cretney, Raven. 2018. "Beyond Public Meetings: Diverse Forms of Community Led Recovery Following Disaster." *International Journal of Disaster Risk Reduction* 28 (June): 122–130. https://doi.org/10.1016/j.ijdrr.2018.02.035

Cullingworth, Jane, Nicholas Watson, Thomas Shakespeare, Richard Brunner, Charlotte Pearson, and Nathaniel Scherer. 2024. "'They Have Been a Saving Grace in All This': The Role of the Third Sector in Disabled People's Experiences of COVID-19 and Implications for Sector–State Relations." *Voluntary Sector Review* 15 (1): 92–109.

Curran, Giorel. 2021. "Community Renewable Energy and Collaborative Governance: Social Entrepreneurialism at the Local Level in Australia." In *Civic Engagement, Community-Based Initiatives and Governance Capacity: An International Perspective*, edited by Jurian Edelenbos, Astrid Molenveld, and Ingmar van Meerkerk, pp. 199–218. New York: Routledge.

Daley, Mick. 2020. "The Amazing World of Our Thriving Co-Operatives, Especially in the Regions." *The Fifth Estate*. https://thefifthestate.com.au/business/investment-deals/business-schools-dont-teach-it-but-community-owned-co-operatives-are-thriving-starting-with-victoria/

Dalton, Russell J. 2005. "The Social Transformation of Trust in Government." *International Review of Sociology* 15 (1): 133–154. https://doi.org/10.1080/03906700500038819

Davis, Fania. 2018. "Whole School Restorative Justice as a Racial Justice and Liberatory Practice: Oakland's Journey." *The International Journal of Restorative Justice* 1 (3): 428–432. DOI: 10.5553/IJRJ/258908912018001003007

de Freytas-tamura, Kimiko. 2021. "How Neighborhood Groups Are Stepping In Where the Government Didn't." *The New York Times*, March 6 update. https://www.nytimes.com/2021/03/03/nyregion/covid-19-mutual-aid-nyc.html

de Souza Briggs, Xavier. 2008. *Democracy as Problem Solving: Civic Capacity in Communities Across the Globe*. Cambridge, MA: MIT Press.

de Swaan, Abram. 1988. *In Care of the State: Health Care, Education and Welfare in Europe and the USA in the Modern Era*. New York: Oxford University Press.

Dean, Jon. 2021. "Informal Volunteering, Inequality, and Illegitimacy." *Nonprofit and Voluntary Sector Quarterly* 51 (3): 527–544. https://doi.org/10.1177/0899764021103458

Dekker, Paul. 2019. "From Pillarized Active Membership to Populist Active Citizenship: The Dutch Do Democracy." *VOLUNTAS: International Journal of Voluntary and Nonprofit Organizations* 30 (1): 74–85. https://doi.org/10.1007/s11266-018-00058-4

della Porta, Donatella and Mario Diani (eds). 2015. *The Oxford Handbook of Social Movements*. Oxford: Oxford University Press.

della Porta, Donatella and Andrea Felicetti. 2019. "Innovating Democracy Against Democratic Stress in Europe: Social Movements and Democratic Experiments." *Representation* 58 (1): 67–84. https://doi.org/10.1080/00344893.2019.1624600

Denters, Bas. 2016. "Community Self-Organization: Potentials and Pitfalls." In *Critical Reflections on Interactive Governance: Self-organization and Participation in Public Governance*, edited by Jurian Edelenbos and Ingmar van Meerkerk, pp. 230–253. Cheltenham: Edward Elgar Publishing.

Dorf, Michael C. and Charles F. Sabel. 1998. "A Constitution of Democratic Experimentalism." *Columbia Law Review* 98 (2): 267–473. https://scholarship.law.cornell.edu/cgi/viewcontent.cgi?article=1119&context=facpub

Dorf, Michael C. and Charles F. Sabel. 2000. "Drug Treatment Courts and Emergent Experimentalist Government." *Vanderbilt Law Review* 53 (3): 831–883. https://scholarship.law.vanderbilt.edu/cgi/viewcontent.cgi?article=1910&context=vlr

Doty, Roxanne Lynn. 2007. "States of Exception on the Mexico–U.S. Border: Security, 'Decisions,' and Civilian Border Patrols." *International Political Sociology* 1 (2): 113–137. https://doi.org/10.1111/j.1749-5687.2007.00008.x

Doucette, Jamie and Laam Hae. 2022. "The Politics of Post-Developmentalist Expertise: Progressive Movements, Strategic Localism, and Urban Governance in Seoul." *Urban Geography* 43 (1): 134–152. DOI: 10.1080/02723638.2021.2003587

Driscoll, Hannah. 2017. "Renewable Energy: Yackandandah Power Play." *The Weekly Times*, November 10, 2017. https://www.weeklytimesnow.com.au/news/national/renewable-energy-yackandandah-power-play/news-story/600813bc6bcc99764a3c4db2fce4dba9

Dryzek, John S. 2010. *Foundations and Frontiers of Deliberative Governance*. New York: Oxford University Press.

Duffy, Bobby, George May, Kirstie Hewlett, James Wright, and Paul Stoneman. 2023a. "Democracy in Theory and Practice: How UK Attitudes Compare Internationally." *World Values Survey*. https://doi.org/10.18742/pub01-127

Duffy, Bobby, George May, Kirstie Hewlett, James Wright, and Paul Stoneman. 2023b. "Trust in Trouble? UK and International Confidence in Institutions." *World Values Survey*. https://www.kcl.ac.uk/policy-institute/assets/confidence-in-institutions.pdf

Duijn, Michael, Arwin van Buuren, Jurian Edelenbos, Jitske van Popering-verkerk, and Ingmar Van Meerkerk. 2019. "Community-Based Initiatives in the Dutch Water Domain: The Challenge of Double Helix Alignment." *International Journal of Water Resources Development* 35 (3): 383–403. https://doi.org/10.1080/07900627.2019.1575189

Dzur, Albert. 2013. "Trench Democracy in Criminal Justice #1: An Interview with Lauren Abramson." *Boston Review*, December 13. http://bostonreview.net/blog/albert-w-dzur-trench-democracy-criminal-justice-interview-lauren-abramson

Dzur, Albert W. 2016. "Conversations on Restorative Justice: A Talk with Kay Pranis." *Restorative Justice* 4 (2): 257–270. https://doi.org/10.1080/20504721.2016.1197535

Dzur, Albert W. 2019. *Democracy Inside: Participatory Innovation in Unlikely Places*. New York: Oxford University Press.

Dzur, Albert W. and Carolyn M. Hendriks. 2024. "Citizens' Governance Spaces." In *The Cambridge Handbook of Community Empowerment*, edited by Brian D. Christens, pp. 193–215. Cambridge: Cambridge University Press.

EA (Elevated Access). 2023. "About Elevated Access" *Elevated Access Website* https://www.elevatedaccess.org/about. Accessed August 22, 2023.

Edelenbos, Jurian and Ingmar van Meerkerk. 2016. "Introduction: Three Reflecting Perspectives on Interactive Governance." In *Critical Reflections on Interactive Governance: Self-organization and Participation in Public Governance*, edited by Jurian Edelenbos and Ingmar van Meerkerk, pp. 1–28. Cheltenham: Edward Elgar Publishing.

Edelenbos, Jurian, Ingmar van Meerkerk, and Todd Schenk. 2018. "The Evolution of Community Self-Organization in Interaction with Government Institutions: Cross-Case Insights from Three Countries." *The American Review of Public Administration* 48 (1): 52–66. https://doi.org/10.1177/0275074016651

Edelenbos, Jurian, Astrid Molenveld, Ingmar van Meerkerk, Patsy Healey, and Anat Gofen. 2021a. "Positioning and Conceptualising Community-Based Initiatives in Waves of Civic Engagement." In *Civic Engagement, Community-Based Initiatives and Governance Capacity: An International Perspective*, edited by Jurian Edelenbos, Astrid Molenveld, and Ingmar van Meerkerk, pp. 1–18. New York: Routledge.

Edelenbos, Jurian, Astrid Molenveld, and Ingmar van Meerkerk (eds). 2021b. *Civic Engagement, Community-Based Initiatives and Governance Capacity: An International Perspective.* New York: Routledge.

Edelenbos, Jurian, Astrid Molenveld, Katerina Mojanchevska, Elena Ensenado, Monserrat Budding Polo Ballinas, Audrey Esteban, et al. 2021c. "Community-Based Initiatives in the Urban Realm What Conditions Their Performance?" *Journal of Environmental Planning and Management* 64 (9): 1689–1712. 10.1080/09640568.2020.1837088

Einstein, Katherine Levine, David M. Glick, and Maxwell Palmer. 2019. *Neighborhood Defenders: Participatory Politics and America's Housing Crisis.* Cambridge: Cambridge University Press.

Elcioglu, Emine F. 2015. "Popular Sovereignty on the Border: Nativist Activism Among Two Border Watch Groups in Southern Arizona." *Ethnography* 16 (4): 438–462. DOI: 10.1177/1466138114552951

Eliasoph, Nina. 2013. *The Politics of Volunteering.* Malden, MA: Polity Press.

Elstub, Stephen and Oliver Escobar (eds). 2019. *Handbook of Democratic Innovation and Governance.* Cheltenham: Edward Elgar Publishing.

Endo, Chikako. 2020. "Creating a Common World Through Action: What Participation in Community Activities Means to Older People." *Ageing & Society* 40 (6): 1175–1194. DOI: https://doi.org/10.1017/S0144686X18001587

Evers, Adalbert and Taco Brandsen. 2016. "Social Innovations as Messages: Democratic Experimentation in Local Welfare Systems." In *Social Innovations in the Urban Context*, edited by Taco Brandsen, Sandro Cattacin, Adalbert Evers, and Annette Zimmer, pp. 161–180. Cham: Springer.

Evers, Adalbert and Johan von Essen. 2019. "Volunteering and Civic Action: Boundaries Blurring, Boundaries Redrawn." *VOLUNTAS: International Journal of Voluntary and Nonprofit Organizations* 30 (1): 1–14. https://www.jstor.org/stable/45147527

Eversole, Robyn. 2011. "Community Agency and Community Engagement: Re-Theorising Participation in Governance." *Journal of Public Policy* 31 (1): 51–71. https://doi.org/10.1017/S0143814X10000206

Feasey, Simon and Patrick Williams. 2009. *An Evaluation of the Sycamore Tree Programme: Based on an Analysis of Crime Pics II Data.* Sheffield, UK: Hallam Centre for Community Justice, Sheffield Hallam University.

Figueroa, Meleiza and Alison Hope Alkon. 2017. "Cooperative Social Practices, Self-Determination, and the Struggle for Food Justice in Oakland and Chicago." In *The New Food Activism: Opposition, Cooperation, and Collective Action*, edited by Alison Alkon and Julie Guthman, pp. 206–231. Berkeley: University of California Press.

Finkel, Eli J., Christopher A. Bail, Mina Cikara, Peter H. Ditto, Shanto Iyengar, Samara Klar, et al. 2020. "Political Sectarianism in America: A Poisonous Cocktail of Othering, Aversion, and Moralization Poses a Threat to Democracy." *Science* 370 (6516): 533–536. https://doi.org/10.1126/SCIENCE.ABE1715

Foa, Robert Stefan and Yascha Mounk. 2016. "The Danger of Deconsolidation: The Democratic Disconnect." *Journal of Democracy* 27 (3): 5–17. DOI: 10.1353/jod.2016.0049

FOG (Friends of Grasslands). 2014. "Field Sites and Talks: Stirling Park, Yarralumla, ACT." In *Grass Half Full or Grass Half Empty? Valuing Native Grassy Landscapes.* Proceedings of the Friends of Grasslands 20th Anniversary Forum. Canberra, Australia: Friends of Grasslands Inc. https://www.fog.org.au/Articles/2014%20forum/Field%20sites%20-%20Stirling%20Park%20ACT,%20FOG%20forum,%20hi%20res.pdf.

FOG (Friends of Grasslands). 2021. *Draft Annual Report 2021*, Friends of Grasslands, https://www.fog.org.au/AGMs/2022%20draft%20Annual%20Report%202021%2020220310.pdf

FOG (Friends of Grasslands). 2022. *News of Friends of Grasslands.* September & October 2022. https://www.fog.org.au/Newsletters/2022-09newsletter.pdf. Accessed September 24, 2022.

FOG (Friends of Grasslands). 2024. "About Us." *Friends of Grasslands Website.* https://www.fog.org.au/Articles/apc15-3-28.htm. Accessed January 19, 2024.

Fogarty, Nick. 2014. "Energy Builds For Yackandandah Renewables Target." *Australian Broadcast Corporation, ABC Local,* June 27. https://www.abc.net.au/local/photos/2014/06/27/4034789.htm

Forkert, Kirsten. 2016. "Austere Creativity and Volunteer-run Public Services: The Case of Lewisham's Libraries." *New Formations* 87: 11–28. https://doi.org/10.3898/NEWF.87.1.2016

Frantzeskaki, Niki, Adina Dumitru, Isabelle Anguelovski, Flor Avelino, Matthew Bach, Benjamin Best, et al. 2016. "Elucidating the Changing Roles of Civil Society in Urban Sustainability Transitions." *Current Opinion in Environmental Sustainability* 22: 41–50. https://doi.org/10.1016/j.cosust.2017.04.008

Fraser, Nancy. 1993. "Rethinking the Public Sphere: A Contribution to the Critique of Actually Existing Democracy." In *Between Borders: Pedagogy and the Politics of Cultural Studies,* edited by Henry A. Giroux and Peter McLaren, pp. 74–98. New York: Routledge.

Fung, Archon. 2006. "Varieties of Participation in Complex Governance." *Public Administration Review* 66 (December): 66–75. https://www.jstor.org/stable/4096571

Fung, Archon. 2012. "Continuous Institutional Innovation and the Pragmatic Conception of Democracy." *Polity* 44 (4): 609–624. https://www.jstor.org/stable/41684506

Fung, Archon and Erik Olin Wright (eds). 2003. *Deepening Democracy: Institutional Innovations in Empowered Participatory Governance.* London: Verso.

Funtowicz, Silvio O. and Jerome R. Ravetz. 1993. "Science for the Post-Normal Age." *Futures* 25 (7): 739–755. https://doi.org/10.1016/0016-3287(93)90022-L

Gaventa, John. 2006. "Finding the Spaces for Change: A Power Analysis." *IDS Bulletin* 37 (6): 23–33. DOI: 10.1111/j.1759-5436.2006.tb00320.x

Gilchrist, Alison and Marilyn Taylor. 2022. *The Short Guide to Community Development.* Bristol: Policy Press.

Gitterman, Alex and Lawrence Shulman (eds). 2005. *Mutual Aid Groups, Vulnerable and Resilient Populations, and the Life Cycle,* 3rd edition. New York: Columbia University Press.

GMRS. 2020. *Goulburn Murray Resilience Strategy: Adapt Transform Thrive.* https://www.rdv.vic.gov.au/__data/assets/pdf_file/0007/1942540/GMID-Resilience-Strategy_6-May-2020.pdf

Gofen, Anat. 2021. "Out of the Governance Capacity Comfort Zone: Noncompliant Community-Based Initiatives in Israel." In *Civic Engagement, Community-Based Initiatives and Governance Capacity: An International Perspective,* edited by Jurian Edelenbos, Astrid Molenveld, and Ingmar van Meerkerk. pp. 69–83. New York: Routledge.

Goodman, Sara Wallace. 2022. *Citizenship in Hard Times: How Ordinary People Respond to Democratic Threat.* Cambridge: Cambridge University Press. https://doi.org/10.1017/9781009058292

Gouillart, Francis and Tina Hallett. 2015. "Co-Creation in Government." *Stanford Social Innovation Review* Spring 2015: 40–47. DOI: 10.48558/d85m-mc53

Grimm, Robert T., Jr. and Nathan Dietz. 2018. "Where Are America's Volunteers? A Look at America's Widespread Decline in Volunteering in Cities and States." *Research Brief: Do Good Institute, University of Maryland.* https://dogood.umd.edu/research-impact/publications/where-are-americas-volunteers

Griswold, Eliza. 2019. "The New Front Line of the Anti-Abortion Movement." *The New Yorker*, November 11. https://www.newyorker.com/magazine/2019/11/18/the-new-front-line-of-the-anti-abortion-movement

Gross, Matthias. 2009. "Collaborative Experiments: Jane Addams, Hull House and Experimental Social Work." *Social Science Information* 48 (1): 81–95. https://doi.org/10.1177/0539018408099638

Guthman, Julie. 2008. "Neoliberalism and the Making of Food Politics in California." *Geoforum* 39 (3): 1171–1183. DOI: 10.1016/j.geoforum.2006.09.002

Halpin, Darren R. 2006. "The Participatory and Democratic Potential and Practice of Interest Groups: Between Solidarity and Representation." *Public Administration* 84 (4): 919–940. https://doi.org/10.1111/j.1467-9299.2006.00618.x

Hanna, Alex and Tina M. Park. 2020. "Against Scale: Provocations and Resistances to Scale Thinking." *arXiv* preprint. 2010.08850

Harvey, David. 2005. *A Brief History of Neoliberalism*. New York: Oxford University Press.

Healey, Patsy. 2015a. "Citizen-Generated Local Development Initiative: Recent English Experience." *International Journal of Urban Sciences* 19 (2): 109–118. https://doi.org/10.1080/12265934.2014.989892

Healey, Patsy. 2015b. "Civil Society Enterprise and Local Development." *Planning Theory & Practice* 16 (1): 11–27. https://doi.org/10.1080/14649357.2014.995212

Hendriks, Carolyn M. 2009. "The Democratic Soup: Mixed Meanings of Political Representation in Governance Networks." *Governance* 22 (4): 689–715. https://doi.org/10.1111/j.1468-0491.2009.01459.x

Hendriks Carolyn M. and Richard Reid. 2023. "Citizen-Led Democratic Change: How Australia's Community Independents Movement Is Reshaping Representative Democracy." *Political Studies*, https://doi.org/10.1177/00323217231219

Hendriks Carolyn M. and Rebecca M. Colvin. 2024. "Spaces of Public Participation in Contemporary Governance." In *Australian Politics and Policy*, edited by Diana Perche, Nicholas Barry, Alan Fenna, Zareh Ghazarian, and Yvonne Haigh, pp. 1281–1315. Sydney: Sydney University Press. https://oercollective.caul.edu.au/aust-politics-policy/chapter/spaces-of-public-participation-in-contemporary-governance/

Hendriks, Carolyn M. and Albert W. Dzur. 2022. "Citizens' Governance Spaces: Democratic Action Through Disruptive Collective Problem-Solving." *Political Studies* 70 (3): 680–700. https://doi.org/10.1177/0032321720980902

Hendriks, Carolyn M., Selen A. Ercan, and Sonya Duus. 2019. "Listening in Polarised Controversies: A Study of Listening Practices in the Public Sphere." *Policy Sciences* 52 (1): 137–151. DOI: 10.1007/s11077-018-9343-3

Hendriks, Frank. 2019. "Democratic Innovation Beyond Deliberative Reflection: The Plebiscitary Rebound and the Advent of Action-Oriented Democracy." *Democratization* 26 (3): 444–464. https://doi.org/10.1080/13510347.2018.1547896

Heylen, Frederik, Evelien Willems, and Jan Beyers. 2020. "Do Professionals Take Over? Professionalisation and Membership Influence in Civil Society Organisations." *VOLUNTAS: International Journal of Voluntary and Nonprofit Organizations* 31: 1226–1238. https://doi.org/10.1007/s11266-020-00214-9

Hicks, Jarra and Nicola Ison. 2018. "An Exploration of the Boundaries of 'Community' in Community Renewable Energy Projects: Navigating Between Motivations and Context". *Energy Policy* 113: 523–534. https://doi.org/10.1016/j.enpol.2017.10.031

HoD. 2023. "Nourishing NYC's Asian Elders with Love and Food Every Week." *Heart of Dinner Website*. https://www.heartofdinner.org/our-story. Accessed December 12, 2023.

Holder, Robyn. 2018. *Just Interests: Victims, Citizens and the Potential for Justice*. Northampton, MA: Edward Elgar.

Hooper, John and Richard Warner. 2013. *Participation and Production: A Resource for Community Enterprise*. Nundah, Queensland: Nundah Community Enterprises Cooperative.

Howell, Angus. 2006. "Warrenbayne Boho Land Protection Group." In *Landcare in Victoria: How Landcare Helped People Government and Business Work Together in Victoria*, edited by Rob Youl, pp. 121–122. South Melbourne: R. Youl. http://www.silc.com.au/wp-content/uploads/2010/10/Landcare-in-Vctoria-R-Youl-cover-and-text.pdf

HREOC. 1997. Juvenile Justice. In *Bringing Them Home. Report of the National Inquiry into the Separation of Aboriginal and Torres Strait Islander Children from Their Families*, Chapter 24. Human Rights and Equal Opportunity Commission. Sydney, NSW: Australian Human Rights Commission. https://humanrights.gov.au/our-work/bringing-them-home-chapter-24

Igalla, Malika, Jurian Edelenbos, and Ingmar van Meerkerk. 2019. "Citizens in Action, What Do They Accomplish? A Systematic Literature Review of Citizen Initiatives, Their Main Characteristics, Outcomes, and Factors." *VOLUNTAS: International Journal of Voluntary and Nonprofit Organizations* 30 (5): 1176–1194. https://doi.org/10.1007/s11266-019-00129-0

Igalla, Malika, Jurian Edelenbos, and Ingmar van Meerkerk. 2020. "What Explains the Performance of Community-Based Initiatives? Testing the Impact of Leadership, Social Capital, Organizational Capacity, and Government Support." *Public Management Review* 22 (4): 602–632. https://doi.org/10.1080/14719037.2019.1604796

Igalla, Malika, Jurian Edelenbos, and Ingmar van Meerkerk. 2021. "Institutionalization or Interaction: Which Organizational Factors Help Community-Based Initiatives Acquire Government Support?" *Public Administration* 99 (4): 803–831. https://doi.org/10.1111/padm.12728

Independent Sector. 2023. *Trust in Civil Society: Headwinds and Opportunities for American Nonprofits and Foundations*. Washington, DC: Independent Sector. https://independentsector.org/resource/trust-in-civil-society/

Interlandi, Jeneen. 2023. "One Year Inside a Radical New Approach to America's Overdose Crisis." Opinion. *The New York Times*, February 22, 2023. https://www.nytimes.com/2023/02/22/opinion/drug-crisis-addiction-harm-reduction.html

Ivsins, Andrew, Vancouver Area Network of Drug Users, Cecilia Benoit, Karen Kobayashi, and Susan Boyd. 2019. "From Risky Places to Safe Spaces: Re-assembling Spaces and Places in Vancouver's Downtown Eastside." *Health and Place* 59 (1) September 2019. https://doi.org/10.1016/j.healthplace.2019.102164

Iyengar, Shanto, Yphtach Lelkes, Matthew Levendusky, Neil Malhotra, and Sean J. Westwood. 2019. "The Origins and Consequences of Affective Polarization in the United States." *Annual Review of Political Science* 22 (1): 129–146. https://doi.org/10.1146/annurev-polisci-051117-073034

Izlar, Joel. 2019. "Radical Social Welfare and Anti-Authoritarian Mutual Aid." *Critical and Radical Social Work* 7 (3): 349–366. https://doi.org/10.1332/204986019X15687131179624

Jacobi, Nadia von, Alex Nicholls, and Enrica Chiappero-Martinetti. 2017. "Theorizing Social Innovation to Address Marginalization." *Journal of Social Entrepreneurship* 8 (3): 265–270. https://doi.org/10.1080/19420676.2017.1380340

Jessop, Bob. 2020. *Putting Civil Society in Its Place: Governance, Metagovernance and Subjectivity*. Bristol: Policy Press.

Johnston, Hank. 2014. *What is a Social Movement?* Cambridge: Polity Press.

Johnstone, Gerry and Daniel Van Ness. 2006. *Handbook of Restorative Justice*. London: Routledge.

Judson, Emily, et al. 2020. "The Centre Cannot (Always) Hold: Examining Pathways Towards Energy System De-centralisation". *Renewable and Sustainable Energy Reviews*, 118, https://doi.org/10.1016/j.rser.2019.109499

Jupp, Eleanor. 2008. "The Feeling of Participation: Everyday Spaces and Urban Change." *Geoforum* 39 (1): 331–343. https://doi.org/10.1016/j.geoforum.2007.07.007

Jurriëns, Edwin. 2009. "Frying the Wires, Freeing the Waves." *Inside Indonesia*, February 15. https://www.insideindonesia.org/frying-the-wires-freeing-the-waves

Just Reinvest NSW. 2019. *Justice Reinvestment: Getting Started in Your Community. A Toolkit*. https://www.indigenousjustice.gov.au/wp-content/uploads/mp/files/resources/files/jr-toolkit-v13-250119-1.pdf

Keane, John. 2009. *The Life and Death of Democracy*. New York: W.W. Norton.

Kelly, Kate and Marisa Schwartz Taylor. 2023. "A Year of Upheaval on Abortion's Front Lines." *The New York Times*, July 20.

Kenny, Sue, Brian McGrath, and Rhonda Phillips (eds). 2017. *The Routledge Handbook of Community Development: Perspectives from Around the Globe*. New York: Routledge.

Kenny, Sue, Marilyn Taylor, Jenny Onyx, and Marjorie Mayo. 2016. *Challenging the Third Sector: Global Prospects for Active Citizenship*. Bristol: Policy Press.

King, Christine and Margaret Cruickshank. 2012. "Building Capacity to Engage: Community Engagement or Government Engagement?" *Community Development Journal* 47 (1): 5–28. https://doi.org/10.1093/cdj/bsq018

Kinna, Ruth. 1995. "Kropotkin's Theory of Mutual Aid in Historical Context." *International Review of Social History* 40 (2): 259–283. https://www.jstor.org/stable/44583751

Klein, Juan-Luis. 2013. "Introduction: Social Innovation at the Crossroads between Science, Economy and Society." In *The International Handbook on Social Innovation: Collective Action, Social Learning and Transdisciplinary Research*, edited by Frank Moulaert, Diana MacCallum, Abid Mehmood, and Abdelillah Hamdouch, pp. 9–12. Cheltenham: Edward Elgar.

Koss, Mary P. 2014. "The RESTORE Program of Restorative Justice for Sex Crimes: Vision, Process, and Outcomes." *Journal of Interpersonal Violence* 29 (9): 1623–1660. https://doi.org/10.1177/0886260513511537

Kretzmann, John P. and John L. McKnight. 1993. *Building Communities from the Inside Out: A Path Toward Finding and Mobilizing a Community's Assets*. Chicago, IL: ACTA Publications.

Kurimoto, Akira and Yurie Kumakura. 2016. "Emergence and Evolution of Co-operatives for Elderly Care in Japan." *International Review of Sociology* 26 (1): 48–68. https://doi.org/10.1080/03906701.2016.1148341

Landcare Australia. 2019. *Thirty Years of Caring for Our Country. The Landcare Story*. Landcare Australia. Accessed February 20, 2024. https://landcareaustralia.org.au/project/thirty-years-of-caring-for-our-country-the-landcare-story/

Lang, Cady. 2020. "BIPOC Entrepreneurs Have Been Hit Hard by the Pandemic—But as They Work to Save Their Businesses, They're Also Giving Back." *Time Magazine*, September 10. https://time.com/5887425/entrepreneurs-of-color-coronavirus/

Larner, Justin and Chris Mason. 2014. "Beyond Box-Ticking: A Study of Stakeholder Involvement in Social Enterprise Governance." *Corporate Governance* 14 (2): 181–196. https://doi.org/10.1108/CG-06-2011-0050

Larner, Wendy J. and David Craig. 2005. "After Neoliberalism? Community Activism and Local Partnerships in Aotearoa New Zealand." *Antipode* 37 (3): 402–424. https://doi.org/10.1111/j.0066-4812.2005.00504.x

Larsson, Ola Segnestam and Taco Brandsen. 2016. "The Implicit Normative Assumptions of Social Innovation Research: Embracing the Dark Side." In *Social Innovations in the Urban*

*Context*, edited by Taco Brandsen, Sandro Cattacin, Adalbert Evers, and Annette Zimmer. pp. 293–302. Heidelberg: Springer Cham.
Laville, Jean-Louis, Dennis Young, and Philippe Eynaud (eds). 2015. *Civil Society, the Third Sector and Social Enterprise: Governance and Democracy*. London: Routledge.
Leadbeater, Anne. 2013. "Community Leadership in Disaster Recovery: A Case Study." *Australian Journal of Emergency Management* 28 (3): 41–47. https://www5.austlii.edu.au/au/journals/AUJlEmMgmt/2013/44.html
Lee, Caroline W., Michael McQuarrie, and Edward T. Walker (eds). 2015. *Democratizing Inequalities: Dilemmas of the New Public Participation*. New York: New York University Press.
Levine, Peter. 2022. *What Should We Do? A Theory of Civic Life*. New York: Oxford University Press.
Lipsky, Michael. 1980. *Street-Level Bureaucracy: Dilemmas of the Individual in Public Services*. New York: Russell Sage Foundation.
Littman, Danielle M., Madi Boyett, Kimberly Bender, Annie Zean Dunbar, Marisa Santarella, Trish Becker-Hafnor, et al. 2022. "Values and Beliefs Underlying Mutual Aid: An Exploration of Collective Care During the COVID-19 Pandemic." *Journal of the Society for Social Work and Research* 13 (1): 89–115. https://www.journals.uchicago.edu/doi/pdf/10.1086/716884
Liu, Helen K. 2021. "Crowdsourcing: Citizens as Coproducers of Public Services." *Policy & Internet* 13 (2): 315–331. https://doi.org/10.1002/poi3.249
Loader, Ian, and Richard Sparks. 2019. "Democratic Experimentalism and the Futures of Crime Control: Resources of Hope for Demotic Times." In *Justice Alternatives*, edited by Pat Carlen and Leandro Ayres Franca, pp. 105–120. London: Routledge
Lockie, Stewart. 2004. "Collective Agency, Non-Human Causality and Environmental Social Movements: A Case Study of the Australian 'Landcare Movement'." *Journal of Sociology* 40 (1): 41–57. https://doi.org/10.1177/1440783304040452
Loeffler, Elke. 2018. "Providing Public Safety and Public Order Through Co-Production." In *Co-Production and Co-Creation: Engaging Citizens in Public Services*, edited by Taco Brandsen, Bram Verschuere, and Trui Steen, pp. 211–222. New York: Routledge.
Lukes, Steven. 2005. *Power: A Radical View*. 2nd edition. New York: Palgrave.
Lupick, Travis. 2017. *Fighting for Space: How a Group of Drug Users Transformed One City's Struggle with Addiction*. Vancouver: Arsenal Pulp Press.
Macy, Beth. 2022. *Raising Lazarus: Hope, Justice, and the Future of America's Opioid Crisis*. New York: Little Brown.
Madsen, Karin Sten. 2004. "Mediation as a Way of Empowering Women Exposed to Sexual Coercion." *NORA: Nordic Journal of Feminist and Gender Research* 12 (1): 58–61. https://doi.org/10.1080/08038740410005776
Manning, Rachael and Phoebe Brook-Rowland. 2023. "'The Bloody WhatsApp Thing': A Qualitative Investigation of Experiences of Social Messaging in a Volunteering Setting." *International Journal of Human–Computer Interaction*, 1–14. https://doi.org/10.1080/10447318.2023.2247557
Mansbridge, Jane and Audrey Latura. 2016. "The Polarization Crisis in the United States and the Future of Listening." In *Strong Democracy in Crisis: Promise or Peril?*, edited by Trevor Norris, pp. 29–54. Lanham, MD: Lexington Books.
Maranguka Community Hub. 2024a. "Bourke Tribal Council." Accessed February 20, 2024. https://maranguka.org.au/about-us/bourke-tribal-council
Maranguka Community Hub. 2024b. "Partnerships." Accessed February 20, 2024. https://maranguka.org.au/partnerships/

Marien, Sofie, Marc Hooghe, and Ellen Quintelier. 2010. "Inequalities in Non-Institutionalised Forms of Political Participation: A Multi-Level Analysis of 25 Countries." *Political Studies* 58 (1): 187–213. https://doi.org/10.1111/j.1467-9248.2009.00801.x

Martin, Victoria Y. 2017. "Citizen Science as a Means for Increasing Public Engagement in Science: Presumption or Possibility." *Science Communication* 39 (2): 142–168. DOI: 10.1177/1075547017696165

Martinelli, Flavia. 2013. "Learning from Case Studies of Social Innovation in the Field of Social Services: Creatively Balancing Top-down Universalism with Bottom-up Democracy." In *The International Handbook. On Social Innovation Collective Action, Social Learning and Transdisciplinary Research*, edited by Frank Moulaert, Diana MacCallum, Abid Mehmood, and Abdelillah Hamdouch, pp. 346–359. Cheltenham: Edward Elgar.

Matarrita-Cascante, David and Mark A. Brennan. 2012. "Conceptualizing Community Development in the Twenty-First Century." *Community Development* 43 (3): 293–305. https://doi.org/10.1080/15575330.2011.593267

Mathie, Alison and John Gaventa (eds). 2015. *Citizen-Led Innovation for a New Economy*. Winnipeg: Fernwood Publishing.

McKnight, John L. 2022. *Associational Life: Democracy's Power Source*. Dayton, Ohio: Kettering Foundation Press.

McLennan, Blythe J. 2020. "Conditions for Effective Coproduction in Community-Led Disaster Risk Management." *VOLUNTAS: International Journal of Voluntary and Nonprofit Organizations* 31 (2): 316–332. https://doi.org/10.1007/s11266-018-9957-2

McMullin, Caitlin. 2023. "'We're Not There to Lead': Professional Roles and Responsibilities in 'Citizen-led' Co-production." *Public Administration Review*. Early view. https://doi.org/10.1111/puar.13770

McQuarrie, Michael, 2013. "No Contest: Participatory Technologies and the Transformation of Urban Authority." *Public Culture* 25 (1): 143–175. DOI: 10.1215/08992363-1890495

Meijer, Albert and Marcel Thaens. 2021. "The Dark Side of Public Innovation." *Public Performance & Management Review* 44 (1): 136–154. https://doi.org/10.1080/15309576.2020.1782954

Milliken, Robert, 2018. "Revival on the Darling." *Inside Story*, 18 September 2018. https://insidestory.org.au/we-are-on-the-road-to-recovery.

Mitlin, Diana. 2008. "With and Beyond the State—Co-Production as a Route to Political Influence, Power and Transformation for Grassroots Organizations." *Environment and Urbanization* 20 (2): 339–360. https://doi.org/10.1177/0956247808096117

Mizrahi, Terry and Jessica Greenawalt. 2017. "Gender Differences and Intersectionality in Community Organizing." *Journal of Community Practice* 25 (3–4): 1–32. DOI: 10.1080/10705422.2017.1356784

Moody-Adams, Michele. 2022. *Making Space for Justice: Social Movements, Collective Imagination, and Political Hope*. New York: Columbia University Press.

Moulaert, Frank, Diana MacCallum, and Jean Hillier. 2013. "Social Innovation: Intuition, Precept, Concept, Theory and Practice." In *The International Handbook on Social Innovation: Collective Action, Social Learning and Transdisciplinary Research*, edited by Frank Moulaert, Diana MacCallum, Abid Mehmood, and Abdelillah Hamdouch, pp. 13–24. Cheltenham: Edward Elgar.

Munday, Bruce. 2017. *Those Wild Rabbits: How They Shaped Australia*. South Australia: Wakefield Press.

Murtagh, Brendan and Niamh Goggin. 2015. "Finance, Social Economics and Community Development." *Community Development Journal* 50 (3): 494–509. https://www.jstor.org/stable/26165004

Nabatchi, Tina, John Gastil, G. Michael Weiksner, and Matt Leighninger (eds). 2012. *Democracy in Motion: Evaluating the Practice and Impact of Deliberative Civic Engagement*. New York: Oxford University Press.
NCEC. 2019. "Community Living Association" *NCEC Website*. https://www.communityliving.org.au/nundah-community-enterprises-co-operative-peoples-organization/
NCEC. 2024. "Nundah Community Enterprises Co-operative" *NCEC Website*. https://ncec.com.au
Newman, Janet and Evelien Tonkens. 2011. "Active Citizenship: Responsibility, Choice and Participation." In *Participation, Responsibility and Choice: Summoning the Active Citizen in Western European Welfare States*, edited by Janet Newman and Evelien Tonkens, pp. 179–200. Amsterdam: Amsterdam University Press. https://doi.org/10.1515/9789048513437-011
Noveck, Beth S. 2021. *Solving Public Problems: How to Fix Our Government and Change Our World*. New Haven: Yale University Press.
Nowland-Foreman, Garth. 2018. "Did Public Policy Kill Community Development?" In *The Routledge Handbook of Community Development: Perspectives from Around the Globe*, edited by Sue Kenny, Brian McGrath, and Rhonda Phillips, pp. 54–69. New York: Routledge.
OCP (Our Community Project). 2021. *Annual Report (FY 2020-2021)* https://www.ourcommunityproject.org.au/s/WEB_221231_v10_AnnualReport_FY20-21_OurCommunityProject_A4.pdf
OECD. 2020. *Innovative Citizen Participation and New Democratic Institutions: Catching the Deliberative Wave*. Paris: OECD Publishing. https://doi.org/10.1787/339306da-en
OECD. 2022. *Building Trust to Reinforce Democracy: Main Findings from the 2021 OECD Survey on Drivers of Trust in Public Institutions*. Paris: OECD Publishing. https://doi.org/10.1787/b407f99c-en
OECD/European Union. 2017. *Boosting Social Enterprise Development: Good Practice Compendium*. Paris: OECD Publishing.
Onyx, Jennifer, 2018. "Governance Issues: An Australian Example." In *The Routledge Handbook of Community Development: Perspectives from Around the Globe*, edited by Sue Kenny, Brian McGrath, and Rhonda Phillips, pp. 40–53. New York: Routledge.
OSA. 2016. *Orange Sky Laundry Annual Report 2015–2016*. Australia: Orange Sky Laundry. https://orangesky.org.au/wp-content/uploads/2018/06/osl_161128_report_annual-2016_a4_cmyk_press_pnl_final.pdf
OSA. 2019. *Orange Sky Australia Annual Report 2018/2019*. Australia: Orange Sky Australia. https://orangesky.org.au/wp-content/uploads/2018/05/annual-report-2019.pdf
OSA. 2021. *Orange Sky Australia Annual Report 2020/2021*. Australia: Orange Sky Australia. https://orangesky.org.au/wp-content/uploads/2021/12/2021_OSA_Annual_Report_FINAL_Financial_Report.pdf
OSA. 2022. *Orange Sky Aotearoa Annual Report 2020/2021*. New Zealand: Orange Sky Aotearoa. https://orangesky.org.nz/wp-content/uploads/2022/02/2021_OSNZ_Annual_Report_FINAL_Financial_Report.pdf
OSA. 2023. *Orange Sky Australia Impact Report 2022/2023*. Australia: Orange Sky Australia. https://orangesky.org.au/wp-content/uploads/2024/02/AU-OrangeSky-ImpactReport-22-23-with-financials.pdf
Ostrander, Susan A. 2013. "Agency and Initiative by Community Associations in Relations of Shared Governance: Between Civil Society and Local State." *Community Development Journal* 48 (4): 511–524. https://doi.org/10.1093/cdj/bss051

Ostrom, Elinor. 1990. *Governing the Commons: The Evolution of Institutions for Collective Action.* Cambridge: Cambridge University Press.

Ostrom, Elinor, 1996. "Crossing the Great Divide: Coproduction, Synergy, and Development." *World Development* 24 (6): 1073–1087. https://doi.org/10.1016/0305-750X(96)00023-X

Ostrom, Elinor. 2010. "Beyond Markets and States: Polycentric Governance of Complex Economic Systems." *American Economic Review* 100 (3): 641–672. DOI: 10.1257/aer.100.3.641

Papadopoulos, Yannis. 2016. "Interactive Governance: Authorization, Representation and Accountability." In *Critical Reflections on Interactive Governance: Self-organization and Participation in Public Governance,* edited by Jurian Edelenbos and Ingmar van Meerkerk, pp. 146–166. Cheltenham: Edward Elgar Publishing.

Parés, Marc, Sonia M. Ospina, and Joan Subirats. 2017. *Social Innovation and Democratic Leadership: Communities and Social Change from Below.* Cheltenham: Edward Elgar Publishing.

Parsell, Cameron and Beth Watts. 2017. "Charity and Justice: A Reflection on New Forms of Homelessness Provision in Australia." *European Journal of Homelessness* 11 (2): 65–76. http://www.feantsaresearch.org/download/think-piece-12032277176126500690.pdf

Parsell, Cameron, Andrew Clarke, and Francisco Perales. 2021. "Poverty by Design: The Role of Charity and the Cultivated Ethical Citizen." *Social Policy and Society* 21 (4): 525–541. DOI: 10.1017/S1474746421000312

Parsons, John R. 2022. "The Power to be Ethical: Controlling Moral Assemblages in Border Militias." *Journal of Contemporary Ethnography* 51 (1): 3–28. DOI: 10.1177/08912416211021897

Patchett, Lucas. 2020. "The Launch of Team Delta." *Orange Sky Australia Website.* https://orangesky.org.au/the-launch-of-team-delta/. Accessed February 1, 2024.

Peck, Jamie and Adam Tickell. 2002. "Neoliberalizing Space." In *Spaces of Neoliberalism: Urban Restructuring in North America and Western Europe,* edited by Neil Brenner and Nik Theodore, pp. 380–404. Malden, MA: Oxford's Blackwell Press.

Pellicer-Sifres, Victoria, Sergio Belda-Miquel, Iván Cuesta-Fernández, and Alejandra Boni. 2018. "Learning, Transformative Action, and Grassroots Innovation: Insights from the Spanish Energy Cooperative Som Energia." *Energy Research & Social Science* 42: 100–111. https://doi.org/10.1016/j.erss.2018.03.001

Pestoff, Victor. 2018. *Co-Production and Public Service Management: Citizenship, Governance and Public Services Management.* New York: Routledge.

Pestoff, Victor Alexis and Lars Hulgård. 2016. "Participatory Governance in Social Enterprise." *VOLUNTAS: International Journal of Voluntary and Nonprofit Organizations* 27 (4): 1742–1759. DOI: 10.1007/s11266-015-9662-3

Pew Research Center. 2021. "Many in U.S., Western Europe Say Their Political System Needs Major Reform." Washington DC: Pew Research Center. https://www.pewresearch.org/global/2021/03/31/many-in-us-western-europe-say-their-political-system-needs-major-reform/

Polletta, Francesca. 1999. "'Free Spaces' in Collective Action." *Theory and Society* 28 (1): 1–38. https://www.jstor.org/stable/3108504

Polletta, Francesca and Kelsy Kretschmer. 2013. "Free Spaces." In *The Wiley-Blackwell Encyclopedia of Social and Political Movements* edited by David A. Snow, Donatella della Porta, Bert Klandermans, and Doug McAdam, pp. 477–480. Malden MA: Wiley,. https://doi.org/10.1002/9780470674871.wbespm094

PoV (Parliament of Victoria). 2020. *Inquiry into Tackling Climate Change in Victorian Communities. Final Report.* Legislative Assembly Environment and Planning Committee, Parliament of Victoria, Melbourne, Australia. http://new.parliament.vic.gov.au/4a4bbb/

contentassets/1f7c789136dd414fb4cf094bacf0d087/laepc-59-01-inquiry-into-tackling-climate-change-in-vic-communities.pdf

Purbo, Onno W. 2015. *The Struggle in Indonesia Computer Network Beginning in the 90's*. Unpublished paper available at https://lms.onnocenter.or.id/pustaka/docs/The-struggle-in-Indonesia-Computer-Network-beginning-in-90/OWP-20150127-the-struggle-in-indonesia-computer-network-in-the-90.pdf

Putnam, Robert D. 2000. *Bowling Alone: The Collapse and Revival of American Community*. New York: Simon and Schuster.

Reiljan, Andres. 2020. "'Fear and Loathing Across Party Lines' (Also) in Europe: Affective Polarisation in European Party Systems." *European Journal of Political Research* 59 (2): 376–396. https://doi.org/10.1111/1475-6765.12351

Rendall, Jack, Maeve Curtin, Michael J. Roy, and Simon Teasdale. 2022. "Relationships Between Community-Led Mutual Aid Groups and the State During the COVID-19 Pandemic: Complementary, Supplementary, or Adversarial?" *Public Management Review* 26 (2): 313–333. https://doi.org/10.1080/14719037.2022.2084769

Renn, Ortwin, Thomas Webler, and Peter Wiedemann. 1995. "A Need for Discourse on Citizen Participation: Objectives and Structure of the Book." In *Fairness and Competence in Citizen Participation: Evaluating Models for Environmental Discourse*, edited by Ortwin Renn, Thomas Webler and Peter Wiedemann, pp. 1–15. Dordrecht: Springer Dordrecht.

Riboldi, Mark and Sarah Hopkins. 2019. "Community-Led Justice Reinvestment: Rethinking Access to Justice." *Precedent (Sydney, NSW)* 154 (2019): 48–51.

Rittel, Horst W. J. and Melvin M. Webber. 1973. "Dilemmas in a General Theory of Planning." *Policy Sciences* 4 (2): 155–169. https://doi.org/10.1007/BF01405730

Riutort Isern, Sebastià. 2015. "The Som Energia Cooperative in Spain." *Planning Theory & Practice* 16 (4): 569–572. DOI: 10.1080/14649357.2015.1083153

Rivera, Sam. 2022. "The Impact of Overdose Prevention Centers." Presentation at the New York Society for Ethical Culture. https://ethical.nyc/rivera-platform/

RMCG. 2019. *Goulburn Murray Irrigation District (GMID) Strategic Plan: Regional Insights*. https://www.rmcg.com.au/app/uploads/2019/07/InsightsPaper_Finalv2_r.pdf

Robins, Lisa. 2018. "More Than 30 Years of 'Landcare' in Australia: Five Phases of Development from 'Childhood' to 'Mid-life' (Crisis or Renewal?)." *Australasian Journal of Environmental Management* 25 (4): 385–397. https://researchers.anu.edu.au/publications/136831

Rosanvallon, Pierre. 2008. *Counter-Democracy: Politics in an Age of Distrust*. Cambridge: Cambridge University Press.

Rosen, Jovanna and Gary Painter. 2019. "From Citizen Control to Co-Production: Moving Beyond a Linear Conception of Citizen Participation." *Journal of the American Planning Association* 85 (3): 335–347. DOI: 10.1080/01944363.2019.1618727

Rosenblatt, Fernanda F. 2015. *The Role of Community in Restorative Justice*. Abingdon: Routledge.

Salathiel, Lauren. 2014. "Community Power." *Ecoportal* August 1, 2014. https://ecoportal.net.au/community-power/

Savy Amira. 2019. Facebook Post. [in Indonesian] Available at https://www.facebook.com/savyamira.sahabatperempuan/posts/2875880952421908. Accessed April 25, 2019.

Savy Amira. 2024. "Profile." *Savy Amira Women's Crisis Centre Website*, [in Indonesian]. http://www.savyamirawcc.com/tentang-kami/profil/. Accessed February 8, 2024.

Schlozman, Kay Lehman, Sidney Verba, and Henry E. Brady. 2012. *The Unheavenly Chorus: Unequal Political Voice and the Broken Promise of American Democracy*. Princeton: Princeton University Press.

# References

Schön, Donald A. and Martin Rein. 1994. *Frame Reflection: Toward the Resolution of Intractable Policy Controversies*. New York: Basic Books.

Scott, James C. 1998. *Seeing Like a State: How Certain Schemes to Improve the Human Condition Have Failed*. New Haven: Yale University Press.

SCRA (Strathewen Community Renewal Association). no date. *Big Stories, Small Towns*. http://bigstories.com.au/story/recovery

Shearing, Clifford and Jennifer Wood. 2003. "Nodal Governance, Democracy, and the New 'Denizens.'" *Journal of Law and Society* 30 (3): 400–419. https://doi.org/10.1111/1467-6478.00263

Simon, Katy, Gradon Diprose, and Amanda C. Thomas. 2020. "Community-Led Initiatives for Climate Adaptation and Mitigation." *Kōtuitui: New Zealand Journal of Social Sciences Online* 15 (1): 93–105. https://doi.org/10.1080/1177083X.2019.1652659

Sirianni, Carmen. 2014. "Bringing the State Back in Through Collaborative Governance: Emergent Mission and Practice at the US Environmental Protection Agency." In *Varieties of Civic Innovation: Deliberative, Collaborative, Network, and Narrative Approaches*, edited by Jennifer Girouard and Carmen Sirianni, pp. 203–238. Nashville: Vanderbilt University Press.

Sirianni, Carmen and Lewis Friedland. 2001. *Civic Innovation in America: Community Empowerment, Public Policy, and the Movement for Civic Renewal*. Oakland: University of California Press.

Skocpol, Theda. 2003. *Diminished Democracy: From Membership to Management in American Civic Life*. Norman: University of Oklahoma Press.

Smith, Adrian and Adrian Ely. 2015. "Green Transformations from Below? The Politics of Grassroots Innovation." In *The Politics of Green Transformations*, edited by Ian Scoones, Melissa Leach, and Peter Newell, pp. 102–118. London: Routledge.

Smith, Adrian and Andrew Stirling. 2018. "Innovation, Sustainability and Democracy: An Analysis of Grassroots Contributions." *Journal of Self-Governance and Management Economics* 6 (1): 64–97. DOI: 10.22381/JSME6120183

Smith, Anna V. 2020. "Oregon Community Program Shows What Defunding the Police Could Look Like." *Christian Century*, July 15. https://www.christiancentury.org/article/news/oregon-community-program-shows-what-defunding-police-could-look

Smith, Belinda. 2022. "How Yackandandah Reached 60 Per Cent Clean Energy Use, and Its Plans To Be Totally Renewable." *Australian Broadcast Corporation ABC News*, September 27. https://www.abc.net.au/news/science/2022-09-27/yackandandah-totally-renewable-energy-electricity-solar-battery/101473306

Soares da Silva, Diogo, Lummina G. Horlings, and Elisabete Figueiredo. 2018. "Citizen Initiatives in the Post-Welfare State." *Social Sciences* 7 (12): 1–21, article no. 252. https://doi.org/10.3390/socsci7120252

Social Enterprise Australia. 2023. Social Enterprise Australia 2023-24 Pre-Budget submission. https://static1.squarespace.com/static/63f3d7bbfd0e4c4dba3d9f6a/t/641c6da7b5d97c1b1d6502f2/1679584683830/Social-Enterprise-Australia-2023-24-Pre-Budget-submission.pdf

Solar Victoria. 2024. "Distributors – What Are They and Why Are They Important?" Webpage of the State Government of Victoria Solar Homes Program. https://www.solar.vic.gov.au/dsnsps-what-are-they-and-why-are-they-important

Sołtan, Karol Edward. 2014. "The Emerging Field of a New Civics." In *Civic Studies: Approaches to the Emerging Field*, edited by Peter Levine and Karol Edward Soltan, pp. 9–19. Washington DC: Bringing Theory to Practice.

Som Energia. 2016. "Synthesis of the Workshop of the School of September 2016 'Begin Process of Strategic and Organizational Reflection,'" [in Spanish]. Document available at https://docs.google.com/document/d/1aBKyh2Z16mWeIe7un804LYqomLQ6rwshQ2D_CPmGgj4/edit# Accessed March 8, 2018.

Som Energia. 2017. *Strategic Framework of Som Energia 2017-2020.* [in Spanish] Document available at https://docs.google.com/document/d/1DMbEYEcowZgmqunZC3i-ZPsOugaG2MV_gVtKy1Mz_3k/edit. Accessed March 8, 2018.

Spade, Dean. 2020a. "Solidarity Not Charity: Mutual Aid for Mobilization and Survival." *Social Text* 38 (1): 131–151. DOI: 10.1215/01642472-7971139

Spade, Dean, 2020b. *Mutual Aid: Building Solidarity During This Crisis (and the Next).* London: Verso Books.

Stall, Susan and Randy Stoecker. 1998. "Community Organizing or Organizing Community: Gender and the Crafts of Empowerment." *Gender & Society* 12 (6): 729–756. DOI: 10.1177/089124398012006008

State Government of Victoria. 2020. "Legislative Assembly Environment and Planning Committee", Transcript of Wednesday, 26 February 2020. *Inquiry into Tackling Climate Change in Victorian Communities*, Melbourne, Victoria. https://www.parliament.vic.gov.au/4b0183/contentassets/624f0ae07f60448aa212ecbfbff80ee5/t052-australian-energy-market-operator.pdf

Stoecker, Randy and Benny Witkovsky. 2021. "From Inclusionary to Exclusionary Populism in the Transformation of US Community Development." In *Populism, Democracy and Community Development*, edited by Sue Kenny, Jim Ife, and Peter Westoby, pp.127–148. Bristol: Policy Press.

Stoker, Gerry, Mark Evans, and Max Halupka. 2018. "Trust and Democracy in Australia: Democratic Decline and Renewal." *Democracy 2025.* https://apo.org.au/sites/default/files/resource-files/2018-12/apo-nid208536.pdf

Suárez, David F. 2011. "Collaboration and Professionalization: The Contours of Public Sector Funding for Nonprofit Organizations." *Journal of Public Administration Research and Theory* 21 (2): 307–326. https://doi.org/10.1093/jpart/muq049

Sunstein, Cass R. 2018. *#Republic: Divided Democracy in the Age of Social Media.* Princeton: Princeton University Press.

Suyatno. 2007. "RT-rw Net and E-Democracy in Indonesia." *Jurnal Global dan Strategis* 1 (2): 108–119. https://journal.unair.ac.id/JGS%40rt-rw-net-and-e-democracy-in-indonesia-article-2191-media-23-category-.html

Sydney Policy Lab. 2021. *Case Study: The Maranguka Cross Sector Leadership Group. Aligning Policy and Resources Towards an Aboriginal Community-Led Agenda.* Sydney: The University of Sydney. https://www.sydney.edu.au/sydney-policy-lab/research-and-policy/maranguka-cross-sector-leadership-group.html

Taylor, Marilyn, 2011. *Public Policy in the Community*, second edition. Basingstoke: Palgrave Macmillan International Higher Education.

Taylor, Marilyn. 2018. "Communities in Governance in a Neoliberal Age." In *The Routledge Handbook of Community Development: Perspectives from Around the Globe*, edited by Sue Kenny, Brian McGrath, and Rhonda Phillips, pp. 12–25. New York: Routledge.

Terzon, Emilia, 2021. "Why Solar Feed-In Tariff Cuts Are Driving a Spike in Household Battery Uptake." *Australian Broadcast Corporation ABC News*, September 29. https://www.abc.net.au/news/2021-09-29/solar-feed-in-tariff-energy-australia-tesla-battery/100498592

TF. 2020. *Tender Funerals Australia and Tender Funerals Illawarra and Sydney IPART Submission.* Online Submission to the "Review of Competition, Costs and Pricing in the NSW Funeral Industry," by NSW Independent Pricing and Regulatory Tribunal (IPART). https://www.ipart.nsw.gov.au/sites/default/files/documents/online-submission-tender-funerals-j.-briscoe-hough-4-dec-2020-120000000.pdf

TF. 2022. *Tender Funerals Annual Report 2021–22.* https://tenderfunerals.com.au/reports/

TF. 2023a. "Homepage." *Tender Funerals Website*. https://tenderfunerals.com.au/. Accessed November 7, 2023

TF. 2023b. "Our Mission, Model, and Impact." *Tender Funerals Website*. https://tenderfunerals.com.au/our-model/

TF. 2023c. *Tender Funerals 2022–23 Annual Report*. https://tenderfunerals.com.au/reports/

Theocharis, Yannis and Jan W. van Deth. 2018. "The Continuous Expansion of Citizen Participation: A New Taxonomy." *European Political Science Review* 10 (1): 139–163. https://doi.org/10.1017/S1755773916000230

Thiery, Harriet, Joanne Cook, Jon Burchell, and Jennifer McNeill. 2022. *Communities Are Doing It For Themselves: Lessons from the Mutual Aid Experience*. Research Report from MoVE: Mobilising Volunteers Effectively. Sheffield, Hull, and Leeds: Universities of Sheffield, Hull, and Leeds. https://d3nag6e3dddgye.cloudfront.net/uploads/milestone_def_file/333/file/MoVE_Mutual_Aid_Report.pdf

Tiarks, Elizabeth. 2019. "Restorative Justice, Consistency and Proportionality: Examining the Trade-Off." *Criminal Justice Ethics* 38 (2): 103–122. https://doi.org/10.1080/0731129X.2019.1638597

Tiratelli, Luca and Simon Kaye. 2020. *Communities vs. Coronavirus. The Rise of Mutual Aid*. New Local. http://newlocal.org.uk/wp-content/uploads/2020/12/Communities-vs-Coronavirus_New-Local.pdf

Tocqueville, Alexis de. 2004. *Democracy in America*, edited by Olivier Zunz and translated by Arthur Goldhammer. New York: The Library of America.

Tolentino, Jia. 2020. "What Mutual Aid Can Do During a Pandemic." *The New Yorker*, May 11. https://www.newyorker.com/magazine/2020/05/18/what-mutual-aid-can-do-during-a-pandemic

TRY. 2017. "Submission to Federal Inquiry into Modernising Australia's Electricity Grid – Building a Yackandandah Community Mini Grid." Federal Parliament of Australia Standing Committee On The Environment And Energy. https://totallyrenewableyack.org.au/kookaburra/wp-content/uploads/2022/02/17-Building-a-Yackandandah-Community-Mini-Grid-TRY-Submission-Inquiry-into-modernising-Australias-electricity-grid.pdf

TRY. 2019. "Submission by Total Renewable Yackandandah to the Inquiry into Tackling Climate Change in Victorian Communities." Parliament of Victoria Legislative Assembly, Environment and Planning Committee. https://www.parliament.vic.gov.au/48eb3d/contentassets/2e7894aa28624abb8476e3df6645bb77/submission-documents/s138-totally-renewable-yackandandah.pdf

Turcu, Catalina and Martina Rotolo. 2022. "Disrupting from the Ground Up: Community-Led and Place-Based Food Governance in London During COVID-19." *Urban Governance* 2 (1): 178–187. https://doi.org/10.1016/j.ugj.2022.04.006

UNV. 2021. *2022 State of the World's Volunteerism Report. Building Equal and Inclusive Societies*. United Nations Volunteers Programme. Bonn. https://swvr2022.unv.org/wp-content/uploads/2022/04/UNV_SWVR_2022.pdf

Valgarðsson, Viktor Orri, Nick Clarke, Will Jennings, and Gerry Stoker. 2021. "The Good Politician and Political Trust: An Authenticity Gap in British Politics?" *Political Studies* 69 (4): 858–880. https://doi.org/10.1177/0032321720928

van Dam, R. I. 2016. *Bonding By Doing: The Dynamics of Self-Organizing Groups of Citizens Taking Charge of Their Living Environment*. Doctoral Dissertation. Wageningen: Wageningen University. https://research.wur.nl/en/publications/bonding-by-doing-the-dynamics-of-self-organizing-groups-of-citize

van der Steen, Martijn, Mark van Twist, and Philip Marcel Karré. 2011. "When Citizens Take Matters into Their Own Hands: How Privately Managed Communities Challenge Government." *Public Integrity* 13 (4): 319–332.

van Meerkerk, Ingmar, Jurian Edelenbos, and Astrid Molenveld. 2021. "Cross-Case Findings and Conclusions: CBI Motivations and Mechanisms Enhancing Governance Capacity." In *Civic Engagement, Community-Based Initiatives and Governance Capacity: An International Perspective* edited by Jurian Edelenbos, Astrid Molenveld, and Ingmar van Meerkerk, pp. 248–272. New York: Routledge.

Varagur, Krithika. 2020. "In Place of Police: The Oregon Experiment." *The New York Review*, September 18. https://www.nybooks.com/online/2020/09/18/who-comes-when-it-shouldnt-be-police-the-oregon-experiment/

Verhoeven, Imrat and Evelien Tonkens. 2013. "Talking Active Citizenship: Framing Welfare State Reform in England and the Netherlands." *Social Policy and Society* 12 (3): 415–427. DOI: 10.1017/S1474746413000158

Viña, Stephen R., Blas Nuñez-Neto, and Alyssa Bartlett Weir. 2006. *Civilian Patrols Along the Border: Legal and Policy Issues*. Washington DC: Congressional Research Service, The Library of Congress. https://sgp.fas.org/crs/homesec/RL33353.pdf

Visscher, Kors, Menno Hurenkamp, and Evelien Tonkens. 2023. "The Democratic Potential of Community-Based Initiatives." *Politics of the Low Countries* 5 (1): 36–57. https://orbilu.uni.lu/bitstream/10993/57597/1/PLC_2023_1_total_v3.pdf

Visser, Vivian, Willem de Koster, and Jeroen van der Waal. 2023. "Understanding Less-Educated Citizens' (Non-)Participation in Citizens' Initiatives: Feelings of Entitlement and a Taste for Politics." *Current Sociology* 71 (5): 924–942. https://doi.org/10.1177/00113921211024700

Voorberg, William, V. J. J. M. Bekkers, and Lars G. Tummers. 2015. "A Systematic Review of Co-Creation and Co-Production: Embarking on the Social Innovation Journey." *Public Management Review* 17 (9): 1333–1357. https://doi.org/10.1080/14719037.2014.930505

Wagenaar, Hendrik. 2007. "Governance, Complexity, and Democratic Participation: How Citizens and Public Officials Harness the Complexities of Neighborhood Decline." *The American Review of Public Administration* 37 (1): 17–50. https://doi.org/10.1177/0275074006296208

Wagenaar, Hendrik. 2016. "Democratic Transfer: Everyday Neoliberalism, Hegemony and the Prospects for Democratic Renewal." In *Critical Reflections on Interactive Governance: Self-organization and Participation in Public Governance*. edited by Jurian Edelenbos and Ingmar van Meerkerk, pp. 93–119. Cheltenham: Edward Elgar Publishing.

Wagenaar, Hendrik. 2019. "Making Sense of Civic Enterprise: Social Innovation, Participatory Democracy and the Administrative State." *Partecipazione e Conflitto* 12 (2): 297–324. DOI: 10.1285/i20356609v12i2p297

Wagenaar, Hendrik, and Patsy Healey. 2015. "The Transformative Potential of Civic Enterprise." *Planning Theory & Practice* 16 (4): 557–561. DOI: 10.1080/14649357.2015.1083153

Wagenaar, Hendrik and Jurgen van der Heijden. 2015. "The Promise of Democracy? Civic Enterprise, Localism and the Transformation of Democratic Capitalism." In *Reconsidering Localism*, edited by Simin Davoudi and Ali Madanipour, pp. 126–146. Milton Park, Abingdon: Routledge.

Wagstaff, Jeremy. 2007. "Digital Deliverance: Asia's Technology Conundrum." Wall Street Journal, July 27. https://www.wsj.com/articles/SB118539630908777946

Wakefield, Sarah, Julie Fleming, Carla Klassen, and Ana Skinner. 2013. "Sweet Charity, Revisited: Organizational Responses to Food Insecurity in Hamilton and Toronto, Canada." *Critical Social Policy* 33 (3): 427–450. https://doi.org/10.1177/0261018312458487

Walker, Brian H., Nick Abel, John M. Anderies, and Paul Ryan. 2009. "Resilience, Adaptability, and Transformability in the Goulburn-Broken Catchment, Australia." *Ecology and Society* 14 (1): Article 12. http://www.ecologyandsociety.org/vol14/iss1/art12

Wallworth, Lynette. 2013. *Tender: A Documentary.* http://www.tenderdocumentary.com.au Accessed November 7, 2023. Adelaide: Adelaide Film Festival.
Warner, Richard. 2016. "Nourishing the Grass Roots: Entrepreneurship Through the Peer-to-Peer Model." *Probono Australia.* Accessed April 23, 2019. https://probonoaustralia.com.au/news/2016/11/nourishing-grass-roots-entrepreneurship-peer-peer-mode/
Warren, Mark E. 2001. *Democracy and Association.* Princeton: Princeton University Press.
Warren, Mark E. 2009. "Governance-Driven Democratization." *Critical Policy Studies* 3 (1): 3–13. https://doi.org/10.1080/19460170903158040
Warren, Mark E. 2011. "Civil Society and Democracy." In *The Oxford Handbook of Civil Society,* edited by Michael Edwards, pp. 377–390. New York: Oxford University Press.
Weir, Margaret. 2010. "Collaborative Government and Civic Empowerment: A Discussion of Investing in Democracy: Engaging Citizens in Collaborative Governance." *Perspectives on Politics* 8 (2): 595–598. https://doi.org/10.1017/S1537592710000411
Whiteley, Paul, Harold D. Clarke, David Sanders, and Marianne Stewart. 2016. "Why Do Voters Lose Trust in Governments? Public Perceptions of Government Honesty and Trustworthiness in Britain 2000–2013." *British Journal of Politics & International Relations* 18 (1): 234–254. DOI: 10.1111/1467-856X.12073
Wilson, Jason. 2020. "Armed Civilian Roadblocks in Oregon Town Fuel Fears Over Vigilantism." *The Guardian,* September 16. https://www.theguardian.com/us-news/2020/sep/16/oregon-fires-armed-civilian-roadblocks-police
Woolvin, Mike and Helen Harper. 2015. "Volunteering 'Below the Radar'? Informal Volunteering in Deprived Urban Scotland: Research Summary." *Volunteer Scotland* https://www.volunteerscotland.net/wp-content/uploads/2022/11/Informal-Volunteering-in-Deprived-Urban-Scotland.pdf
World Bank. 2016. *Economic and Social Rationales for Government Support of the Social Enterprise Sector. The Case for Public Stewardship.* Washington, DC: World Bank Group. https://www.innovationpolicyplatform.org/www.innovationpolicyplatform.org/system/files/SE%20Policy%20Note_Jun20/index.pdf
World Bank. 2018. *Engaging Citizens for Better Development.* Independent Evaluation Group, Washington, DC: World Bank.
Yates, Luke. 2015. "Rethinking Prefiguration: Alternatives, Micropolitics and Goals in Social Movements." *Social Movement Studies* 14 (1): 1–21. https://doi.org/10.1080/14742837.2013.870883
Young, Dennis R. 2000. "Alternative Models of Government-Nonprofit Sector Relations: Theoretical and International Perspectives." *Nonprofit and Voluntary Sector Quarterly* 29 (1): 149–172. https://doi.org/10.1177/0899764000291009
Zigon, Jarrett. 2018. *A War on People: Drug User Politics and a New Ethics of Community.* Oakland: University of California Press.
Zinsstag, Estelle and Inge Vanfraechem (eds). 2012. *Conferencing and Restorative Justice: International Practices and Perspectives.* New York: Oxford University Press.

# Index

*For the benefit of digital users, indexed terms that span two pages (e.g., 52–53) may, on occasion, appear on only one of those pages.*

accountability, 9, 12–13, 115, 133, 135–138, 149–151, 169, 171
activism, 12, 14–15, 30 n.6, 155. *see also* protest
advocacy
 experiential, 37, 52–53, 103–105
 policy, 56, 73, 99, 121–122, 128–129, 138
agency (citizen), 78, 104, 117–118, 136–137, 139, 164
Alinksy, Saul, 41–42
Ansell, Christopher, 159
anti-intellectualism, 108
associations. *see* civil society organizations (CSOs)
austerity measures, 10, 14–16, 132, 153–154
autonomy, 22, 38–39, 117–119, 125–126, 131, 133, 136, 138–139, 164, 168

Baltimore Community Conferencing Center, 1–2, 4–5, 7–8, 59–60, 63, 144, 160
Bang, Henrik, 6–7, 109, 161
border patrols, 21, 65–67
Border Watch, 66–67
Boyte, Harry, 6–7, 161
boundary spanning, 144–145, 150, 166
Bourke Tribal Council, 122–124
Boyd, Susan, 101–102
Brandsen, Taco, 152

CAHOOTS (Crisis Assistance Helping Out On The Streets), 64–65, 86, 95–96, 160
care. *see* social welfare
charities, 1, 12–13, 25, 30–31, 46, 73–74, 132, 134, 147, 154–155, 164
citizen governance. *see* citizens' governance spaces
citizen spaces. *see* citizens' governance spaces

citizen-led initiatives. *see* citizens' governance spaces
citizens' governance spaces
 accountability of, 115, 133, 135–136, 149–151, 169
 capacity building in, 73–76, 84–85, 159, 167–168, 171
 characteristics of, 26–39
 citizen voice in, 18, 73, 78, 88, 94–96, 98, 103, 142
 critiques of, 14–15, 30–31, 107, 115–116, 145–155
 definition of, 1, 4–8
 democratic attributes, 19, 70–77, 165–166
 disruptive effects of, 1–2, 7–8, 25, 33–36, 43–44, 46–47, 49, 55, 60–61, 105–106, 110, 139, 141–142
 experimentation and innovation in, 26–28, 31–36, 59–60, 78, 85, 93–94, 152, 159–161
 functional policy work of, 29–31, 60–70
 gendered effects, 134, 148
 hybridity in, 39, 137–138, 152
 knowledge in. *see* knowledge
 leadership in, 27–28, 71, 109
 legitimacy of, 110, 115, 129
 lessons from, 111–112, 163–165
 motivations, 26–27, 52–60
 non-compliant, 18, 61–63, 65–67, 69–70
 normative considerations (good and bad), 18–21, 65, 105–110, 165–166
 participatory processes in, 36–37, 44, 70–72, 76–79, 95–96, 111–112, 142
 public outreach of, 5, 37, 76–77, 142
 risks of, 105–110, 145–155
 self-governing arrangements of, 70–72, 94–95
 social connection in, 32–34, 37, 74–75, 107, 164–165

citizens' governance spaces (*Continued*)
support from government and NGOs for, 166–168
civic studies, 162
civil society, 3–4, 6, 9–10, 17–18, 20–21, 137–138, 145–148, 167, 170–171
civil society organizations (CSOs) (conventional), 26–27, 29, 56, 164–165, 171
   partnerships with, 122–124
   tensions with, 34–35, 126, 131–132, 135
   trust in, 12–13
climate change, 2, 10, 57–58, 68–69, 75–77, 87–88, 99–100, 125
co-creation, 47–48
Common Unity Project Aotearoa (CUPA), 75–76
community conferencing, 1–2, 7–8, 59–60, 63–67, 72, 93–94, 144
community development, 40 n.13, 41, 119, 132, 134. *see also* community organizing
community energy. *see* renewable energy
community gardens, 43, 75–76, 151
community organizing, 7–8, 40–42, 108, 132
community-based initiative, 5–6
complexity, 2, 18, 45–46, 67, 89–90, 97, 99–100, 104, 134–135, 137–138, 157
congruence, 117–132, 134–135, 137–138
cooperatives, 1, 34–35, 54, 126–127, 133–135, 137
co-option, 115, 117–118, 125–127, 132–133, 170–171
co-production, 32–33, 46–49, 131, 138–139
COVID-19 (community response groups), 2, 44–45, 53–54, 120, 126, 147, 167–169
criminal justice, 59–60, 63–67, 90–91, 93–94, 100, 122–124, 142–143, 157–160, 163
Crisis Assistance Helping Out On The Streets (CAHOOTS), 64–65, 86, 95–96

Dekker, Paul, 92–93
deliberative forums. *see* participatory forums
democratic experimentalism, 141–145, 171
democratic innovations (citizen-led), 7, 44
democratic renewal, 3 n.5, 7, 14–15, 47–48, 148, 170

democratic theory, 3–4, 3 n.5, 6–8, 6 n.9, 7 n.10, 14–16, 18–21, 29, 44, 47–48, 105–110, 141–163, 170
depoliticization, 115, 132–133, 153–154
Dewey, John, 22–23, 156, 160
disaster recovery, 3, 94–95, 131–132
distrust, 10–13, 58, 64, 75–76, 101, 161. *see also* trust
diversity, 73, 85–86, 109, 145–148
division. *see* polarization
do-democracy, 10
drug usage. *see* substance use and recovery

Edelenbos, Jurian, 146, 148–149
elder care, 34–35, 53–54
electoral politics. *see also* polarization
   political parties, 11, 13
   politicians, 11–14, 77, 99–101, 108, 129–130, 161
   voting, 11, 141, 146, 156, 161, 164
Elevated Access, 89
energy. *see* renewable energy
environmental protection, 67–70, 121–122, 127–128
everyday making, 6–7, 29, 161–162
exclusion, 19–20, 108–109, 145–146
experimentation. *see* citizens' governance spaces

First Nations people. *see* Indigenous people
Friends of Canberra Grasslands (FOG), 121–122, 137–138
funding, 27–28, 33, 57, 68–69, 75, 107, 117–118, 134, 169
   crowdfunding, 55
   hybrid, 39
   loss of autonomy due to, 34, 127–129, 133
   pressures due to, 135
   seed, 55, 57, 68–69
   transparency of, 169
funeral services, 1–2, 55–56, 73–74, 76–77, 95, 102, 105, 110, 143
Fung, Archon, 2 n.1, 7, 7 n.10

gender-based violence, 52–53, 144
Glendale Gateway Trust, 68, 97
Goulburn Murray Resilience Taskforce, 68–69, 87–88, 98, 107, 109, 134 n.11, 143, 167–168

governance. *see also* citizens' governance spaces (functional policy work)
  decentered, 9–10
  definition of, 4 n.6, 29–30
  implications for, 105–110
  ineffective, 151–152
  shared. *see* congruence

harm reduction, 90–91, 103–104, 106, 129–130, 142–143, 160. *see also* CAHOOTS, Serenity Café, VANDU
Healey, Patsy, 68, 92–93, 97, 135
health care, 34–35, 54, 89, 130
Heart of Dinner (HoD), 53–54
Hendriks, Frank, 3 n.5, 30 n.6
homelessness, 25, 30–31, 43–44, 49, 59, 64, 74, 90–91, 129–130, 150, 154–155

Igalla, Malika, 26 n.2, 29, 38
inclusion, 7, 36–37, 70–73, 93–100, 108–109, 142, 166
Indigenous people, 28, 122–124
inequality, 2, 10, 57, 107, 118–119, 145–148
informality, 5, 130–131, 164, 168
innovation. *see* citizens' governance spaces (experimentation and innovation in)

knowledge
  about governance systems (systemic), 96–98
  about the needs and capacities of the "needy," 90–91
  about networks, 92–93, 97, 110
  citizen/expert distinction, 109–112
  place-based, 91–93, 110
  procedural, 93–98
  production of, 82–98
  sharing of, 81–82, 99–103, 112 n.10
  street-level, 85–86
  substantive, 85–93, 100

labor, 107, 134
Landcare, 127–128, 133
leadership. *see* citizen's governance spaces, leadership in
listening, 13–14, 106–107
lobbying. *see* insisted spaces

market. *see* private sector
marketization, 2, 9–10, 124. *see also* neoliberalism

mini-publics. *see* participatory forums
misinformation, 106
mutual aid, 25–26, 35–36, 44–46, 48, 110, 120, 126, 130–131, 147, 167–169

needle exchange. *see* syringe exchange
neoliberalism, 9–10, 115–116, 115–116 n.1, 148, 154–155
non-governmental organization (NGO). *see* not-for-profit sector
not-for-profit sector, 12–13, 56, 129, 134
Nundah Community Enterprises Cooperative (NCEC), 126–127, 136–137

off-loading (state), 57, 106–107, 121–122, 132–133, 139, 148–149
OnPoint, Safe Injection, 129–130
Orange Sky Australia (OSA), 25, 28, 30–33, 37–38, 38 n.12, 43–44, 49, 74, 90, 142, 154–155
Ostrom, Elinor, 46–47, 46–47 n.16

participatory forums (structured), 7, 78–79, 83–84, 111–112, 141, 144, 170
participatory practices. *see* citizens' governance spaces (participatory processes in)
partisanship. *see* polarization
partnerships
  multi-sector, 9, 14–15, 38–39, 40 n.13, 117–119, 121, 121 n.4, 135, 138–139, 144–145
  private sector, 124–125
  public sector, 128, 133
philanthropy, 12–13, 135–136
planning (local and regional), 40 n13, 67–70, 88
polarization, 13–14, 13 n.17, 146
policing, 7 n.10, 57–61, 64–65, 86–87, 158–160
power
  empowerment, 19, 36–37, 55–56, 71–72, 74, 148, 158, 165
  power-over, 101–102, 119
  power-sharing, 36–37, 70–72, 94, 142
pragmatism, 156–159, 159 n.4
Pranis, Kay, 163
prefigurative politics, 43, 45, 48, 57 n.3, 104
pre-natal support, 20–21, 89

private sector, 7–8, 38–39, 85, 107
protest, 7–8, 14–15, 30 n.6, 30, 41–44, 43–44 n.14, 49, 78, 83–84, 106, 155–156, 165. *see also* activism
public engagement. *see* citizens' governance spaces
public sector, 9–10, 123–124, 132, 134 n.11, 167
public work, 6–7, 29, 161–162
Putnam, Robert, 15

reframing, 55–56, 81, 106, 142–143
regulation, 62, 105, 133, 149–151
renewable energy, 38, 46–47 n.16, 57–58, 77, 99–100, 107, 124, 153–154
representation, 94–95, 103–105
restorative justice, 7–8, 46–47 n.16, 59–60, 88, 90–91, 93–94, 112 n.10, 144, 163
Restorative Justice for Oakland Youth, 59–60, 100
rural issues, 68, 107, 127, 133

Savy Amira, 52–53, 144, 155
scale
 scaling-up, 135–137, 168
 small-scale, 1–2, 27, 49, 92, 107, 115, 152
Serenity Café, 33–39, 71–74, 106, 110, 129
social capital, 15–16, 145–146
social enterprise, 5–6, 54–55, 75, 78 n.12, 120, 153–154
social entrepreneurship. *see* social enterprise
social fragmentation, 154–155
social innovation. *see* social enterprise
social isolation, 31, 54
social media, 14, 27
social movements, 6, 41–44, 43–44 n.14, 48–49, 52, 57 n.3, 83–84, 104, 109, 138, 145, 152, 154
social welfare, 14–15, 54, 64, 148, 152, 155
solidarity, 14–16, 19, 45, 53
Soltan, Karol, 162
Som Energia, 1–2, 8, 60–61, 71, 73–74, 77, 142
Sørensen, Eva, 6–7, 161
spaces. *see also* citizens' governance spaces
 definition of, 5, 5 n.7
 insisted, 30, 30 n.7, 106
 invited, 5 n.7, 77, 83, 97

Spade, Dean, 132–133
Squatters in Lingewaard, 69–70
stakeholders, 72, 123, 150–151, 159
state. *see* public sector
Strathewen Community Renewal Association, 94–95
substance use and recovery, 37, 86, 90–91, 101–102, 150–151, 157. *see also* OnPoint, Serenity Café, syringe exchange, VANDU
syringe exchange, 34–35, 58, 62, 130

Taylor, Marilyn, 134–135, 152 n.3
Tender Funerals Australia, 1–2, 55–56, 55 n.2, 73–74, 76–77, 95, 102, 102 n.5, 105, 110, 143
Tocqueville, Alexis de, 15
Totally Renewable Yackandandah (TRY), 57–58, 58 n.4, 73, 77, 99–100, 124–125, 145
transparency, 20, 169
trust, 11, 11 n.13, 12–13, 15, 27, 101, 107, 121–122, 168. *see also* distrust

van Meerkerk, Ingmar, 146, 149
Vancouver Area Network of Drug Users (VANDU), 34 n.8, 34–35 n.9, 58–59, 61–62, 71, 86–88, 101–104, 106, 129, 141–143
vigilantism, 65–67, 66–67 n.9, 106
voluntary organisations. *see* civil society organizations
volunteers
 conventional, 6, 12–13
 informal, 6, 33, 147

Wabash Valley Crisis Pregnancy Center, 20–21
Wagenaar, Hendrik, 3 n.5, 89–90, 97, 137, 151 n.2
Warren, Mark E., 170
wildfires, 94–95, 106, 131–132
Wright, Eric Olin, 7, 7 n.10

Yackandandah Community Development Company (YCDCo), 54–55, 57

Zigon, Jarrett, 43–44 n.14, 104
Zwelethemba, 160